David

Deca

July 75

World
Literary Anecdotes

World Literary Anecdotes

Robert Hendrickson

Facts On File
New York • Oxford • Sydney

For my granddaughter, Erin

Facts On File, Inc.
460 Park Avenue South
New York NY 10016
USA

Facts On File Limited
Collins Street
Oxford OX4 1XJ
United Kingdom

Facts On File Pty Ltd
Talavera & Khartoum Rds
North Ryde NSW 2113
Australia

Library of Congress Cataloging-in-Publication Data

Hendrickson, Robert, 1933-
    World literary anecdotes / Robert Hendrickson.
        p. cm.
    Includes index.
    ISBN 0-8160-2248-8
    1. literature—Anecdotes. I. Title.
PN165.H35   1990
808.88′2—dc20   89-34089

British and Australian CIP data available on request from Facts On File.

Facts On File books are available at special discounts when
purchased in bulk quantities for businesses, associations,
institutions or sales promotion. Please contact the Special
Sales Department of our New York office at 212/683- 2244
(dial 800/322-8755 except in NY, AK or HI).

Text design by Ron Monteleone
Jacket design by Victore Design Works
Composition by Facts On File, Inc.
Manufactured by the Maple-Vail Book Manufacturing Group
Printed in the United States of America

10 9 8 7 6 5 4 3 2 1

This book is printed on acid-free paper.

CONTENTS

INTRODUCTION

While various books of American and British literary anecdotes have appeared over the years it is hard to think of one book in English collecting literary anecdotes from other nations of the world. In fact, with the exception of a number of much-repeated French anecdotes, most dating back to the age of Voltaire, and some stories of Tolstoy, Dostoyevsky and several other literary giants, very few stories about non-English speaking (or writing) authors have appeared even in general anthologies. This book, the result of over ten years of combing hundreds of millions of words, is an attempt to correct that situation and is probably the first of its kind. In it the reader will find not only the bon mots of great literary wits from Austria to Zaire, but oddities and curiosities of world literature and touching stories as well. However, while these pages provide a unique and extensive introduction to the literatures of the world, the scope of the anthology is so wide that some readers will doubtless find omissions, which I would be glad to add in future editions if brought to my attention.

The basic ground rules for this collection are the same as for its companion volumes, *American Literary Anecdotes* and *British Literary Anecdotes* (which covers writers from countries belonging to the Commonwealth). First, I've scrupulously tried to exclude either anecdotes of living writers or anecdotes of deceased writers that could hurt living friends and relations. Writers and their relatives have troubles enough and John Aubrey is generally right, I think, when he says of his marvelous "rude and hastie collection," *Brief Lives*, that before literary anecdotes are "fitt to lett flie abroad" the "author and the Persons...ought to be rotten first." Second, I should say that my collection too is "rude and hastie," though I hope hastier than rude; in any case, I tried to be as brief as possible with each entry so that there could be more entries. This meant sometimes condensing or paraphrasing what I could have preferred to quote at length, but I hope that in most cases I've managed to get the essence of the author and anecdote. Third, I've tried to indicate when a story is doubtful, or when it has been told about several writers, though I doubtless missed some anecdotes I should have labeled apocryphal (despite checking one or more biographies for most stories). Finally, I've tried to include stories and very brief sketches of all the major world literary figures and represent all the noted literary wits among them with an ample selection of their quips, but I haven't hestitated to include literary anecdotes concerning people who weren't writers, or to include authors noteworthy or remembered solely today for one good story regarding them, such as a few remembered just for their last words or epitaphs. I hope in the last case that the stories may lead readers to the forgotten work of some very deserving writers.

It should be added that this book, which ranges from prehistoric to present times, is arranged alphabetically by authors but has a name and place index, which includes writers mentioned in these pages who haven't an entry to themselves, as well as a topic index enabling readers to find one or more anecdotes about certain subjects, such as accidentally destroyed manuscripts, literary hoaxes, love affairs, hard-drinking authors, strange deaths etc. etc.

My thanks to my editor, Gerry Helferich, and copy editor, Gloria Mc-Darrah, both of whom made valuable contributions to this work. I would also like to thank the many people, too numerous to mention here, who suggested anecdotes to me through the years, particularly those correspondents who wrote from all over the world (including one from Saudi Arabia whose address I've lost and can't write to thank) providing me with more literary hors d'oeuvres after my *The Literary Life and Other Curiosities* was published in 1980. But, of course, all of the errors herein are my responsibility. I can't even blame them on my wife, Marilyn, who worked as hard on this book as I did but who would be she who hung the moon and stars to me if she neither worked upon nor even read a word of my deathless prose.

Robert Hendrickson
Far Rockaway, New York

Ivar Andreas Aasen (1813–1896)

Aasen, a Norwegian philologist and lexicographer, is the only person known to have created a national language. The author had collected all of his country's difficult regional speech for the books he had written on Norwegian dialects. Out of these he fashioned a popular language, or *folk-maal*, which replaced the Dano-Norwegian his countrymen had previously used, to enable all the nation's different dialect users to understand each other. Aasen has been hailed as having "an isolated place in history as the one man who has invented or at least selected and constructed a [national] language." In order to do this, he not only constructed the new composite language but also wrote poems and plays in the *folk-maal* to help popularize it. (See also VUK STEFANOVITCH KARAFICH.)

∇ ∇ ∇

Abbad al-Motadid (d. 1069)

This great figure in Spanish Mohammedan history was a noted poet and patron of the arts, but a drunkard, poisoner, and treacherous warrior as well. He killed with his own hand a son who rebelled against him. Another time he tricked his Berber enemies into visiting him at Seville and smothered them all to death in a steam room of the palace. As was his custom, he used the skulls of the poorest of these dead men as flowerpots, and put the skulls of the richest to use as containers for his gold, jewels and poems.

∇ ∇ ∇

Shah Abbas I (1557–1628?)

The Persian ruler, accomplished poet and magnanimous patron of the arts, despised tobacco and tried to trick his courtiers into abandoning their smoking habits. Drying some horse manure, he substituted it for the tobacco kept in the palace tobacco cans and told them it was a rare, costly blend presented to him by the vizier of Hamadan. However, his courtiers relished it. "It smells like a thousand flowers!" one poet exulted. Replied Shah Abbas: "Cursed be that drug that cannot be distinguished from the dung of horses!"

∇ ∇ ∇

Peter Abelard (1079–1142)

Abelard was a French philosopher hired by Fulbert, a canon at Notre Dame, to educate his brilliant niece Heloise. When Abelard fell in love with the girl and instructed her in the arts of love, making her pregnant, Fulbert took his revenge. He hired a gang of toughs to assault Abelard on the street and emasculate him with their knives. After this the philosopher became a monk, living for another 25 years, and Heloise became a nun.

Bernardo Accolti (1465–1536)
Sometimes called Unico because of his great skill as an improvisational poet, Accolti's unequaled prowess in impromptu poetry was rewarded lavishly by Pope Leo. The Italian *improvisatore* earned so much in fees from the pope that he was actually able to buy the little duchy of Nepi.

∇ ∇ ∇

Achiacharus (5th century B.C.)
The Eastern sage's wise sayings became proverbial in many languages, and the legend of his life influenced much world literature. Achiacharus is said to have been a magician who built castles in the air and made twisted ropes out of sand. His fables, in which he employed animals and birds, anticipated Aesop's.

∇ ∇ ∇

Uriel Acosta (c. 1591–1647?)
Born into the Roman Catholic faith, to which his Jewish family had been forced to convert, the Portuguese author converted back to Judaism, exchanging his baptismal name of Gabriel for Uriel. But he found no satisfaction in either religion, switching back and forth all his life—he was twice excommunicated from the Catholic church and twice readmitted to the synagogue at Amsterdam. Finally, he recanted his severe criticism of Judaism, a criticism that did not take into account the persecution of the Jews over the ages, and was required to do penance. After being scourged, Acosta was made to lie across the doorway to the synagogue, and the congregation, including his brother Joseph, who had strongly condemned him, all stepped over him on the way out. It is said that Spinoza, then a boy of 15, may have watched his humiliation. In any case, Acosta went home and again bitterly denounced his religion in his intellectual autobiography *Exemplar Humanae Vitae*, which he wrote in several days and nights. Having finished the book and seeing nowhere to turn, he decided to commit suicide. After loading two pistols, he waited by the window until his brother passed. He fired at Joseph, missed him, and then turned the other pistol on himself. His autobiography, first published 40 years after he committed suicide, became the basis of K. F. Gutzkow's tragedy *Uriel Acosta* (1847).

∇ ∇ ∇

Arthur Adamov (1908–1970)
In a 1962 speech at Edinburgh the brilliant playwright of the Theatre of the Absurd advised: "The reason why most Absurdist plays take place in No Man's Land with only two characters is mainly financial."

Alfred Adler (1870–1937)

One evening the Austrian psychiatrist and author, an associate of Freud, was lecturing about his theory that people's handicaps lead to their choice of work. Stutterers often become actors, he maintained, fat boys distance runners, visually deficient people painters, etc. "Dr. Adler," someone asked after his lecture, "wouldn't your theory indicate that weak-minded people tend to become psychiatrists?"

∇ ∇ ∇

Aeschines (c. 390–314? B.C.)

The famous Athenian orator and unsuccessful rival of the great Demosthenes was a tragic actor before he turned political speaker. Though a highly regarded thespian he very nearly didn't live out his career, performing before audiences who expressed their displeasure by throwing olives, figs or stones at actors. One time he appeared in a play that the audience regarded as highly offensive and was almost stoned to death, which is perhaps why he turned to oratory.

∇ ∇ ∇

Aeschylus (525–456 B.C.)

One of the few qreat writers who was also a great war hero, the founder of Greek drama fought as a soldier in the war against Persia. He saw action at Marathon, Artemisium, Salamis and Plataea, and his brother Cynaegirus, fighting beside him at Marathon, was killed while attempting a conspicuously gallant act. The Athenians revered Aeschylus as a war hero as well as a great tragedian, placing portraits of the brothers in the picture that served as the national memorial of the battle in Athens' *Stoa Poecile* (pictured porch). In his epitaph, probably written by himself, the poet is represented as fighting at Marathon

Aeschylus is said to have been acting in one of his own plays when a reference to Demeter, the goddess of agriculture, was made and the audience accused him of revealing the secrets of that "earth mother," who had the power to make the earth barren. The audience rose up in fury, cursing the poet and charging toward him. Aeschylus saved himself only by fleeing to the altar of Dionysus in the orchestra, which even the angry crowd respected as an inviolable sanctuary. Later, when tried for his crime, he pleaded that "he did not know that what he said was secret" and was freed, probably largely because of his heroism as a soldier at Marathon.

Though he came from a noble family, bravely fought for his country, and was noted for his dignity, sublimity and eloquence, Aeschylus died a quite undignified death far removed from the themes of utmost grandeur that he chose for his plays. According to legend, at least, the Greek poet was killed when an eagle dropped a tortoise on his bald head, mistaking it for a rock to break its meal upon.

∇ ∇ ∇

Aesop (c. 620–c. 560 B.C.)

Stories abound about Aesop, who may be a legendary figure. The author of the noted animal fables is said to have been the freed black slave of Iadmon of Samos who was killed by the people of Delphi as a sacrifice when a pestilence came upon them. The reasons suggested for Aesop's offending the gods included his insulting sarcasm, the embezzlement of money entrusted to him by King Croesus, and the theft of a rare silver cup. One account describes him as an ugly, deformed man, and it is said that during the reign of Peisistratus he told his fable of "The Frogs Asking for a King" to persuade the people not to change Peisistratus for another ruler. But of Aesop's life only the fables are known to be real.

In the first issue of his magazine *Le Festin d'Ésope (Aesop's Feast)*, published in 1903, the French writer Guillaume Apollinaire reprinted this old anecdote about the Greek fabulist:

> His master, Xantus, who was giving a banquet for his friends, ordered him one day to compose a meal of the best ingredients he could buy. Aesop served a banquet in which every dish, from the soup to the dessert, was made of tongues prepared in various ways. When Xantus reproved him, Aesop replied that he had followed his orders to the letter, since the tongue (French *langue*) being the organ of language, is also the vehicle of truth, reason, science, social life and all things that make life precious. The next day Xantus ordered Aesop to prepare a meal consisting of all the worst ingredients. Aesop again served the same dishes, explaining that the tongue, as the organ of language, is also responsible for all the worst things in the world— quarrels, dissensions, lawsuits, strife, war, lies, slander, blasphemy and all manner of things evil.

∇ ∇ ∇

Clodius Aesopus (fl. 1st century B.C.)

Aesopus, a Roman tragedian and friend of Cicero, was considered as great an actor as the comic player Roscius, his artful facial expressions and gestures said to be unrivaled. The old tale about Cleopatra dissolving an expensive pearl in vinegar may have as its origin a story about Aesopus taking a pearl from the earring of Caecilia Metella and dissolving it in vinegar so that, according to a British writer, "he might have the satisfaction of swallowing £800 at a gulp."

Denis Auguste Affre (1793–1848)

The French Catholic archbishop and author, who wrote a noted study of Egyptian hieroglyphics, among other works, tried to restore peace during the riots of June 1848. Despite warnings he mounted the barricades at the entrance to the Faubourg St. Antoine in his robes, waving a green branch as a symbol of peace. But the insurgents, hearing shots in the distance, believed they had been betrayed, and opened fire wildly—a stray bullet killing the archbishop.

∇ ∇ ∇

Alexander Nikolayevich Afinogenov (1904–1941)

On the Eve (1941), the Russian dramatist's final play, depicted a German attack on the Soviet Union. A month after its first performance he himself was killed in a German air raid on Moscow.

∇ ∇ ∇

Jean Louis Rodolphe Agassiz (1807–1873)

The Swiss-born naturalist, author and educator taught for 25 years at Harvard, and in that time had more offers to give public lectures than he had time for without detracting from his scientific studies. One lyceum repeatedly asked him to speak, and when he kept refusing, assured him that he would be very well paid for his lecture. "That is no inducement to me," Agassiz replied. "I cannot afford to waste my time making money."

At the start of each year at Harvard, Agassiz would tell his classes: "Gentlemen, the world is older than we have been taught to think. Its age is as if one were gently to rub a silk handkerchief across Plymouth Rock once a year until it were reduced to a pebble."

∇ ∇ ∇

Marcus Vipsanius Agrippa (c. 62–12 B.C.)

The Roman general and author of a lost autobiography was convinced by the emperor to take the promiscuous Julia as his third wife. According to a traditional tale, when Julia was later asked why despite all her adulteries each of her five children resembled Agrippa, she replied, "I never take on a passenger unless the vessel is already full."

∇ ∇ ∇

Akutagawa Ryunosuke (1892–1927)

The author of *Rashomon*, perhaps schizophrenic, killed himself with an overdose of sleeping pills after an attack of severe paranoia. It is said that the Japanese author felt guilty of plagiarism for basing his fiction on traditional tales, even though they dated as far back as the 10th century.

∇ ∇ ∇

Alcaeus (fl. c. 600 B.C.)

A nobleman who fled from battle after losing his shield in the war against the Athenians, Alcaeus was forced into exile by his political enemies. Many of the lyric poems written by this inventor of Alcaic verse were drinking songs. According to Alcaeus and other Greek writers, literary cocktail parties in ancient Greece were more lively than their present-day counterparts. In one game, called *cottalus*, the object was for the recumbent player to drink most of his wine and cast the remainder from his drinking cup in such a way that it would sail through the air as one intact mass and hit a mark, making a distinct noise. In one of many variations, shallow saucers were floated in a huge basin; the object was to cast the wine into the saucers and sink them, with the competitor who sank the most saucers receiving a prize.

∇ ∇ ∇

Marianna Alcoforado (1640–1723)

When she was about 25 the lovely Portuguese nun met the Marquis de Chamilly, a handsome marshal of France then serving in Portugal's army. She fell in love with him and Chamilly, aided by his prestige and her naiveté, seduced her before clandestinely deserting to France when their affair was discovered and a scandal arose. Between December 1667 and June 1668 Marianne wrote to her lover the five short letters known as *Letters of a Portuguese Nun*, that have become a classic translated into many languages, including a German edition by Rilke. Only Rousseau doubted the epistles' veracity—he thought they were written by a man.

∇ ∇ ∇

Ulisse Aldrovandi (Lat. Ulysses Aldrovandus; 1523?–1605?)

"Cock-and-bull" has its rightful place beside "fish story" and "pescatorial prevarication," but this scientist, not a sportsman, is responsible for the phrase. Aldrovandus had the profession of naturalist and an imagination as lively as any fisherman's. The phrase cock-and-bull derives from his story of the cockatrice, or basilisk: the mythical, crown-headed king of serpents. Aldrovandus swore that this creature, produced from a cock's egg hatched by a snake, withered plants and poisoned men by its look. The sound of crowing killed the monster, he said, and he persuaded many of his contemporaries to carry roosters with them when they traveled. Cynics, however, proved Aldrovandus wrong, and although the 16th century naturalist filled 13 or 14 folio volumes with a wealth of valuable material, he is remembered for the "big one that got away."

Aldrovandus was so ample on the subject of cock-and-bull and cockatrice, that a new phrase was added to the language. All rambling, gossiping tales of doubtful credibility have since been called cock-and-bull stories.

▽ ▽ ▽

Sholom Aleichem (Solomon Rabinowitz; 1859–1916)

The Russian-born Yiddish author took his penname from the traditional greeting of Jews, meaning "peace unto you." Aleichem suffered from triskaidekaphobia, fear of the number 13, and his manuscripts never had a page 13. Ironically, he died on a May 13, but the date on his headstone in Mount Carmel Cemetery, Glendale, New York, reads "May 12a, 1916." According to one tale, Aleichem, called "The Jewish Mark Twain," chanced to meet Mark Twain in New York. "I am The American *Sholom Aleichem*," Twain modestly told him.

While a tutor of Russian to 12-year-old Olga Loeff, Aleichem fell in love with his pupil. Her wealthy father fired him, but he waited four years until he was 21, then married Olga. Her father soon died and left them a large fortune, much of which Aleichem used to encourage Yiddish writers.

▽ ▽ ▽

Jean d'Alembert (1717–1783)

The brilliant French scientist and encyclopedist was the illegitimate child of Claudine Alexandrine de Tencin, a former nun, and artillery officer, the Chevalier Destouches. Having escaped from the nunnery in which her father had enrolled her 16 years before, Claudine hid in the bed of the chevalier, where the two of them soon produced Jean. When he was born, however, his mother abandoned him on the steps of the Church of St-Jean-le-Rond, where he was found and eventually adopted. His enterprising mother went from the bed of the chevalier to the beds of Matthew Prior and Lord Bolingbroke. Improving herself all the time, she added Richelieu, Fontenelle and the head of the Paris police to her long list of lovers. This interesting woman influenced history with her famous salon as well as her choice of beds, but she is best remembered for her romantic escapades. It is said that she became the regent's mistress by posing as a nude statue in his palace and coming to life when he touched her.

"You will never be anything but a philosopher," d'Alembert's adoptive mother once told him sadly. "And what is a philosopher? 'Tis a madman who torments himself all his life so that people may talk about him when he is dead."

While writing his contribution to the great French *Encyclopédie*, d'Alembert lived in poverty in a Parisian garret. On receiving a letter from Voltaire describing a majestic view, he replied, "You write to me from your bed, where you command ten leagues of lake, and I answer you from my hole, whence I command a patch of sky three ells long."

∇ ∇ ∇

Alexander the Great (356–323 B.C.)
Legend says Alexander the Great always carried a treasured edition of Homer corrected by his tutor Aristotle, and that he put it under his pillow at night along with his sword. When Alexander found a golden casket studded with gems in the tent of Darius after he defeated the Persian king, he placed his edition of Homer inside and kept it there, whenever he wasn't reading it, for the rest of his life, frequently saying, "There is but one thing in life worthy of so precious a casket."

∇ ∇ ∇

Alfonso the Learned (1226?–1284)
As Carlyle observed, nothing is remembered of the many sayings of this Spanish king and author except his remark about Ptolemy's astronomy: "Had I been present at the creation, I would have given some useful hints for the better ordering of the universe."

∇ ∇ ∇

Alphonse Allais (1854–1905)
This French humorist and dramatist admired himself or pretended to admire himself more than history has admired him or pretended to admire him. "I have been asked to talk to you on the subject of the theater," he once said, in words that have also been attributed to Mark Twain, "but I feel that my talk will make you sad. For Shakespeare is dead, Molière is dead, Racine is dead, Marivaux is dead—and I am not feeling too well myself."

∇ ∇ ∇

Karl Jonas Ludwig Almquist (1793–1866)
Almquist was a famous writer in Sweden when he fled to the United States in 1851 after being convicted of forgery and charged with murder. Nothing was heard of him for years, though it is now known that he settled in St. Louis. While on a journey through Texas the novelist was held up at gunpoint by robbers who stole all his manuscripts, including several unpublished novels of which he had no copies. Almquist appealed in person to President Lincoln for help in retrieving his manuscripts, but the robbers were never found. This was the author's only

punishment for his crimes, however; he soon left America for Germany, where he died the next year in Bremen while posing as a Professor Westerman.

▽ ▽ ▽

Anacreon (fl. 6th century B.C.)
A Greek lyric poet, Anacreon wrote light poems praising wine and love that were imitated by Jonson, Herrick and other early English bards. A drinking club in London used his name, and its club song, "Anacreon in Heaven," provided the music for Francis Scott Key's "Star Spangled Banner," the American national anthem.

▽ ▽ ▽

Anaxagoras (c. 500–c. 430 B.C.)
The Greek philosopher and scientist was brought a ram with a single unicornlike horn in the center of its forehead and told that a soothsayer had claimed the single horn was a supernatural omen. Anaxagoras killed the animal, cleft its skull and showed that the brain had grown upward toward the center rather than filling both sides of the cranium, thus producing the single horn.

On his deathbed a man of ill repute complained to the philosopher that he was dying in a foreign land. "The descent to Hades," Anaxagoras replied, "is the same from any place."

Anaxagoras was condemned to death in absentia by the Athenians on charges of impiety because he had described the sun as "a mass of stone on fire." When he was told of the condemnation, he replied, "Nature has long since condemned both them and me."

▽ ▽ ▽

Hans Christian Andersen (1805–1875)
Never a healthy man (he died as a result of falling out of bed) and viewed as a lunatic by many in his early years when he wanted to become an opera singer, Andersen had little confidence in himself and always disdained his immortal fairy tales. The Danish fabulist was so ashamed of his body that before going out he would pad his shirt with newspapers to make himself appear more muscular.

Andersen didn't enroll in grammar school until he was 17 years old. He was over six years older and fully a head taller than the 11-year-olds in whose class he was placed.

The nightingale in Andersen's "The Nightingale" (1843) was based on Jenny Lind, with whom the writer fell in love early in her career when she was an unknown opera singer. The diva spurned his love, though she remained his friend, and later became famous as P. T. Barnum's "Swedish Nightingale."

While traveling in Europe, Andersen, still an unknown writer, met Victor Hugo and asked him for his autograph. A suspicious Hugo, afraid that his signature might be used as acknowledgment of a debt that might be inserted above it, signed "Victor Hugo" in the right-hand corner at the very top of Andersen's blank piece of paper.

Andersen submitted his immortal *Fairy Tales* to every publisher in Copenhagen. All of them turned it down and he was forced to publish the book himself.

In his *A Visit to Germany, Italy and Malta, 1840–1841*, the Danish writer told this story:

> I was walking through one of the Munich streets and came to a bookshop where, among the books on display, I saw a German edition of my *Improvvisatore*...I went in and asked for it. A young man handed me a small volume, which comprised just the first part.
> "But I want the whole novel," I said.
> "It is the whole," he answered. "There are no other parts. I have read it myself, sir."
> "But did you not think," I asked, "that it ends rather abruptly and that one really does not have a proper solution?"
> "Well, yes," he said, "but it is like those French novels. The writer hints at a conclusion and one has to fill it in for oneself."
> "But that is not the case here," I interrupted. "This is only the first part you have given me."
> "But I tell you," he said, half angry, "I have *read* it!"
> "But I *wrote* it!" I replied
> The man looked me up and down. He did not contradict me, but I could see from his face that he did not believe me.

Before Andersen died, he arranged for a composer to write his funeral march. "Most of the people who will walk after me will be children," he instructed, "so make the beat keep time with little steps."

∇ ∇ ∇

Jerzy Andrzejewski (b. 1909)
The Polish author's *Gates of Paradise* (1962), a novel about the Children's Crusade, appears to be the longest literary work written without punctuation. The novel amounts to one long sentence with no punctuation for the first 40,000 words.

Anonymous
No one knows how many authors have used the byline "Anonymous" or "Anon." over the ages. A French dictionary published in 1822–23 alone listed over 23,000 anonymous entries. Often these were prominent authors forced to conceal their names for one reason or another.

Ancient Greek actors and dramatists were sometimes frightened off the stage by audiences who threw figs, olives or stones when they disliked a performance. One anonymous dramatist-actor, apparently a poor one, borrowed a supply of stones to build a house and promised to return the loan with the stones he expected to collect from his next performance.

The longest poem in the world is the *Mahabharata,* which tells the story of the descendants of the Hindu king Bharata. *Mahabharata* means "the great Bharata," and the poem's 110,000 couplets, or 220,000 lines, make it four times longer than the Bible and eight times longer than Homer's *Iliad* and *Odyssey* combined. The Indian poem is really the combined work of many generations of anonymous writers, written between the years 400 B.C. and 150 B.C. Though its main theme is the war between descendants of Kuru and Pandu, it is a vast repository of philosophy and legend. The *Ramayana,* named after the god Rama, is another great Indian epic poem, containing 24,000 stanzas in seven books as we know it today.

In ancient times "word contests" were often quite literally wars with words. The most colorful examples of this were those poets who led pre-Islamic Arabs into combat, hurling curses at the enemy, who usually had poets who cursed back.

Only monks did more copying of manuscripts than the medieval private or professional scribes, who were hired by rich men or booksellers. Often the scribes ended their wearisome labor with strange or humorous requests on the last page—these colophons including:

> This completes the whole;
> For Christ's sake give me a drink.
> For the work of this pen let the writer
> receive a beautiful girl.

The *Missae ac Missalis Anatomia,* published in 1561, has been called the world's worst printed book, its 172 pages including 15 pages of errata. In any event, its anonymous author claimed that Satan had soaked his manuscript, making it splotched and illegible in many places and causing the printer to make so many mistakes.

Something one canardly believe, said a punster in defining "canard." In French *canard* means "duck," and the word for a ridiculously false story comes from the French expression *vendre un canard à moitié*—literally, "to half-sell a duck." As a duck, or anything else, can't be half-sold, the expression figuratively means to make a fool out of a buyer, or anyone else, with a false story. Tellers of "half-ducks," or canards, were known in France three centuries ago, and the word probably gained a firmer foothold with a hoax played by an anonymous French writer. The author, testing the gullibility of the public, published a story that he had 30 ducks, one of which he killed and threw to the other 29, which ate it. Then he cut up a second, then a third, until the 29th duck was eaten by the survivor—an excellent bull, duck or canard story.

No one knows the names of the publisher or authors of the off-color French books called *La Bibliothèque Bleue* that contributed to the coining of the word "blue" for obscene, as in pornographic "blue movies." An actually nonexistent book is responsible for what are called "blue laws." This term usually means never-on-Sunday moral laws and may take its name from a nonexistent Connecticut "blue book" rumored to contain fanatical laws. The vengeful rumor was spread by the Reverend Samuel Peters, an American Tory who returned to England after the Revolution. Peters claimed that the fictitious blue-bound book contained laws prohibiting such activities as kissing one's wife on Sunday.

There are many examples of books bound in human skin, sometimes the author's (as in the case of an American murderer who wrote a posthumously published autobiography), but in a small volume at Bhutan's Taktsang monastery every other page is written in a white "ink" made from the bones of a great lama who had lived and died there.

Pango Pango should be the name of the Pacific island Pago Pago, the chief harbor of American Samoa, and that, in fact, is the way the locals pronounce the name. An old story, which may be true, explains that the island is called Pago Pago because several unknown missionaries transliterating the local speech into the Latin alphabet found that there were many sounds that had to be "represented by *n* in combination with a following consonant." So many, in fact, that there weren't enough *n*'s in their type fonts to enable them to set all such words in type. So they quite arbitrarily eliminated the *n* from some words—leaving us with *Pago Pago* instead of *Pango Pango*.

A German burgomaster said that he cared nothing for such trifles as commas. Hearing this, the village schoolteacher had a pupil write on the blackboard: "The burgomaster of R—— says the teacher is an ass."

He then told the boy to add commas so that the sentence read: "The burgomaster of R——, says the teacher, is an ass."

If the Japanese word *mokusatsu* hadn't been misinterpreted by an anonymous translator, World War II might have ended sooner, atomic power might never have been used in warfare, and tens of thousands of lives might have been saved. *Mokusatsu* has two meanings: (1) to ignore, and (2) to refrain from comment. As historian Stuart Chase has written:

> The release of a press statement using the second meaning in July 1945 might have ended the war then. The Emperor was ready to end it, and had the power to do so. The cabinet was preparing to accede to the Potsdam ultimatum of the Allies— surrender or be crushed—but wanted a little more time to discuss the terms. A press release was prepared announcing a policy of *mokusatsu*, with the "no comment" implication. But it got on the foreign wires with the "ignore" implication through a mixup in translation: "The cabinet ignores the demand to surrender." To recall the release would have entailed an unthinkable loss of face. Had the intended meaning been publicized, the cabinet might have backed up the Emperor's decision to surrender.

Instead there came Hiroshima and Nagasaki.

Traduttore tradittore (the translator is a betrayer), goes an Italian proverb. A case in point is the anonymous Japanese translator who was asked to translate back from the Japanese the phrase in the new Japanese constitution that represented the American "life, liberty, and the pursuit of happiness." He came up with "license to commit lustful pleasure."

A writer who in the late 1960s researched the film *De Sade* in Hamburg's notorious red-light district submitted an expense account including such items as a "party for 69 prostitutes, $430...a farewell dinner for 21 masochists and 21 sadists, $300...and a rest cure in Garmisch-Partenkirchen, $1850..."

In pre-glasnost 1979, the editor of the Russian humor magazine *Niangi* was fired for not being serious enough.

∇ ∇ ∇

Abraham Hyacinthe Anquetil-Duperron (1731–1805)
Determined to translate the sacred books of the East, but too poor to travel there, the French scholar enlisted in the army and spent eight years in India, where he

learned Persian, Sanskrit, Pahlavi and Zend and collected hundreds of manuscripts. Returning to Paris, he lived on bread, cheese and water while translating the Zend-Avesta and other Parsee books into French for the first time.

∇ ∇ ∇

Antiphanes (c. 408–334 B.C.)
Some 365 comedies are attributed to the ancient playwright, apparently a foreigner who settled in Athens. Plutarch credits him for originating an anecdote that has been told by many writers, including Rabelais, and is even told of the Texas Panhandle. "Antiphanes said merrily," Plutarch assures us, "that in a certain city the cold was so intense that words were congealed as soon as spoken, but that after some time they thawed and became audible; so that the words spoken in winter were articulated next summer."

∇ ∇ ∇

Marcus Gavius Apicius (fl. 1st century A.D.)
Apicius might be called the world's first gourmand and bon vivant as well as the author of the earliest cookbook. His *Of Culinary Matters* has gone through countless editions since first written about 1,500 years ago. Some historians claim that Apicius was a rich Roman merchant who collected recipes wherever he traveled, others that his name is a nom de plume deriving from the word "epicure," but most authorities believe that he was the Roman nobleman Marcus Gavius Apicius, who lived under Tiberius in the first century A.D. Whatever his identity, an "Apicius" still brings to mind a chef and gastronome without peer, one who went to such lengths as spraying his garden lettuce with mead in the evening so that it would taste like "green cheesecakes" the next morning, one who concocted Apician dishes that remain, in the words of Mark Twain, "as delicious as the less conventional forms of sin."

Apicius, perhaps the world's first cookbook author, spent a huge sum—a hundred million sesterces, according to one source—on a fabulous banquet and then took a lethal dose of poison when he realized that he had only about ten million sesterces left (over half a million dollars), hardly enough to support a wealthy Roman in style.

∇ ∇ ∇

Apellicon (d. 84 B.C.)
This wealthy Athenian was not only one of the world's earliest and most famous book collectors, but an infamous book thief as well. Apellicon, in fact, stole books and original documents from the archives of Athens and other Greek cities; when detected he fled his country for a time. But it was Apellicon who purchased the

dilapidated manuscripts of Aristotle, hidden for many years in a cellar, that became the basis of an important early edition of Aristotle's works.

∇ ∇ ∇

Guillaume Apollinaire (1880–1918)

The French avant-garde poet was as unconventional in his personal life as in his art, but was obsessively orderly, especially about his bed, which was strictly for sleeping and dreaming and which he would never even make love in. "The living room [in his flat] was too small for guests," Apollinaire's friend Fernande Olivier once recalled. "It opened into a bedroom, where we would go to be a little more comfortable. We would sit down in there, being careful not to disarrange anything—Guillaume wouldn't have liked that. We had to be especially careful never to touch the bed. The slightest wrinkle, the slightest sign of its having been sat on, made him frown and look irritated. I was a friend of his mistress, who told me that their love-frolics were restricted to an armchair: his bed was sacred."

Apollinaris water takes its name from the St. Apollinaris shrine located near the mineral spring at Bad Neuenahr where the water is found. One story circulating through Paris, however, had it that the poet Apollinaire entered a café a little drunk and called for Apollinaris water, crying "C'est mon eau! C'est mon eau!" The tale is probably apocryphal, for Apollinaire challenged the author of the story (first printed in a Paris newspaper) to a duel if he did not issue a formal retraction. The author never answered his letter and the duel was never fought, though no retraction was ever made.

Among the poet's basic themes was food, one explanation for why he grew paunchier with each passing year, as Picasso's famous bookplate drawing of him as a gargantuan king at table shows so well. Indeed, according to a contemporary, Apollinaire often ate "*two* entire meals in rapid succession" as he sat at the groaning board.

Jean Sevé, a friend of the poet, is thought to have financed Apollinaire's first magazine, *Festin d'Ésope* (*Aesop's Feast*). To show his gratitude Apollinaire signed the name Jean Sevé to a small paragraph he printed in the magazine satirizing the grandiose paintings of the illustrious Gérôme, a much respected member of the Academy. After the piece was published Apollinaire met his friend in a bar. "Have you read the magazine?" he asked, beaming. "Are you pleased with your bit about Gérôme?"

"Yes, I've read it," Sevé said, more sorrowful than angry. "Didn't you know that Gérôme is my uncle?"

Like Gertrude Stein, who found commas "servile" and refused to use them, Apollinaire disdained punctuation, as he demonstrated in his book of poems, *Alcools*. But Apollinaire did explain himself. "As for punctuation, I have eliminated it only because it seemed to me useless," he wrote of his book, "and it actually is useless; the rhythm itself and the division into lines provide the real punctuation and no other is needed."

Apollinaire wrote a literary gossip column consisting only of anecdotes for the bimonthly *Mercure de France*. His column, entitled "La Vie Anecdotique," was wide-ranging and written entirely by himself. Its best-known anecdote, which appeared on April 1, 1913, was a scabrously funny bit on the funeral of Walt Whitman years before. Americans in Paris were outraged, writing indignant letters to the magazine, but Apollinaire insisted that the story was "indisputably known in America" and told to him in the presence of a poet "knowledgeable of the United States." Still the letters kept coming in—no one apparently noticing the date of Apollinaire's column.

Following is an example of an anecdote from Apollinaire's "La Vie Anecdotique":
"The painter Picasso was looking at a canvas by a Futurist painter. It presented a very confused appearance—a mixture of disparate objects, a bottle, a collar, the head of a jovial-looking man, etc. This chaos was entitled 'Laughed.'
"'It ought to be called 'Pell-Mell,' said Picasso, with a smile."

Apollinaire's volume of poetry *Le Bestiaire, ou Cortège d'Orphée*, illustrated by Raoul Dufy, was certainly one of the most beautiful books of its time. As he often did, the poet wrote the blurb for his own book, praising it in the most extravagant terms. He was right, but only 50 of the 120 copies printed sold; the rest of them were remaindered at 40 francs each. Today a good copy of *Le Bestiaire* fetches at least several thousand dollars.

As Apollinaire lay dying of pneumonia in his Paris flat, he begged his doctor to cure him. His last words (or at least nearly his last words) would have been an appropriate poem to end his last book: "Save me, doctor! I want to live! I still have so many things to say!"

This excerpt from the journal of French author Paul Leautaud, a friend and early supporter of Apollinaire, is significant only if one knows that Guillaume was the French name for Wilhelm II, the German kaiser during World War I:

"Interesting detail concerning Apollinaire's death: The Armistice was signed this morning. The news reached Paris immediately, and everyone went wild.

Crowds filled the Rue de Rennes, the Place Saint-Germain-des-Prés, and the Boulevard Saint-Germain. On the boulevard, under the very windows of the small room where Apollinaire was lying dead on his flower-covered bed, crowds were shouting 'Down with Guillaume! Down with Guillaume!'"

In his *Le Poète Assassiné* Apollinaire envisioned the assassination of "the greatest living poet," clearly based on himself, and described the erection of a monument to that poet by a great painter-sculptor, clearly based on his good friend Picasso. His vision of the latter proved true when after Apollinaire's death Picasso built a sculpture memorial in the little park at Saint-Germain-des-Prés on the street now called Rue Guillaume Apollinaire.

∇ ∇ ∇

Michael Apostolius (d. c. 1480)

This Greek philosopher and author had to earn his very meagre livelihood by copying the manuscripts of others. In one of them still surviving, the *Icones* of Philostratus, he penned the inscription: "The king of the poor of this world has written this book for his living."

∇ ∇ ∇

Hari Narayan Apte (1864–1919)

Apte, the first major Marathi-language novelist in India, was lucky enough to have a rich uncle who appointed him to a sinecure so that he could comfortably devote all his time to writing, even giving him enough money to publish his own monthly magazine from 1890 to 1917. This would seem to be a writer's dream and Apte did publish his novels serially in the magazine. But his self-publishing and editing encouraged a self-indulgent laziness that was reflected in his construction and repetition. And whenever Apte tired of the plot of a novel, he would simply stop writing it—no matter how far along it was in serialization—and start another one. As a result of this capriciousness, only half of his two dozen novels were ever finished.

∇ ∇ ∇

Lucius Apuleius (fl. c. 155 A.D.)

Apuleius's novel *Metamorphoses*, or *The Golden Ass*, is the source for a number of incidents in the later works of Cervantes, Boccaccio and other authors. The North African author married a rich widow, whose greedy relatives quickly accused him of having won her hand by casting a magic spell over her. Apuleius, who was deeply interested in magic and had written of it, finally persuaded the proconsul Claudius Maximus that he was innocent of the charge.

Louis Aragon (1897–1982)

The surrealist French poet, who became a communist in 1937, fought against the advancing Nazi armies at the beginning of World War II. One time his orders were to establish a medical detachment in a building 300 meters ahead of the farthest advance post. The captain in charge of the post, Count Alphonse de Rothschild, of the fabulously wealthy French Rothschilds, refused to let him proceed. "You can't pass beyond this point," Rothschild said. "The German fire is too close."

"My instructions are to get to that building," Aragon insisted.

"My orders are that you are not to go on. You must stay right here!" the captain commanded.

As Aragon's friend the Chilean poet Pablo Neruda later put it: "Knowing Aragon as well as I do, I am sure that during the argument sparks flew like hand grenades, answers like sword thrusts. But it didn't even last ten minutes. Suddenly, before the startled eyes of Rothschild and Aragon, a grenade from a German mortar struck the building, converting it instantly to smoke, rubble and smoldering ashes. And so France's first poet was saved, thanks to the stubbornness of a Rothschild."

∇ ∇ ∇

Archestratus (fl. c. 330 B.C.)

This Greek poet and gourmet traveled far and wide seeking foreign delicacies for the table. He was so obsessed with food in his poems that he came to be known as the Glutton or the Hesiod of Gluttons.

∇ ∇ ∇

Archilochus (fl. 7th century B.C.)

The great Greek critic Alexander of Byzantium, head of the Alexandrian library, in two words paid the poet the supreme compliment when asked which of Archilochus' poems he liked best. "The longest," he replied.

It is said that the impoverished Archilochus fell in love with a rich girl named Neobule, writing many love poems to her. But her father insisted she end their affair and she obeyed him. In "raging iambics," as the emperor Hadrian described his lines, the "scorpion-tongued" Greek poet, the bastard son of a slave woman, satirized both the father and his beloved, his satires so savage and biting, tradition has it, that both father and daughter hanged themselves. But the celebrated poet didn't come to a good end himself, or have a good life. Pressed by poverty all his days, he threw away his shield and fled the battlefield in one minor war and was later banished from Sparta for his cowardice and the licentiousness of his works. He was finally killed in another small war, uncon-soled by the story that his slayer was cursed by the oracle for having slain a servant of the Muses.

∇ ∇ ∇

Archimedes (c. 287–212 B.C.)
Archimedes is best remembered for his inadvertent coining of an expression. One day he was asked to determine the amount of silver an allegedly dishonest goldsmith had used for the king's crown, which was supposed to have been made of pure gold. While pondering the solution in his bath, he observed that the quantity of water displaced by a body will equal in bulk the bulk of the immersed body (the Archimedean Principle). All he had to do then was to weigh an amount of gold equal in weight to the crown, put crown and gold in separate basins of water, and weigh the overflow to determine how much gold the crown really contained. According to one story, he was so overjoyed with his discovery that he forgot his clothes and ran out into the streets naked, astounding passersby with his shouts of "*Eureka, eureka!*" ("I have found it, I have found it!")

When he wrote *The Sphere and the Cylinder*, the great mathematician purposely included several false propositions in order to trick his friends and trap those who might claim his work as their own.

"Give me a place to stand on and I will move the earth," said Archimedes of a fixed fulcrum. When King Heiron challenged him to prove his theory by moving a large ship that had to be beached for repairs, Archimedes arranged a series of cogs and pulleys with which he alone drew the huge vessel out of the water.

The traditional story of his death gives evidence of Archimedes's mythical quality. It seems that Archimedes's giant burning-mirrors, or lenses—not to mention his grapnels and improved catapults—held the Roman ships besieging Syracuse at bay for three years by setting them on fire from a distance. When the Romans finally took the town in 212 B.C., strict orders were given that Ar-chimedes should not be harmed. Bu legend tells us that he was run through by a soldier, unaware of his identity, after refusing to follow the soldier because he was intent upon solving a problem he had etched in the sand.

∇ ∇ ∇

Pietro Aretino (1492–1556)
The Italian poet, whom Thomas Nash called "one of the wittiest knaves God ever made" and Milton called "that notorious ribald of Arezzo," wrote many licen-

tious works, including *Sonnetti Lussuriosi* (roughly *Sonnets of the Lustful*), a collection of verses and erotic drawings showing positions of sexual intercourse. *Sonnetti* was an underground favorite in Europe for centuries, though the English poet John Donne observed that some "postures" were not included. Aretino makes modern sex authorities look flaccid by comparison. At least six Italian courtesans were so proud of having slept with him that they called themselves Aretines. But he had his detractors, one of whom wrote this mock epitaph on the satirist:

> Here lies the Tuscan poet Aretine
> Who evil spoke of everyone but God,
> Giving as his excuse, "I never knew him."

The original title page of the ribald *Ragionamenti* read in part: "The Dialogues of Nanna and Antonia…composed by the divine Aretino for his pet monkey Capricio…"

By clever politics, such as dedicating poems to powerful people, Aretino managed to stay in favor and dress in "shirts worked with gold," despite his lewd sonnets. Wrote a contemporary of him: "He walks through Rome dressed like a duke. He takes part in all the wild doings of the lords. He pays his way with insults couched in tricked-up words. He talks well and knows every libelous anecdote in the city. The d'Estes and the Gonzagas walk arm in arm with him, and listen to his prattle. He treats them with respect, and is haughty to everyone else. He lives on what they give him. His gifts as a satirist make people afraid of him, and he revels in hearing himself called a cynical, impudent slanderer. All that he needed was a pension. He got one by dedicating to the pope a second-rate poem."

Literary legend has it that Aretino went out as he had lived, laughing so hard at a dirty story his sister told him that he died of apoplexy. Another tale claims that Aretino first regained consciousness to see a priest giving him extreme unction. "Well, now that I'm oiled, protect me from the rats!" were his last words.

∇ ∇ ∇

Arion (fl. 700 B.C.)

The semimythical Greek poet, a pupil of Alcman, is said to have made a great fortune in Italy. On his return the sailors on his ship robbed him and threw him overboard. But they had allowed him to sing a last song before casting him into the sea and a dolphin, charmed by his beautiful song, carried him safely home on its back.

Lodovico Ariosto (1474–1533)

While he labored on *Orlando Furioso*, Ariosto lived in a little house still standing in what is now Ferrara's Via Ariosto. Above the door were inscribed the proud, simple words: "Small but suitable for me, hurtful to no one, not mean, yet acquired by my friends: home."

Only the Duke of Gloucester's famous "Scribble, scribble, scribble…" remark to Edward Gibbon surpasses in obtuseness Cardinal Ippolito d'Este's alleged remark to Ariosto after the author showed him the huge manuscript of *Orlando Furioso*, which Ariosto had spent 26 years writing and polishing. "Where, Messer Lodovico," his patron asked, "have you found so much nonsense?" It is said that Ippolito only had the masterpiece published because he liked its dedication to him.

∇ ∇ ∇

Aristarchus of Samos (fl. 270 B.C.)

Long before Copernicus, this Greek astronomer and author maintained that the earth revolved around the sun, and Copernicus apparently was clearly aware of his theory, although he tried to conceal his knowledge of it. The enemies of Aristarchus, like those of Copernicus, declared that he should be tried for impiety, though he never was.

∇ ∇ ∇

Aristippus (435?–356? B.C.)

The Cyrene philosopher and student of Socrates was a handsome, refined man who felt at home wherever he went. Shipwrecked and destitute in Rhodes, he so charmed the inhabitants that they provided him with all the comforts he needed. "Parents," he observed, "should arm their children with such wealth that even after a shipwreck it should be able to swim to shore with its owner."

None of his works have survived, but there are many anecdotes about Aristippus and his ready wit. When Dionysius I, whom he was trying to win over to his side, spat upon him, he quickly quipped, "A fisherman must put up with more moisture than this to catch an even smaller fish."

On another occasion the philosopher did the spitting. Aristippus despised the ostentatious display of wealth. One time the wealthy Phrygian Simus led him through his ornate marble house. The philosopher spat in his face and when the rich man protested, he replied, "I could not find, amid all this expensive marble, a more suitable place to spit."

A friend reproved Aristippus for living with a courtesan who had slept with many men. "Why not?" he replied. "I have no objection to living in a house, or sailing in a ship, that other men have used before me."

"I am in a family way by you," his mistress told him.

"You can no more tell that it was I," he replied, "than you could tell, after going through a thicket, which thorn had scratched you."

∇ ∇ ∇

Aristotle (384–322 B.C.)

One legend says the immortal Greek philosopher, the pupil of Plato and tutor of Alexander the Great, drowned himself in a channel of water on the island of Euboea in the Aegean when he studied the channel and couldn't explain why its current changed direction some 14 times a day. The phenomenon remains a mystery to scientists.

So far as is known Aristotle's collection of books was the first extensive private library. Just the portion of it that he bought from Plato's successor Speusippus is said to have been worth about $100,000 in today's money. Aristotle's books were passed down from generation to generation until they were finally buried in Asia Minor to prevent their misuse by the Pergamene kings. A century later, damaged by the dampness, they were sold to the philosopher Appellicon of Teos, who repaired them and filled in missing words as best he could. They eventually wound up in Rome.

Aristotle's habit of giving his lectures in the *peripatos*, or walking place, of the Athenian Lyceum gave his school of philosophy the name Peripatetic, which centuries later yielded the English word peripatetic, "walking about or carried on while walking about from place to place."

Aristotle's pupil Hermias, ruler of Atarneus, was put to death by the Persians, dying with these words on his lips, "Tell my friends and companions that I have done nothing unworthy of philosophy." It is said that when Aristotle heard this he not only wrote an ode to Hermias, but also inspired another of his pupils, Alexander the Great, to attack and defeat the Persians and go on to conquer the world.

When asked how much educated men were superior to those who were uneducated, he replied, "As much as the living to the dead."

∇ ∇ ∇

Antoine Arnauld (1612–1694)

One of the French author's associates complained that he was tired. "Tired!" echoed the inexhaustible Arnauld. "Why, you have all of eternity to rest in!"

An adversary complained that the great savant had misunderstood his argument, but the poet and critic Nicolas Boileau-Despréau silenced him with the question, "My dear sir, whom do you expect to understand you if Arnauld does not?"

▽ ▽ ▽

Antonin Artaud (1896–1948)

When *La Nouvelle Revue Française* rejected a batch of his poems in 1923 the French avant-garde poet and theorist rejected the rejection. He wrote back:

> The question of the acceptability of these poems is a problem which concerns you as much as it does me. I am speaking, of course, of their absolute acceptability, of their literary existence. I suffer from a horrible sickness of the mind. My thought abandons me at every level. From the simple fact of thought to the external fact of its materialization in words. Words, shapes of sentences, internal directions of thought, simple reactions of the mind—I am in constant pursuit of my intellectual being. Thus as soon as I can grasp a form, however imperfect, I pin it down, for fear of losing the whole thought. I lower myself, I know, and I suffer from it, but I consent to it for fear of dying altogether...This is why, out of respect for the central feeling which dictates my poems to me and for those strong images or figures of speech which I have been able to find, in spite of everything I propose these poems for existence.

▽ ▽ ▽

King Ashurbanipal (fl. 7th century B.C.)

King Ashurbanipal, possibly the prototype of the semilegendary Sardanapalus of Greek fable, whose name has become a synonym for excessive luxury, is said to have been a poet and great patron of the arts; his library of over 30,000 clay tablets is now in the British Museum. Legend has it that the Assyrian king committed suicide by making his magnificent palace a funeral pyre and leaping into it with all his 15 wives. He left behind the epitaph "Eat, drink and love, the rest's not worth this!" and a longer epitaph for his burial mound in Nineveh:

> I was the king and while I lived on
>   earth,
> And saw the bright rays of the genial sun,
> I ate, and drank, and loved; and knew
>   full well
> The time that men do live on earth was brief
> And liable to many sudden changes,
> Reverses and calamities. Now others
> Will have the enjoyment of luxuries
> Which I do leave behind me. For these
>   reasons,

I have never ceased one single day from
   pleasure.

$$\triangledown \ \triangledown \ \triangledown$$

Athanasius the Great (c. 298–373)

Though it is rarely used anymore in everyday speech, the 18th-century slang *Athanasian wench* for "a forward girl, ready to oblige any man that shall ask her" has an amusing origin. It alludes to the ecumenical Athanasian Creed, which, although he did not author it, takes its name from St. Athanasius, or Athanasius the Great, an exiled third-century Alexandrian bishop and author who was a pioneer in scientific theology. The English Book of Common Prayer includes the Athanasian Creed, and the term Athanasian wench arose when some wit pointed out that the familiar first words of the creed read *quicumque vult*, "Whosoever desires…"

$$\triangledown \ \triangledown \ \triangledown$$

Farid ud-Din Attar (1119–1229)

"The Pearl of Religion," as the Persian poet was called, was a prolific writer who penned more than 120,000 couplets over his career. He loved to write, but he stopped writing altogether in his later years because he became so ascetic in his religious beliefs that he refused to let himself enjoy the pleasures of poetical composition. He lived to the age of 110.

$$\triangledown \ \triangledown \ \triangledown$$

Titus Pomponius Atticus (109–32 B.C.)

The rich Roman aristocrat was also an author and publisher who kept a large staff of slaves trained in copying and binding manuscripts. Atticus served as Cicero's publisher and advised him on both literary and personal matters. He was stricken with an incurable illness in his 77th year and starved himself to death.

$$\triangledown \ \triangledown \ \triangledown$$

Giovanni Augurelli (1441–1524)

When the Italian poet dedicated a rhyming treatise called *Chrysopoeia*, or the art of making gold by alchemy, to Pope Leo X, he hoped for a handsome gift in return. But the witty Leo sent him an empty purse.

$$\triangledown \ \triangledown \ \triangledown$$

Augustus (Gaius Julius Caesar Octavianus (63 B.C.–14 A.D.)

The first Roman emperor was a man of letters and an author, writing a 13-book autobiography, among other works, and originating the saying "to pay on the Greek kalends" (to never pay). He was very generous to poets and as a result swarms of them surrounded him whenever he left the palace. One Greek poet pressed poems upon him day after day, until even Augustus's patience wore thin and he decided not to reward the man with money. Instead, he stopped in the street, composed a poem of his own and gave it to the poet. The witty Greek, however, handed the emperor a few denarii and said he wished it could be much more. Augustus gave him 100,000 sesterces.

For his last words, before he embraced his wife Livia and died, Augustus chose a phrase often used at the conclusion of Roman comedies: "Since well I've played my part, clap now your hands, and with applause dismiss me from the stage."

∇ ∇ ∇

Decimus Magnus Ausonius (c. 310–400)
This talented poet of Gaul's Silver Age and his young wife lost their first child at a tragically early age and he never forgot the sad loss. When an old man, Ausonius touchingly commemorated the child: "I will not leave you unwept, my first-born child, called by my name. Just as you were practicing to change your babbling into the first words of childhood…we had to mourn your death. You lie on your great-grandfather's bosom, sharing his grave."

∇ ∇ ∇

Marcel Aymé (1902–1967)
The French novelist and dramatist told a reporter that he felt perfectly free in this world, but for one exception: "From time to time I find myself terribly limited by the dictionary."

∇ ∇ ∇

Marchese Massimo Taparelli d'Azeglio (1798–1866)
A novelist and pamphleteer before he became a statesman, d'Azeglio, whose aristocratic Italian family hated his artistic endeavors, took as his second wife Luisa Blondel, a vain, headstrong woman from whom he separated. As he lay dying, however, Luisa hurried to his deathbed. "Ah, Luisa," he told her, "you are always arriving just as I am leaving."

∇ ∇ ∇ ∇ ∇ ∇ ∇ ∇ ∇

Babur (Zahir ud-Din Muhammad; 1483–1530)
This ruler of the Mogul dynasty, a descendant of Tamerlane, won great military victories that laid the foundations for the Mogul Empire in India. Also a noted

poet and man of letters, he warred and wrote poetry from the time he assumed the throne at 14. All five of his children were accomplished poets and all the later rulers of the Mogul dynasty also excelled as poets, more so than perhaps any royal family in history.

∇ ∇ ∇

Hermann Bahr (1863–1934)
The Austrian dramatist was asked to criticize the work of a young playwright. Just tell me the truth, the aspiring author wrote him: "Words of criticism from a source so judicious would make me feel ennobled."

"I'd like to make you at least an archduke," Bahr scribbled on the manuscript.

∇ ∇ ∇

Bakin (1767–1848)
The Japanese author probably holds the record for the longest novel with his 106-volume *Hakkenden* (*The Tale of Eight Dogs*). The popular author wrote more than 200 other novels as well.

∇ ∇ ∇

Mikhail Bakunin (1814–1876)
His colleague Nechaieff grew bitter about Russia's leading anarchist, the progenitor of Nihilism. "For him," Nechaieff said of Bakunin, "truth, mutual confidence, real strict solidarity only exist between a dozen individuals who form the *sanctum sanctorum* of the society. All the rest are to serve as blind instruments…they are conspiracy-fodder…In the name of the cause it is his duty to gain possession of your whole person without your knowledge…If your friend has a wife or a daughter, he will manage to seduce her and give her a baby in order to force her to break away from official morality and into a revolutionary protest against society."

∇ ∇ ∇

Honoré de Balzac (1799–1850)
Honoré de Balzac assumed the particle in his name only after 1830. Before that he called himself merely Balzac. His fascination with the aristocracy can be seen even in one of his early pseudonyms—Lord R'hoone, an anagram of Honoré—and he may have adopted the "de" to associate himself with the aristocratic French author Jean-Louis Guez de Balzac (1594–1654). Actually Balzac had no known aristocratic forebears. In fact, though it was probably unknown to him, his name wasn't even Balzac. His true name, before his father changed it, was

Balssa; his family for more than a century before his birth had been day laborers and very small peasant proprietors.

Balzac had great ambitions from the beginning. In 1819 after he quit his law clerk job to begin his career as a writer, he wrote under a picture of Napoleon: "What Napoleon could not do with the sword, I shall accomplish with the pen."

In his beginning years as a writer Balzac lived in an empty unheated garret, but he furnished it with his imagination. On one wall he wrote "Rosewood paneling with commode," and on another "Gobelin tapestry with Venetian mirror." In the center of the small room over the fireplace was the inscription "Picture by Raphael." (See also *IKKU*.)

He summed up his religious belief in an 1837 letter to Madame Hanska: "I believe in the incomprehensibility of God."

He contracted with French publisher Urbain Canel for *Les Chouans*, the first work to appear under his own name. Canel spent months trying to get him to deliver the manuscript, so anxious was the author to have it perfect.

Balzac thought he had a surefire publicity stunt for his play *Les Ressources* (1842). On opening night he spread a rumor that tickets were scarce, hoping to create a stampede to the box office. But the rumor backfired when most people on their way to the play heard it and turned back home, thinking it would be hopeless to get tickets.

Of authors who consistently burned the midnight oil, Balzac is perhaps the best example. Like Pliny the Elder before him, Balzac liked to begin work at midnight and write for 18 hours at a stretch. He did this for weeks on end and was so meticulous a craftsman that he several times completely rewrote his novels in proof. Often, he kept himself awake by drinking 50 cups of coffee a night, and he was so poor while writing the *Comédie Humaine* that he had to lock himself up in a secret writing room to hide from creditors.

The caffiene-loaded sludge-like coffee he drank stimulated his mind, he claimed; after he drank it ideas "pour out like the regiments of the Grand Army over the battlefield, and the battle begins. Memories come charging in with flags flying: the light cavalry of comparisons extends itself in a magnificent gallop; the artillery of logic hurries along with its ammunition train, and flashes of wit bob up like sharpshooters."

It's said that Balzac awoke one night to find a thief ransacking his desk and began laughing uncontrollably. "What are you laughing at?" the startled thief asked. "I am laughing," Balzac replied, "to think what pains and risks you are taking in the hope of finding money by night in a desk where the lawful owner can never find any by day."

The German naturalist and author Alexander von Humboldt (1769–1859), for whom the Humboldt Current is named, asked a French doctor friend who specialized in mental disorders to let him observe a lunatic at close quarters. The doctor arranged for them to dine with two men: one well-dressed and quiet, the other a wild-haired, flamboyantly dressed man who incessantly talked and gestured as he ate. Toward the meal's end, Humboldt nodded toward the frenetic man and whispered to his friend, "I like your lunatic, he amuses me." His host replied, "But the other one is the lunatic. The man you're looking at is Monsieur Honoré de Balzac."

Charlie Chaplin wrote in his autobiography: "Like Balzac, who believed that a night of sex meant the loss of a good page of his novel, so I believe that it meant the loss of a good day's work at the studio." Chaplin was right about Balzac, though Balzac may not have been right about sex and writing, but Balzac did believe that the two acts of love were incompatible and that his writing prowess depended on how much sperm he retained in his body while writing. He once "suffered" an uncontrollable nocturnal emission and claimed that it cost him a masterpiece the following day. One story has it that after one of his rare visits to a brothel Balzac could be heard muttering when he left: "Ah, j'ai perdu un livre! J'ai perdu un livre!" ("I've lost a book!")

Balzac kept Evelina Hanska as his mistress for 17 years before he finally married her in 1850. "It is easier," he observed after a month or so of marriage, "to be a lover than a husband, for the same reason that it is more difficult to show a ready wit all day than to produce an occasional *bon mot*."

Unfamiliar with the language and currency on his first visit to Vienna, Balzac could not understand the local cab drivers and never knew how much fare to pay. So each time he reached a destination he handed his driver a single coin. If the man's hand remained outstretched, he added another coin. Adding one coin after another, he kept his eyes on the driver's face. As soon as a smile appeared there, Balzac knew he'd given one coin too many, took back his last coin and left the cab.

No novelist ever contemplated such a giant fictional scheme as Balzac's *Comédie Humaine*. Balzac planned to write 137 works forming a grand design that would authentically depict French life from the late 18th through the first half of the 19th centuries. Commonly working 16 hours a day from 1827 to 1847, he managed to complete 97 of these novels, peopled by more than 2,000 characters, before death ended his efforts. At least a dozen of these books are masterpieces and earned Balzac the reputation of the greatest of novelists.

Many novels have been written in less time, but Balzac's masterpiece *Le Père Goriot* (1834) is probably the best of all rapidly written books. Balzac wrote the well-constructed novel in just 40 days, working 24 hours a day most of the time. He was so rundown mentally and physically at the end of his labors, and poisoned by coffee, that his doctor ordered a complete rest. However, he soon went back to his old ways. In fact, his novel *Le Secret des Ruggieri* (1836) is traditionally said to have been written in a single night, though this seems unlikely.

Life seemed to be all work. He wrote in a letter to a friend:

> I must tell you that I am submerged in excessive labour. The mechanics of my life have altered. I go to bed at six or seven in the evening, like the hens. I am awakened at one o'clock in the morning and work till eight. At eight I sleep for an hour and a half. Then I have something light to eat, and a cup of black coffee, and harness my wagon until four. I receive callers, I take a bath or go out, and after dinner I go back to bed. I have to live like this for months on end if I am not to be overwhelmed by my obligations. The profits accrue slowly; the debts are inexorable and fixed. It is now certain that I shall make a great fortune; but I need to go on writing and working for another three years.

He was never properly recognized by the literary establishment in his country. Often taking steps to become a member of the French Academy, Balzac usually withdrew his name when it became apparent that he had no chance of being elected. On the one occasion that he did actually stand for election, in 1849, he obtained only two votes.

Few literary characters, even Gargantua or Trimalchio, ate more within books than Balzac did in real life. A typical meal for the French novelist consisted of a hundred oysters for starters, twelve lamb cutlets; a duckling with turnips, two roast partridges; sole à la Normande; various fruits; and wines, coffee and liqueurs to wash it all down. Thackeray, who died of overeating, never consumed as much at one sitting.

$$\nabla \ \nabla \ \nabla$$

Mahmud Abdu'l-Baqi (1526–1600)
Such was the Turkish lyric poet's great fame in his time that his country's ruler, Sultan Suleiman the Magnificent, wrote a poem praising the excellence of his verses (an almost unimaginable idea today).

Barbad (fl. c. 600)

Persian king Khosru Parvez ("Victorious") loved song almost as much as his 3,000 wives. Tradition holds that at his command his favorite poet and singer Barbad composed 360 songs, singing one each night to his sovereign for a full (Persian) year. Despite Barbad, however, Khosru did not end his life so happily. When his generals revolted against him, 18 of his sons were killed before his eyes and another son was forced to kill him.

∇ ∇ ∇

Chand Bardai (fl. c. 1200 A.D.)

The Hindu poet's *Prithiraj Rasau*, a poem written in ballad form chronicling his sovereign's deeds, contains over 100,000 stanzas. Parts of it are still sung today, and it remains a valuable history of northwestern India.

∇ ∇ ∇

Giusseppe Baretti (1719–1789)

A member of Dr. Johnson's circle in England, the Italian critic stabbed and killed a man who attacked him in the street. He was acquitted on the grounds of self-defense after Dr. Johnson testified as a character witness at his 1769 trial. Several years later, however, the irascible Baretti broke with his friend Johnson when they quarreled over a move in a chess game.

∇ ∇ ∇

Joa de Barvios (1496–1570)

This Portuguese writer wrote a history of Asia for the king of Portugal. He wasn't in a position to dicker with his monarch when it came to payment and had to accept an unusual arrangement. The king gave him 130,000 acres of land in Brazil for his fee— doubtless the most land ever paid to a writer for his work.

∇ ∇ ∇

Charles Baudelaire (1821–1867)

Convinced that he was cursed to be unhappy from the day of his birth, Baudelaire often pointed out, only half jokingly, that he had been born at 13 Rue Hautefeuille in Paris. However, in the life of this poet, who shared a mother-son relationship probably as morbid as any in literary history, there stands one often overlooked fact that much better explains his temperament: Baudelaire believed that his father was a priest and once confided that he had seen him wearing a cassock. Recent research indicates that this was apparently no figment of the poet's imagination, as many critics have believed. It seems certain that François Baudelaire was a Roman Catholic priest who had renounced his office in 1793.

Though this was years before Baudelaire's birth, the poet perhaps believed, as many people did in his day, that the civil act permitting his father to shed his robes did not release him from the holy vow of celibacy he had taken and therefore his son was living proof of his sacrilege, "an offense in the eyes of God," as one biographer put it.

One of the most persistent stories about Baudelaire's strange relationship with his mother has him, as a boy of seven, locking his mother alone in her bedroom on the night she wed his stepfather and throwing away the key. Though he deeply resented the marriage, the story is untrue—his mother and stepfather had left Paris without their young son immediately after their marriage ceremony.

Baudelaire was expelled from school as a youth of 18 when caught receiving a note passed by a classmate. When the teacher demanded that he reveal the contents of the note, Baudelaire ripped it into little pieces which he swallowed. He later broke into hysterical laughter when the principal told him that by keeping silent he was placing the worst possible construction on the affair, and was expelled. There is absolutely no proof for the old tale that he and the boy were carrying on an amorous affair.

Strange as it may seem, Baudelaire at 20 was a dandy as well as a bohemian, "with the whole theory of elegance at his fingernails," as a contemporary put it. The poet went through an inherited fortune living the high life in Paris. According to a friend: "Every fold in his jacket was the subject of earnest study…The dress coat, so gracefully and graciously cut, its lapels constantly fingered by the carefully manicured hand; the beautifully knotted cravat; the long waistcoat, fastened very high by the top button of the twelve and negligently gaping lower down to reveal a fine white shirt with pleated cuffs, and the corkscrew trousers fitting into a pair of immaculately polished shoes…the thin cane with a little gold top…" Baudelaire played the romantic dandy or Beau Brummel for almost seven years, and during this time he even designed all his own clothes.

Baudelaire told a friend about his first publication: "On the day when a young writer corrects his first proofsheet he is as proud as a young schoolboy who has just gotten his first dose of the pox."

As his favorite French word the poet chose *hemorroïdes* (hemorrhoids).

Baudelaire's *Les Fleurs du Mal* (*Flowers of Evil*) was prosecuted by the French government when published in 1857, mainly, it was rumored, because the government wished to win its case to avenge the action it had lost against

Flaubert's *Madame Bovary*. In any case, the government did win the case, and six of the 13 poems were ordered removed from all future editions on the grounds that they were "indecent" (they were not published in France for almost 150 years). As for Baudelaire, he acted at the end of the affair as he had at the beginning. At that time, he was seen walking the streets of Paris dressed in funereal black clothes and was asked if he wore his black suit in honor of a friend who had died the day before. "I am in mourning for *Les Fleurs du Mal*," he replied; "it was seized yesterday evening at five o'clock."

Les Fleurs du Mal probably received the most uniformly vicious reviews of any book written in the 19th century. Wrote a reviewer in *Le Figaro*: "All of these coldly displayed charnelhouse horrors, these abysses of filth into which both hands are plunged to the elbows, should rot in a drawer." Wrote another critic in the same pages: "There are times when one doubts Monsieur Baudelaire's sanity: there are times when there is no longer any doubt...the odious is cheek by jowl with the ignoble—and the repulsive joins the disgusting. You have never seen so many bosoms being bitten, chewed even, in so few pages; never has there been such a procession of demons, fetuses, devils, cats and vermin. The book is a hospital open to all forms of mental derangements and emotional putrefactions..."

Baudelaire originally chose the title *Les Limbes* for *Les Fleurs du Mal*, possibly feeling that the hopeless longing or desperation described in the original 11 poems suggested Dante's Limbo on the outskirts of hell. The critic Hippolyte Babou suggested the title *Les Fleurs du Mal* while Baudelaire and his friends were drinking at a café one night, this title indicating not only that the poems were a blossoming of evil, but that the artistry of the poems turned evil into beauty.

He earned an average of about 600 francs a year over his 25 years of literary labors. Toward the end of his life he fled to Brussels, where he would be safe from his creditors. There he stayed, unable to leave for a long time because he couldn't pay his hotel bill. He wrote in his sparsely furnished room, where he had no way to tell the time because he had pawned his watch; but at least he was provided with the companionship of the most unusual of literary pets. Baudelaire had captured a bat in a nearby graveyard and kept it in a cage on his desk, feeding it milk and bread.

When he was only 20 and keeping company with a woman called Squint-eyed Sara, who possibly infected him with a venereal disease, Baudelaire, who would die of syphilis, composed and quoted to his friends a cynical epitaph he had composed for his own gravestone:

Here lieth one whose weakness for loose ladies
Cut him off young and sent him down to Hades.

Baudelaire had tried to kill himself at the age of 24, leaving a note that read in part, "I kill myself without unhappiness…" He died, as a result of syphilis, in his mother's arms. Mme. Aupick recalled that he died while she murmured endearments to him, "a smile on his lips." By a stroke of irony he was laid to rest next to his hated stepfather in the Cimetière Montparnasse, where Mme. Aupick joined them four years later.

∇ ∇ ∇

Vissarion Grigoryevich Belinsky (1810—1848)
Ideas were the sustenance of the Russian literary critic. One time he and his guest Turgenev vehemently discussed God, social injustice and the future of the world for hours, even after dinner awaited them for some time on the table. The novelist, famished, couldn't conceal his desire to get at the food and Belinsky soon noticed this. "Here we haven't even settled the question of the existence of God," he bellowed, "and you think about eating!"

∇ ∇ ∇

Bellincione (fl. 1480)
The Tuscan poet was so bitterly and constantly argumentative that when he died a rival poet wrote an inscription for his tomb, warning any passerby to walk softly—so that the corpse wouldn't rise up and bite him.

∇ ∇ ∇

Karl Mikael Bellman (1740–1795)
This impoverished Swedish poet would sit in a Stockholm tavern with his friends and suddenly announce the muse was about to visit him. Leaning back he would take his zither, close his eyes, and improvise the words and music to long Bacchic odes in praise of love or wine. It is said that much of his best poetry was so written.

"The Anacreon of the North," as Sweden's Gustavus III called him, was thrown into prison for debt and developed the consumption that killed him far too young. Even knowing that he would soon die of consumption, "the last of the troubadours" could not be stopped from visiting his favorite tavern, where he drank and sang his songs until he went hoarse. He died soon after.

Pietro Bembo (1470–1547)

The great Italian stylist wrote a letter to a friend telling of the death of his lover and mother of his three children: "I have lost the dearest heart in the world, a heart which tenderly watched over my life—which loved it and sustained it neglectful of its own; a heart so much the master of itself, so disdainful of vain embellishments and adornments of silk and gold, of jewels and treasures of price, that it was content with the single and (so she assured me) supreme joy of the love I bore it…[Her dying words were:] 'I commend our children to you, and beseech you to have care of them, both for my sake and yours. Be sure they are your own, for I have never deceived you; that is why I take Our Lord's body just now with a soul at peace.' Then, after a long pause she added, 'Rest with God,' and a few moments afterward closed her eyes forever, those eyes that had been the clear-shining faithful stars of my weary pilgrimage through life."

Style was more important to Bembo than anything in life. "It is far better to speak like Cicero," he wrote to a friend, "than to be pope."

∇ ∇ ∇

Pierre-Jean de Béranger (1780–1857)

Béranger's satirical songs against Napoleon and other authorities cost him his university teaching post and two long imprisonments, but he refused to compromise. So popular was his work that many of his songs were circulated in manuscript copies throughout France when they could not be printed; in fact, he is said to be the only poet of modern times who could altogether have dispensed with printing. When he died the streets of Paris were lined with mourners, the cry often rising: "Honneur, honneur à Béranger!"

∇ ∇ ∇

Tristan Bernard (1866–1947)

The French author got his start as a newspaper and magazine writer turning out sketches and stories. He once won a newspaper contest for the best answer to the question, "If a fire broke out in the Louvre and you could save only one painting, which one would it be?" His answer: "The one nearest the exit."
Bernard wrote what is the world's shortest play with dialogue. Following is the complete text of *The Exile*:

Exile: Whoever you are, have pity on a hunted man. There is a price on my head.
Mountaineer: How much?

Like many writers, Bernard did not care to write— despite his tremendous output, which included vaudevilles, satires, comedies, stories and novels—and he put off writing whenever he could find an excuse. As a standard reply when someone suggested visiting him, he would say: "Please do. And preferably in the morning. That's when I work."

∇ ∇ ∇

Sarah Bernhardt (1844–1923)

The immortal actress, who acted for the great part of her stage career with a wooden leg, died in 1923, aged 79, but had prepared herself for death long before then. During her adolescence, Sarah had conquered a morbid fear of death by persuading her mother to buy her a silk-lined rosewood coffin, which she kept in her bedroom for the rest of her life and often slept in, she said, "to get used to her final resting-place."

Sarah Bernhardt never lost her sense of humor, not even after her leg was amputated. When the boorish manager of the San Francisco Pan-American Exposition wired, offering her $100,000 to exhibit her leg at the exposition, she cabled back, "Which leg?"

Playing Cleopatra, she stabbed the slave who brought news of Anthony's defeat at Actium, storming, raving and wrecking scenery before dropping in a heap on the stage. Soon after a middle-aged British matron remarked to her companion: "How different, how very different from the home life of our own dear Queen [Victoria]."

When a reporter asked her where she and the man she had been living with had been married (they hadn't been), Sarah punned, "Naturellement, à l'autel." The words mean "Naturally, at the altar," but the same pronunciation means, "Naturally, at the hotel."

One tradition has it that "break a leg!" means "good luck" in theatrical circles because the Divine Sarah "had but one good leg and it would be good luck to be like her." There is no proof for this, but neither is there proof for any other theory about the origins of the phrase.

Francesco Berni (1497–1536)
Byron imitated this Italian author's facetious burlesque style in *Don Juan*. The wittiest of a club of Roman literary men who, as an English critic later put it, "devoted themselves to light and sparkling effusions," Berni's name, in the form of *poesie bernesca* or Bernesque poetry, became a synonym for seriocomic poetry. The poet was poisoned by Duke Alessandro de' Medici when he refused to poison the duke's cousin. He had not yet turned 39.

∇ ∇ ∇

Hayyim Nahman Bialik (1873–1934)
The Russian-born Bialik (or Byalik) has been called the greatest Hebrew poet of modern times, but he ceased to write during World War I. Poets weren't needed, he contended, and Jews should learn to face the harsh realities of life. He soon established a publishing firm in Tel Aviv, writing no more poems.

∇ ∇ ∇

The Bible
Anonymous printers have made disastrous mistakes in various Bibles printed over the years. Here are seven of the most outrageous:

• The Sin On Bible, printed in 1716: *John 5:14* contains the printer's error "sin on more," instead of "sin no more."

• The Bug Bible, 1535, reads: "Thou shalt not nede to be afrayed for eny bugges [instead of 'terror'] by night" in *Psalm 91:5*.

• The Fool Bible, printed in the reign of Charles I, reads: "The fool hath said in his heart there is a God" in *Psalm 14*; for this mistake the printers were fined 3,000 pounds.

• The Idle Bible, 1809: The "idole shepherd" (*Zechariah 11:17*) is printed "the idle shepherd."

• The Large Family Bible, 1820, *Isaiah 66:9* reads: "Shall I bring to the birth and not cease [instead of 'cause'] to bring forth."

• The Unrighteous Bible, 1653, *I Corinthians 6:9* reads: "Know ye not that the unrighteous shall inherit [for 'shall not inherit'] the Kingdom of God."

• The Wicked Bible, 1632: The word *not* in the seventh commandment is omitted, making it read: "Thou shalt commit adultery."

∇ ∇ ∇

Bilhana (fl. 11th century A.D.)
Bilhana, born in Kashmir, served his king as court poet. Romantic legend has it that he fell in love with the king's daughter, had a secret affair with her, and was condemned to death when her father discovered them. While in prison awaiting death he wrote and recited a series of quatrains, each beginning with the words

"even now," to evoke the princess's presence. The king chanced to overhear these verses (which survive today) and granted him his life and his true love.

∇ ∇ ∇

Bion (fl. 3rd century B.C.)

The slave of a Greek rhetorician, who recognized his genius and not only freed him but made him his heir, Bion wrote many satires and was famous as a prolific literary wit at the court of Antigonus Gonatas. He also had abundant wit under pressure. When a sudden storm frightened the wicked crew on a ship he was sailing, the dissolute sailors fell down on their knees and waved their arms, praying for the gods to save them. "Keep quiet," Bion advised them. "Better for the gods *not* to see you."

∇ ∇ ∇

Birbal (fl. 1600)

Few if any generals have come from the ranks of poets like the Hindu poet Birbal. Birbal was the court poet of the great Mogul ruler Akbar, who liked him so much that he made him a general and paid him a gold piece worth 16 rupees for each couplet of the 700 couplet *Sat-sei* that he wrote. Birbal, however, proved a dismal failure as a soldier, making a mess of his last campaign and being slaughtered by the enemy as he tried to flee the battlefield. One of his Muslim enemies at court wrote with pleasure: "Birbal, who had fled from fear of his life, was slain, and entered the row of dogs in Hell."

∇ ∇ ∇

Blondel de Nesle (fl. late 12th century)

Legend says that the French troubadour, attendant and friend of England's Richard the Lionhearted, discovered that Richard was imprisoned in the castle of Durrenstein by singing beneath the tower window a song he and Richard had composed. When Richard Coeur de Lion responded midway through the song and sang the remainder of the lyrics, Blondel knew he had found him and returned to England with the news.

∇ ∇ ∇

Giovanni Boccaccio (1313–1375)

Though his *Decameron* became one of the most famous books in all literature, the Italian author always regretted that he wrote prose and not poetry. He felt that this was because his father had forced him to waste six years as an apprentice to a merchant at a time when he should have ben studying poetical techniques. "If my father had dealt wisely with me," he said in bitterly reproaching him, "I might have been among the great poets."

He was bitter too about being born out of wedlock to a French mother known to history only as Jeanne and for whom he was named. Following his birth in Paris his banker father took him back to Florence and married a local woman who paid little attention to him once she gave birth to a child of her own.

Like Petrarch (q.v.) with his Laura, Boccaccio first caught sight of the woman who was to profoundly influence all his work while he attended church one morning. This was Maria d'Aquino, a young married woman and the illegitimate daughter of King Robert. Boccaccio would immortalize her under the name Fiammetta, but after he gave himself to her she betrayed him. Many of his future works were written, as he put it in a letter to her, "thinking of past joy in present misery."

Late in life Boccaccio turned from creative writing and became a scholar. It is said that the Western world owes the restoration of Homer to him because he hired a Greek named Leon Pilatus to translate Homer's work into Italian. Boccaccio saw to it that Pilatus was given a Chair of Greek at the University of Florence and took the man into his house, gallantly putting up with his barbarous, repellent manners and ferocious temper until the translation was finished.

His last years were so impoverished that his friends had to help him. Poverty hastened his end, and a quack doctor ensured it. Yet it is said that the last thing he wrote, his swan song, was a letter full of love for his friend Petrarch and concern about the poet's work.

∇ ∇ ∇

Jehan Bodel (d. c. 1210)

Little is known about this French author of one of the first miracle plays. Apparently he was about to embark on a crusade to the Holy Land when he was stricken by leprosy. He wrote a touching last poem to his friends and entered a leper hospital, where he died at an early age.

∇ ∇ ∇

Hermann Boerhaave (1668–1738)

When the Dutch physician died, he left among his effects one sealed copy of his self-published book entitled *The Onliest and Deepest Secrets of the Medical Art*. The book was sold for the equivalent of an unheard of $20,000 at auction, and when the eager buyer opened it, he found that all of the pages except the title page were blank. Written in hand on the title page was the advice: "Keep your head cool, your feet warm, and you'll make the best doctor poor."

∇ ∇ ∇

Anicius Manlius Severinus Boethius (475?–524?)

Roman King Theodoric sentenced the author to death for treason, though Boethius denied the charges. While in prison Boethius wrote his famous medical book, *De Consolatione Philosophiae,* accepting his fate stoically. His death was a horrible one, however. His executioners tighened a cord around his head until his eyes burst from their sockets; they then beat him to death with clubs.

∇ ∇ ∇

Nicholas Boileau-Despréaux (1636–1711)

France's most diplomatic critic was surely the poet Nicholas Boileau-Despréaux. One time the court poet criticized a sonnet written by France's Louis XIV. "Sire," Boileau said, "nothing is impossible for Your Majesty. You set out to write some bad verses and you have succeeded."

In October 1677 Louis XIV told Boileau and Racine that he had narrowly missed being hit by a cannonball. "Sire," Boileau-Despréaux said, "as your Historians Royal, we beg you not to finish our history so soon."

Boileau-Despréaux once introduced a starving poet to a prospective patron, saying: "Sir, I present to you a person who will give you immortality; but you must give him something to live upon in the meantime."

As his last words the arbiter of good taste said: "It is a great consolation to a poet on the point of death that he has never written a line injurious to good morals."

∇ ∇ ∇

François Le Métel de Boisrobert (1592–1662)

Work by the Académie Française on the great *Dictionary* progressed so slowly that the poet wrote:

> Six months they've been engaged on F;
> Oh, that my fate would guarantee
> That I should keep alive till G.

Count Joseph Boruwalski (fl. early 19th century)

Spoonerisms, the transposing of sounds at the beginnings of words (for example, "It is customary to kiss the bride" becomes "It is kisstomary to cuss the bride"), were first called marrowskis, a word said to derive from the name of Polish Count Joseph Boruwalski, a writer who suffered the same affliction as the more famous Reverend W. A. Spooner, an English professor. The word is first recorded in 1863, and soon after intentional marrowskis became the basis for a kind of slang called marrowski language. Metathesis, the process of transposing letters or sounds, is responsible for a number of English words, including *dirt*, which was earlier *drit*.

∇ ∇ ∇

Georg Bose (fl. 1742)

A professor at the university of Leipzig and writer on scientific subjects, Bose was a practical joker. He was also one of the first to experiment with electricity. One time he introduced his dinner guests to an attractive woman who had been charged with electricity but whose shoes insulated her from the floor. Bose invited his unknowing guests to kiss the young woman. Those who did so received shocks that in his words almost "knocked their teeth out."

∇ ∇ ∇

Stanislas Jean de Boufflers (1738–1815)

The French statesman and man of letters was an idol of the Parisian salons. But he was a paradoxical man, his character best summed up by Antoine de Rivaral, who called him "Abbé libertin, militaire philosophe, diplomate chansonnier, émigré patriote, républicain courtisan (Libertine priest, military philosopher, diplomat songwriter, patriotic emigrant, republican courtier)."

∇ ∇ ∇

Dominique Bouhours (fl. 18th century)

Bouhours, a French grammarian, uttered as his last words on earth: "I am about to—or I am going to—die. Either expression is used."

∇ ∇ ∇

Tycho Brahe (1546–1601)

Brahe, the most prominent astronomer of the late 16th century, built his own castle observatory on the island of Ven. The Danish astronomer and author was as noted in his lifetime for his nose as for his astronomical discoveries. He had lost his nose in a duel and wore a golden one attached to his face with glue.

Louis Braille (1810–1852)

When only three years old Louis Braille was blinded by an awl driven into his eye while he was playing in his father's leather-working shop. Total blindness extended to both eyes, but young Louis attended the village school in Coupvray outside of Paris, where he learned his alphabet by feeling twigs in the shape of letters, and then the *Institution Nationale des Jeunes Aveugles*, where he learned to read from three huge 400-pound books engraved with large embossed letters. This last method had been invented by Valentin Hauy, Father and Apostle of the Blind, the institute's founder, but it could not be easily written by the blind and was thus inadequate. At about the time that Louis Braille was made a junior instructor at the institute, French army officer Captain Charles Barbier introduced his "night writing," a system of 12 raised dots and dashes that fingers could "read," enabling brief orders—like one dot for advance, or two dots for retreat—to be written with a simple instrument and understood in total darkness. Barbier demonstrated his invention at the institute and it fired young Braille's imagination. When only 15 he began work on the improved system that bears his name. Louis Braille, highly regarded as an organist and composer in his own right, also invented a braille musical notation, but braille was not officially adopted at the institute where he taught until 1854, two years after his death. Tradition has it that a blind organist performing at a fashionable salon told her audience that she owed everything to Louis Braille, who had died young and unheralded of tuberculosis, and that her touching story finally led to universal recognition of his system.

∇ ∇ ∇

Georg Morris Brandes (George Morris Cohen; 1842–1927)

The Danish literary critic and historian made so many enemies with his revolutionary activities and slashing pen that he carried a pistol at all times to protect himself from their retaliation.

∇ ∇ ∇

Georges Braque (1882–1963)

Braque was asked if the avant-garde poet Guillaume Apollinaire did not sometimes write "Cubist poetry" due to his close association with the cubists. He replied: "I suppose that when he printed his poems in the shape of guitars and other objects that we used to use in our canvases, that could be called Cubist poetry." The French artist replied, "though personally I should prefer to call it Cubist typography!"

Bertolt Brecht (1898–1956)

The German dramatist and poet is said to have created the role of the dumb girl in his *Mother Courage* for his wife, Helene Weigel, solely because the play was first performed in Sweden and she didn't speak Swedish.

∇ ∇ ∇

Clarin de Breujère (early 20th century)

A madwoman who wrote *Sordid Amok*! (1901), an incoherent chronicle of six months in a Paris insane asylum, the French author designed her own coat-of-arms, on which she emblazoned her motto: "My Rights or I Bite," which, strangely enough, no writer has adapted and displayed to his publisher since.

∇ ∇ ∇

Anthelme Brillat-Savarin (1755–1826)

Anthelme Brillat-Savarin's classic *Physiologie du Goût* (*Physiology of Taste*), still in print today, had to be published at the author's expense in 1825, after he had spent 30 years writing it. And when Brillat-Savarin's brother later sold the rights to a publisher, he got only $120—after throwing in a genuine Stradivarius as well! As for the great gourmet, appropriately enough born in the town of Belley, he frequently had to support his food-oriented life (he was admittedly something of an eccentric, often carrying around dead birds in his pocket until they became "high" enough for cooking) by scrounging from his relatives and writing pornographic novels. *Brillat* was actually Anthelme's real name—he took on the hyphen and *Savarin* when his great-aunt left him her entire fortune on the condition that he add her name to his.

Love of food seemed to run in the Brillat family. Anthelme's youngest sister, Pierrette, for instance, died at the dinner table. She was almost 100 years old and her last words are among the most unusual in history: "And now, girl, bring me the dessert."

∇ ∇ ∇

Herman Broch (1886–1951)

The Austrian author, 40 years old and a prosperous textile factory director, was being driven to work in Vienna one morning when he felt a sudden compulsion to tell his chauffeur to stop and take him back home. Though he had never considered quitting work before, Broch never returned to the factory again, but devoted the rest of his life to writing.

Giordano Bruno (1548–1600)

"Bruno the Nolan [from the town of Nola], Graduate of the Academy, called the Nuisance," the Italian philosopher signed one of his plays. Convicted of heresy by the Inquisition, "The Nuisance" was stripped naked, bound to a stake over a pyre, his tongue tied so that he could make no speeches, and burned alive before a huge crowd.

∇ ∇ ∇

Comte de Buffon, Georges-Louis Leclerc (1707–1788)

The great French naturalist argued with Thomas Jefferson about the appearance of the North American moose. To settle the argument Jefferson had a moose killed in New Hampshire and its skeleton shipped whole to France. On seeing the specimen, Buffon was quick to admit he had been wrong. "I should have consulted you, Monsieur," he told Jefferson, "before publishing my book on natural history, and then I should have been sure of my facts."

∇ ∇ ∇

Luis Buñuel (1900-1983)

Asked if he had changed his views on religion, the Spanish author and film director replied, "I am an atheist still, thank God."

∇ ∇ ∇

By A Lady

Strange as it may seem this is the world's commonest pseudonym or anonym. There are about 1,000 literary works in English alone of which the author is identified as "By A Lady."

∇ ∇ ∇ ∇ ∇ ∇ ∇ ∇

Guilhen da Cabestan (fl. 13th century)

This Provençal troubadour suffered an end similar to the tale of King Tereus in Greek mythology, who was served the flesh of his son by his vengeful wife, Procne. According to one story, Cabestan was killed by a jealous husband, who had the poet's heart cooked as a delicacy and served to his unfaithful wife. After his wife finished her meal the husband informed her that she had eaten the heart of her lover and she threw herself out the window to her death.

Gaius Julius Caesar (102–44 B.C.)

The first of the Caesars, a writer of great lucidity as his Gallic War *Commentaries* proves, wasn't brought into the world by the Caesarean section operation named in his honor, as is popularly believed. Caesar probably wasn't extracted from his mother's womb by the sectioning, or cutting through, of the abdominal walls, but the operation was commonly practiced on dead mothers in early times. Caesar, whose mother, Julia, lived many years after his death, possibly had his name confused with the operation because it was mandatory under the *lex Cesare*, the Roman law of the time, just as it had been under the *lex regia* before it. Roman law prescribed that every woman dying in advanced pregnancy should be so treated. The first known Caesarean on a *live* woman was performed about the year A.D. 1500.

In his secret communications Caesar would simply write down the third letter following the one he meant (thus in English today the letter *A* would be *D* and the word dog would be *GRJ*). Though this simple cipher or substitution code was used long before him, cryptologists still call it the Caesar cipher. His successor, Augustus Caesar, made the process even simpler, merely substituting the letter immediately following the one he meant, which enabled him to write in code as quickly as he could in normal letters.

Whether he said *"Et tu, Brute?"* (You, too Brutus?) when Brutus stabbed him is not known. Shakespeare, who put these words in his mouth, quoted either a lost Latin play or "The True Tragedie of Richard Duke of York." Suetonius noted: "Some have written that as M. Brutus came running upon him, he said, 'And you, my son.'" As for the famous *"Veni, vidi, vici"* (I came, I saw, I conquered), Suetonius says this was the inscription displayed after his Pontic triumph, while Plutarch says he first used the words in a letter announcing this triumph. Suetonius also says he uttered the words *"Iacta alea est"* (The die is cast) at the crossing of the Rubicon, and Plutarch attributes to him the traditional proverb "Caesar's wife must be above suspicion."

$$\nabla \ \nabla \ \nabla$$

Caesarius of Heiterbach (c. 1170–c. 1240)

The medieval chronicler tells of one of his fellow Cistercian monks who angrily prayed to Christ: "Lord, if Thou free me not from this temptation, I will complain of Thee to Thy mother."

Caesarius also told of a fellow abbot and a young monk out riding together. The monk saw the first women he had ever seen and asked, "What are they?"

"They be demons," the abbot said.

"I thought," said the monk, "that they were the fairest things that ever I saw."

Ambrogio Calepino (1435–1511)
In 1502 the Italian Augustine friar and linguist Ambrogio Calepino published a famous Latin dictionary that went through many editions and was *the* Latin dictionary of the day. Apparently this dictionary of Calepino's was published in an "octoglot" edition. *Calepin* was used for "a polyglot dictionary, a dictionary or any book of authority or reference" until well into the 18th century, and has had limited use ever since.

∇ ∇ ∇

Callimachus (fl. 3rd century B.C.)
The Greek poet Callimachus, who may have been head of the famed Alexandrian library, immortalized the term Berenice's hair, the lock of a woman's hair that became a constellation. Callimachus made the term famous in the five surviving lines of his poem *The Lock of Berenice*, which is said to be based on a true story. The real Berenice was married to Ptolemy III, king of Egypt, and when he invaded Syria in 246 B.C. to avenge the murder of his sister, she dedicated a lock of her hair to the gods as an offering for his safe return. The hair mysteriously disappeared, but the court astronomer, Conon of Samos, perhaps to assuage her, pretended to discover that it had been carried to heaven and transformed into a constellation of the northern hemisphere, which has been known ever since as Coma Berenices. A coma is the hazy envelope around a comet, and the word comet itself derives from the Greek and Latin words for hair, alluding to a fancied resemblance between the tails of comets and hair blowing in the wind. Ptolemy returned from the wars safely, but soon after his death in 221 B.C. the fabled Berenice was murdered at the instigation of her son.

Unlike his rival poet Apollonius Rhodius, a former student of his, Callimachus preferred to write short poems. After reading Apollonius' epic *Argonautica*, he quipped, "A big book is a big evil" (which I hope isn't true).

∇ ∇ ∇

Callisthenes (d. 327 B.C.)
A nephew and pupil of Aristotle, Callisthenes offended Alexander the Great, publicly criticizing his Oriental ways and refusing to prostrate himself before him. Finally he told the king, "Alexander will be known to posterity only through Callisthenes the historian," and the enraged conqueror had him thrown in prison for plotting against him. Callisthenes died seven months later.

Augustin Calmet (1672–1757)

The great French Benedictine scholar and author, who refused an appointment as a bishop, devoted all his time to his books, happily ignoring the outside world. "Who is this Madame Pompadour?" he once asked Voltaire in all seriousness. His self-composed epitaph reads: "Here lies one who read much, wrote much, prayed much; may it have been well! Amen."

∇ ∇ ∇

John Calvin (1509–1564)

Calvin gave the word *libertine* its modern connotation when he charged Geneva's party called the *Libertins*, or Liberals, with moral laxity. Though he was excessive in his condemnations he was preaching in a city where, for example, one entire district was occupied by prostitutes, who were ruled by their own *Reine du bordel*, or Brothel Queen.

∇ ∇ ∇

Giraldus Cambrensis (1165?–1220?)

This early English churchman and author, son of the Welsh Princess Nesta, had a sharp tongue that got him in trouble throughout his stormy but fruitful career. He may well have been the first in a long line of sardonic English literary critics, judging by his story about Geoffrey of Monmouth's Latin *History of the Britons* (c. 1136), a book that greatly contributed to the popularity of the Arthurian legends in England but which some writers of the day called pure invention. In his story Giraldus tells of a Welshman who "has the knowledge of occult events", but one night finds "a hairy, rough and hideous creature" in his arms in place of the beautiful damsel he is making love to. He goes mad, but is restored to health "through the merits of the saints," yet still has occult powers because of his familiarity with the evil spirits. Among other powers, Giraldus says, the Welshman "If he looked on a book faultily or falsely written or containing a false passage, although wholly illiterate he would point out the place with his finger…[being] directed by the demon's finger at the place." Giraldus ends his fantastic tale with the following anecdote: "If the spirits oppressed him [the Welshman] too much, the Gospel of St. John was placed on his bosom [and] like birds, they immediately vanished; but when the book was removed, and the *History of the Britons* by Geoffrey [of Monmouth] was substituted in its place, they instantly reappeared in greater numbers, and remained a longer time than usual on his body and on the book."

Luiz Vaz de Camöens (1524–1580)

Camôens is best remembered for his epic poem the *Lusiads*, which celebrates Portugal herself. The poet, who had lost an eye at war, was forced to join the army again after he stabbed a courtier in a street fight. Known as the Swashbuckler to his comrades, he fought in many battles, from Arabia to China, claiming that he held a sword in one hand, a pen in the other, all the while writing his epic. One story has it that the ship he sailed home on—after he was arrested for some unknown reason—was wrecked off Cambodia. His beloved Chinese mistress drowned, but he swam to shore with his masterpiece clenched between his teeth.

Camöens died of the plague in a Lisbon hospital, the friar who blessed him bemoaning, "So great a genius without even so much as a sheet to cover him." He was buried in a Potters Field common grave with other victims of the plague.

∇ ∇ ∇

Campantar (fl. 7th century)

Legend holds that this Tamil poet saved his country from Jainism with the eloquence of his poems. An earlier story has it that when he was a baby Campantar was suckled by the goddess Parvati and immediately after sang his first song.

∇ ∇ ∇

Cesare Cantù (1804–1895)

The Italian historian lived until age 91, despite a hard life. As a child he had to support his whole family after his father died. In jail or running from the authorities for political reasons for much of his adult life, he never made much money, though his 35-volume universal history, *Storia Universale* (1846), made his publisher a fortune. Cantù's first novel, *Margherita Pusterla* (1838), takes the prize for the book written with tools least resembling a word processor. The full-length novel was written on scrap paper in an Austrian prison, and Cantù used a toothpick as a pen and candle-smoke for ink.

∇ ∇ ∇

Marc-Antoine Carême (1784–1833)

"The king of cooks and the cook of kings," author of *La Cuisine Française*, founded classic French cooking as we know it today. In his own words "one of the twenty-five children of one of the poorest families in France," he was eventually granted by Louis XVIII the right to call himself "Carême of Paris." But his motto was "One master: Talleyrand. One mistress: Cooking." He was always faithful to his first benefactor and as a result is the only noted chef in history who was also a spy, relaying information he overheard at important dinner tables all over Europe to the French minister of foreign affairs. The great chef died on January 12, 1833, while sampling a quenelle of sole prepared by a student in his cooking school. "These are good," he is supposed to have murmured critically, "but prepared too hastily. You must shake the saucepan lightly—see, like this…" These were his last words, for, as he lifted the saucepan, he collapsed and fell to the floor dead. Someone wrote that he had died "burnt out by the flame of his genius and the heat of his ovens."

∇ ∇ ∇

Count Guglielmo Carucci ("Libri"; fl. late 19th century)

"Libri," the inspector general of French libraries under Louis Philippe, was actually an infamous book thief who stole hundreds of thousands of dollars' worth of rare books from the libraries he inspected. Count Guglielmo "Libri" Carucci was sentenced to 10 years in prison after a long trial but fled to England. By 1890 he had sold back all the stolen books to the French government.

∇ ∇ ∇

Isaac Casaubon (1559–1614)

The great scholar Joseph Justus Scaliger called Casaubon "the most learned of living men," but King Henry IV's finance minister considered him worthless. As curator of the Bibliothèque Royale, Casaubon made 1,200 livres a year. "You cost the king too much, sir," the finance minister told him. "Your pay exceeds that of two good captains, and you are of no use to your country."

When Casaubon left France for England he marveled at the good pay and respect given scholars there. In Germany, he pointed out, professors often had to sell wine and beer to their students or operate freewheeling taverns catering to them in order to make a living.

∇ ∇ ∇

Lodovico Castelvetro (1505–1571)

A poem by Caro failed to attain an adequately Petrarchan style, 16th-century Italian critic Lodovico Castelvetro charged. Caro and his defenders disagreed, and a literary feud broke out during which the classical critic apparently murdered one of the poet's supporters. Excommunicated from the Church, Castelvetro fled Rome and wandered Europe in exile for the rest of his life, the only critic known to have literally murdered someone.

Baldassare Castiglione (1478–1529)

It is hard for us to understand the author of *The Courtier*, one of the most famous books of the Renaissance, for the author was a true gentleman, of which we may have no living example today. In any case, Castiglione is said to have been successful in diplomacy by "the sheer charm of his integrity," an impossibility today. Castiglione mourned for his wife for 10 years or so after she died in childbirth. When the gentlest of gentlemen was finally laid to rest in his own tomb, the bones of his wife were brought there to lie beside his own under the following inscription he had written while he grieved for her: "I do not live now, o sweetest wife, for fate has taken my life from your body; but I shall live when I am laid in the same tomb with you, and my bones are joined with yours."

∇ ∇ ∇

Catherine the Great (1729–1796)

The Russian empress, a friend of Voltaire, was an accomplished playwright whose historical tragedies and comedies usually pleased her audiences, even if they were not masterpieces. Catherine rose at five and often worked 20 hours a day. She wrote her work under pseudonyms so as not to influence critical opinion. Catherine also edited a satirical magazine and wrote poems, librettos, historical articles and a fairy tale, *Prince Khlor*, that became a Russian classic. She did have secretaries to correct her poor spelling and grammar.

∇ ∇ ∇

Marcus Porcius Cato (Cato the Censor/Cato the Elder; 234–149 B.C.)

Cato the Censor, a fearsome man with wild red hair and a scar-covered face, was the first great Roman orator and writer of Latin prose, though relatively little of his written work has survived. A stern moralist, he once expelled a senator for killing his wife in public. He himself never embraced his wife except when it thundered, he said, though he did add that he was glad when storms came.

It is said that when the Roman author married a young woman on the death of his first wife, his son asked him: "Sir, in what have I offended you that you have brought a stepmother into our house?"

"Quite the contrary," Cato replied. "You have pleased me so well that I want to have more such."

"The father of Roman prose" had as his motto *Rem tene, verba sequentur*, "Know your facts and the words will come."

There were too many statues in Rome, Cato once observed, in vetoing the idea of having one built in his honor. "I would rather people ask why is there not a statue to Cato than why there is," he said.

▽ ▽ ▽

Jacob Cats (1577–1660)
"Father Cats," as he is called by his Dutch countrymen, came down with a tertian fever on the night he was to be married The poet and humorist had to cancel the ceremony and traveled for two years throughout Europe seeking a cure, consulting the most eminent medical authorities. All seemed hopeless and Cats returned to Zeeland to die, when he was mysteriously cured on his deathbed by a wandering quack. He lived over 50 years more.

▽ ▽ ▽

Catullus (c. 84–54 B.C.)
In about 57 B.C. the Roman poet traveled to Asia and found the tomb of his brother, who had died near Troy. After he performed the ancient Greek burial rites over the grave, there came to him the famous "Ave atque vale" poem that contains a phrase still common to dozens of languages over 2,000 years after he invented it:

> Dear brother, through many states and seas
> Have I come to this sorrowful sacrifice,
> Bringing you the last gift for the dead…
> Accept these offerings wet with fraternal tears;
> And forever, brother, hail and farewell.

▽ ▽ ▽

Benvenuto Cellini (1500–1571)
The Florentine sculptor, and author of one of the best autobiographies ever written, was as arrogant as he was brilliant. When he became a priest in 1558 he had three illegitimate children by his mistress Piera. Two years later he got himself released from his vows, took up with Piera again and they had another three children before he finally married her.

▽ ▽ ▽

Miguel de Cervantes Saavedra (1547–1616)
The great Spanish author served as a private in Spain's regular army in 1571. On October 7th of that year he was with the Armada aboard the *Marquesa* in the thickest action at the battle of Lepanto. As the fleet was about to go into action, Cervantes lay below burning up with a fever, but despite the pleas of his

comrades he insisted on fighting with them. He commanded twelve men in a boat by the galley's side and suffered three gunshot wounds, two in the chest and one that maimed his left hand—"for the greater glory of the right," as he put it. Despite his wounds, he fought in at least two naval battles the following year.

After his service in the army Cervantes started home to Spain carrying letters of recommendation to Philip II from his superiors. Barbary pirates captured his ship and he became the slave of the Greek renegade Dali Mami. Mami, thinking he was a man of importance because of the letter, held Cervantes for a high ransom. Though he tried to escape several times, Cervantes spent over five years as Mami's slave before his family finally freed him by paying the pirate 500 gold ducats.

Cervantes made numerous slips in his immortal *Don Quixote,* as when he has Sancho Panza sell his ass, and shortly afterward, inexplicably, has him riding the animal. Among other mistakes, Cervantes has Sancho lose his wallet and then use it again with no mention of his having found it; has Sancho lose his greatcoat with food in it and later says the food remained in Sancho's possession; makes the party at the Crescent Tavern eat two suppers in one night; and has Don Quixote's helmet broken to pieces, only to make it whole and sound again later in the book.

He was greatly admired in his own time. Traveling through the Spanish countryside King Philip II saw a man reading by the side of the road and laughing so hard that tears coursed down his cheeks. "That man," the king observed, "is either crazy or he is reading *Don Quixote.*"

When the French ambassador to Spain complimented Cervantes on *Don Quixote,* Cervantes whispered in his ear: "Had it not been for the Inquisition, I should have made my book much more entertaining."

Cervantes, so poor that he had to borrow money to buy a suit of clothes, signed one of the worst contracts in literary history. In September 1592, he contracted with a producer to write six plays at 50 ducats each—but no payment was to be made unless the producers considered that each of these plays "was one of the best ever produced in Spain." If any of these plays were ever written or Cervantes was ever paid for one, it has gone unrecorded.

A few days before he died he dedicated his new romance, *Pérsiles y Sigismunda,* to his friend the Count of Lemos: "Yesterday I received extreme unction and today I pen this dedication. The time is short, my agony increases, hopes diminish...and so farewell to jesting, farewell my merry humors, farewell my gay friends; for I feel that I am dying, and have no desire but to see you happy in the other life."

∇ ∇ ∇

Sebastien-Roch-Nicholas Chamfort (1741–1794)

Royalty were always glad to give the witty French author room and board in exchange for the pleasure of his conversation. But Chamfort, long a republican, became a dedicted revolutionary with the outbreak of the French Revolution. Then he himself was imprisoned briefly during the Terror. Fearing he'd be jailed again he committed suicide, writing his message in his own blood: "I Sebastien-Roch-Nicholas Chamfort, would rather die a free man than die a prisoner."

His famous maxims reflected his disillusioned view of life. "Whenever I had a conversation with Chamfort in the morning," said Madame Helvétius, his longtime friend, "I was saddened for the rest of the day."

His last words could have come from his *Maximes*. Just before he died he turned to his friend Abbé Sieyès and said: "I go at last out of this world, where the heart must break or make itself bronze."

∇ ∇ ∇

Charles, Duke of Orleans (1391–1465)

The finest French poet of his age, the Duke of Orleans was taken prisoner at Agincourt and held in captivity for 25 years before he was allowed to return home. In one of his last poems he said farewell to his young friends, whose revels he could join in no longer:

> Salute for me all the company
> Where now you meet in comradery,
> And say how gladly I would be
> One of their band if it could be;
> Age holds me in captivity…

Yet for all that he held out longer than most against the ravages of time. He is said to have fathered the future Louis XII of France when over 70.

∇ ∇ ∇

Charondas (fl. 6th century B.C.)

The laws Charondas gave to Catana were written a full generation before Solon wrote his laws and they set a precedent for much of Sicily and Italy. A law he made forbade citizens to be armed in the assembly. One day he himself forgot and entered the public meeting wearing a sword. A citizen scolded him for breaking his own law and Charondas replied, "I will rather confirm it," immediately slaying himself with his sword.

▽ ▽ ▽

Vicomte François-Auguste-René de Chateaubriand (1768–1848)

An old story tells us that Brillat-Savarin dined in Paris with Chateaubriand on the night that an anonymous restaurant proprietor invented steak Chateaubriand in his honor. The occasion, according to this tale, was the publication of the French author's *La Génie du Christianisme* and the succulent tenderloin was encased between two flank steaks (later discarded) symbolizing Christ and the thieves. But the novelist's great chef, Montmeril, could just as well have invented the dish.

The romantic author once wrote a pamphlet so critical of Napoleon that the emperor, fearful that others might read his copy, slept with it under his pillow at night and had his wife hide it under her dress during the day.

Louis XVIII said that the 50 pages Chateaubriand had written against Napoleon in his pamphlet *De Buonaparte et des Bourbons* (1792) was worth 100,000 troops. He had good reason to hate Napoleon, for the emperor had refused to save his brother Armand from execution for carrying Bourbon dispatches. Chateaubriand had arrived just after his brother was shot, to find "a butcher's dog licking up his blood and his brains." He, in fact, wrote the pamphlet on the fifth anniversary of Armand's death.

Chateaubriand never recovered from the pessimism of a youth strongly influenced by the early death of four brothers and sisters. Late in life he remarked, "I ought never to have been born."

Yet he was among the most vain of men. "He thinks himself deaf," Talleyrand once said of him in his old age, "because he no longer hears himself talked of."

▽ ▽ ▽

Marquise du Châtelet (Émilie de Breteuil; 1706–1749)

The brilliant Marquise du Châtelet, a scientist, musician, author and the first to translate Newton's *Principia Mathematica* into French, became Voltaire's mistress in 1734, and for the next 15 years they lived together at her husband's château in Champagne, which became Voltaire's refuge from the Paris police so often on his trail. But in 1749 Madame met the younger, handsome Jean-François de Saint-Lambert, a vain, vastly overrated poet, who had nonetheless been elected to the French Academy and had a reputation as a great lover, having stolen the Marquise de Boufflers from the Duke of Lorraine. Madame du Châtelet became pregnant and later that year died in childbirth. When she died, Voltaire and her husband took the locket she always wore and anxiously opened it, each hoping that it would contain a memento of himself. All they found was Saint-Lambert's portrait. "This story reflects no credit on either of us," Voltaire said to Monsieur du Châtelet when he recovered his wit. As for Saint-Lambert, he immediately left for Paris, where his reputation preceded him and he became the lover of still another famous literary figure, Madame d'Houdetot, the Sophie about whom Rousseau describes his unreciprocated passion in his *Confessions*. Madame d'Houdetot remained Saint-Lambert's mistress for over 50 years, until he died in 1803 at 87, a poet who had beaten both Voltaire and Rousseau at love if not literature.

∇ ∇ ∇

Anton Chekhov (1860–1904)

"All things considered, I'm a mediocre playwright," Chekhov wrote to a friend after finishing *The Seagull* in less than a month. On opening night, the audience more than agreed with his assessment. Most had come expecting a farce and booed and hissed when the final curtain came down, after having laughed and whistled through the entire performance. Chekhov put his collar up, bent over and hurried out of the theater, unable to leave fast enough. However, several days later the play's second performance, which Chekhov did not attend, was a resounding success, with encores after each act and cries of "Author! Author!" This was mainly because the audience had not come expecting a comedy.

The image of the seagull brought down by a thoughtless hunter so central to Chekhov's *The Seagull* was suggested by a woodcock winged by the author's friend Isaak Levitan while they were hunting together. Levitan could not finish off the bird staring at them with bright black eyes and begged Chekhov to do so. Chekhov finally agreed and smashed its head with the butt of his rifle. Later he wrote to a friend: "And while two idiots went home and sat down to dinner, there was one less beautiful, infatuated creature in the world."

Chekhov's major story "The Black Monk" is another tale—like Stevenson's "Dr. Jekyll and Mr. Hyde" and Coleridge's poem "Kubla Khan"—that was inspired by a dream. One afternoon while taking a nap he awoke with a start and ran into the next room. "I've just had the most awful dream!" he shouted to his brother, his face contorted. "I was visited by a black monk!" The dream became an obsession that he could only escape by writing about it.

That the realism of Ibsen and Strindberg wasn't intentionally emulated by Chekhov, despite all the naturalistic Stanislavskian interpretations of his plays, is evidenced by a letter the author sent to a friend in 1888. "The modern theatre is a skin disease," Dr. Chekhov wrote, "a sinful disease of the cities. It must be swept away with a broom; it is unwholesome to love it."

When a friend implored him to drop medicine and give all his time to writing, he piquantly replied, "Medicine is my lawful wife and literature is my mistress. When I get tired of one, I spend the night with the other."

Essentially a short story writer and playwright he longed to write a fine long novel and never did. Before he wrote *The Steppe*, really a series of separate episodes without much organic structure, he despaired, "I wish I could write a novel a thousand verses long!"

"Critics are like horsefiles which prevent the horse from ploughing," he wrote to a friend. "For over twenty years I have read criticisms of my stories, and I do not remember a single remark of any value or one word of valuable advice. Only once Skabichevsky wrote something which made an impression on me. He said I would die in a ditch drunk."

Chekhov's worst words for his afflictions weren't for his heart trouble or the tuberculosis that eventually killed him at so young an age, but for the "vile, loathsome" hemorrhoids that plagued him as they had another great Russian author, Nikolai Gogol. (Gogol had written his mother in 1831 that "not one man in St. Petersburg [is] free from this nuisance.") Wrote Chekhov to a friend early in 1893: "It's not syphilis, it's worse—hemorrhoids...pain, itching, tension. I can't sit, can't walk; my whole body is so sore I feel like hanging myself."

As the playwright lay dying, Chekhov's doctor sent for a bottle of champagne. It was hopeless, there was no chance he would live. The doctor poured him a glass and Chekhov took it, turning to his wife Olga and smiling. His last words were, "It's been so long since I've had champagne," and after slowly draining the glass, he rolled over on his left side and in a few moments stopped breathing. It was a week before his body reached Moscow from Germany and the group of friends led by Maxim Gorky who met the train were furious that his coffin had been carried in a filthy green van with the words "For Oysters" printed on the door.

∇ ∇ ∇

Ch'en Tzu-ang (661–702)

The Chinese poet was a brilliant man of wild temperament who became a doctor before he was 18, with little or no study. Ch'en came from a wealthy family and could afford to introduce the empress to his poetry in the strange way he chose. Inviting her and the public to a *hu-ch'in* musical recital featuring himself, he smashed his expensive instrument to pieces as soon as all were seated. He then handed out copies of his poems to the audience, declaring that they were far more valuable and worthy of attention than any musical instrument, no matter how expensive.

∇ ∇ ∇

André-Marie de Chénier (1762–1794)
Imprisoned as a Girondist during the French Revolution, the poet, known as the Keats of French literature, fell in love with Mademoiselle de Coigny, a prisoner in a cell close by, and wrote for her in his dungeon the poem "The Young Captive." Its last stanza implored:

> O Death you need not haste!—begone! begone!
> Go solace hearts that shame and fear have known,
>   And hopeless woes beset.
> For me Pales [goddess of flocks] still has her grassy ways
> Love has its kisses, and the Nurse her lap;
>   I would not die yet.

But he was condemned to death at his trial and guillotined soon after.

∇ ∇ ∇

Agostino Chigi (1465–1520)
One of the greatest patrons of the arts in Renaissance Italy, Chigi went so far as to set up a printing press in his home to publish scholarly and poetic works of merit. At one dinner he gave, each guest was served his meal on a gold plate bearing his own motto and coat of arms, and the guests were given the plates. But he could be clever as well. At another Chigi feast hundreds of silver plates were thrown into the Tiber to assure his guests that no dish would be used twice. His servants, however, had set up nets in the river from which they later retrieved the silver.

∇ ∇ ∇

Chikamatsu Monzaemon (Sugimori Nobunori; 1653–1725)
This Japanese dramatist, widely regarded as "The Shakespeare of Japan," probably took the pen name Chikamatsu Monzaemon because his prominent samurai family objected to his writing for the plebeian *joruri* or puppet theater of Japan. Chikamatsu himself liked to write for puppets because they could not distort the meaning of his work, as he felt actors did in the plays he wrote for

Kabuki theater. In any case, this one dramatist alone for three-quarters of a century made puppet theater more popular than any theater of living actors in Japan, something unique in theatrical history.

"Audiences nowadays will not accept plays unless they are realistic and logical," someone told him. "The old plots are full of nonsense that nobody will tolerate any more. The reputation of Kabuki actors depends on just how realistic their acting seems."

"What you say seems plausible," he replied, "but it does not take into account the true methods of art. Art is something that lies in between reality and unreality. Of course it seems desirable, in view of the current taste for realism, for the actor playing a retainer to copy the gestures and speech of a real retainer, but would a real retainer rouge and powder his face the way actors do? Or, would the audiences like it if an actor, on the grounds that real retainers pay no attention to how they look, were to perform unshaven or display a bald head? The theatre is unreal, and yet not unreal, real and yet not real. Entertainment lies between the two."

∇ ∇ ∇

Ch'in Shih Huang Ti (259–210 B.C.)

The emperor who unified China was the illegitimate son of the Queen of Ch'in and her minister Lu, a poet who considered his poems so good that he left dangling at his gate a thousand pieces of gold for anyone who could improve them by a single word. Shih, however, hated his father and forced him to commit suicide when he became emperor. He hated poetry and all literature as well, ordering that with few exceptions all books in China except scientific works be burned. Literati who failed to comply were put to death, hundreds of them were buried alive, or sent to labor on the Great Wall. Shih reasoned that if all records were destroyed, history would begin with him. Some scholars, however, memorized the complete works of Confucius and other books and passed them on in this way. Shih grew more hated with each passing year of his reign until finally he took to sleeping in different rooms of his many palaces every night so that no assassin could find him. For generations after his death the people expressed their hatred of him by urinating on his grave.

∇ ∇ ∇

Chrysippus (c. 280–204 B.C.)

The Greek Stoic philosopher held that bedbugs were of great service to humans, as they prevented us from oversleeping. Better than burying relatives, he said, would be to use their flesh as food.

Dio Chrysostom (40–120)

Dio of the Golden Mouth's orations were so eloquent that his countrymen were said to interrupt wars to hear them. Not that many knew what Dio was talking about; his was a triumph of style. "I don't know what you mean," the emperor Trajan told him, "but I love you as myself."

∇ ∇ ∇

Marcus Tullius Cicero (206–43 B.C.)

The eloquent Roman statesman, orator and writer, "the father of his country," epitomized knowledge, honesty and style, which is the reason travel guides in Italy were first called cicerones. According to Plutarch, Cicero got his name from the Latin *cicer* (a wart), due to the "flat excrescence on the tip of his nose."

Cicero's brother Quintus drew up a campaign manual when the great orator stood against the dissolute Catiline for the consulate in 63 B.C. Among the instructions, honored through the ages: "Be lavish in your promises; men prefer a false promise to a flat refusal...Contrive to get some new scandal aired against your rivals for crime, corruption or immorality." Whether he used the manual or not, Cicero defeated Catiline and drove him from the city with his great speech "In Catilinam."

Cicero once punned that the man who ploughed his family graveyard was cultivating his father's memory.

It is said that the Emperor Augustus, Cicero's political enemy, caught his young grandson reading Cicero. Augustus took the dangerous document the boy tried to conceal and carefully studied it. He finally returned it, saying, "An eloquent man, my boy, eloquent and a patriot."

Rufus Marcus Caelius, the Roman orator, letter writer and friend of Cicero, was accused by Clodia, wife of the consul Metellus, of trying to poison her. In open court Caelius called her a *quadrantaria*, a ½-cent woman, or the commonest of prostitutes. Cicero, his lawyer, insisted that Caelius was "not the enemy of women, still less of one who was the friend of all men." Caelius was acquitted, whatever the merits of Clodia's case.

∇ ∇ ∇

Gaius Helvius Cinna (d. 44 B.C.)

The Roman poet, a good friend of Catullus, unfortunately had the same name as one of the conspirators (Cornelius Cinna) who assassinated Casesar. As

Shakespeare wrote in *Julius Caesar*, devoting an entire scene to the incident, the poet attended Caesar's funeral and was mistaken for the assassin by the mob of plebeians, who beat him to death. Shakespeare has the mob tear him apart. "I am Cinna the poet, I am Cinna the poet!" he protests. "Tear him for his bad verses, tear him for his bad verses!" a plebeian cries. In fact, according to a modern critic, he *was* a rather bad poet, his work "showing the learning and obscurity of the Alexandrian influence at its worst."

∇ ∇ ∇

Cleanthes (fl. 3rd century B.C.)
On turning 70, the Greek Stoic philosopher began a long fast. When asked to stop, he replied that he "would not go back after coming halfway" and continued his fast until he died.

∇ ∇ ∇

John Climax (c. 525–600 A.D.)
The Christian ascetic and mystic wrote his *Ladder to Paradise*, which instructs readers how to attain holiness, while living 40 years in a cave at the foot of Mount Sinai.

∇ ∇ ∇

Jean Cocteau (1889–1963)
The French author and film director was called a collaborator by some during World War II, and he certainly managed to walk a thin line between the Germans and the Resistance. A master of survival, he years before told Ezra Pound that "The tact of audacity [in art] consists in knowing how far to go too far."

Proust complained to Cocteau that his model for the Duchesse de Guermantes, the witty Comtesse Adhéaume de Chevigné, a descendant of the Marquis de Sade, refused to read his masterwork. "You might as well have asked an ant to read Fabre," replied Cocteau. "One does not invite an ant to read entomology."

Surveying Cocteau's admirable art and book collections, someone asked what he would remove if his house were on fire and he was allowed to take only one thing. "I would remove the fire," he replied.

Charles Cogniard (1806–1872) and Jean Cogniard (1807–1882)

Nicolas Chauvin of Rochefort was a genuine hero, wounded 17 times in service of the French Grand' Armée and retiring only when so scarred that he could no longer lift a sword. How then did his name become associated with excessive nationalism or superpatriotism? Chauvin actually was left with little after his war service. For his wounds and valor he received a medal, a ceremonial saber and a pension of about $40 a year. Instead of growing bitter, the old soldier turned in the opposite direction, for, after all, his sacrifices had to mean something. Chauvin became an idolator of the Little Corporal; even after Waterloo and Napoleon's exile, he spoke of nothing but his hero's infallibility and the glory of France. The veteran became a laughingstock in his village, but he would have escaped national attention if dramatists Charles Cogniard and his brother Jean hadn't heard of him and used him as a character in their comedy *La Cocarde Tricolore* (1831). The play truthfully represented Chauvin as an almost idolatrous worshipper of Napoleon and was followed by at least four more comedies by other authors caricaturing the old soldier. As a result the French word *chauvinisme*, or chauvinism, became synonymous with fanatical, unreasoning patriotism and all that such blind, bellicose worship of national prowess implies.

∇ ∇ ∇

Jean-Baptiste Colbert (1619–1683)

The French statesman and patron of the arts is responsible for "The Forty Immortals" becoming a synonym for the Académie Française. Colbert, chief minister to Louis XIV and a member of the academy himself, thought it unfair that a rich member had an easy chair installed in the academy for himself while the other members sat on hard chairs. So he ordered 39 more chairs installed to maintain equality among the members.

∇ ∇ ∇

Louise Colet (1810–1870)

Flaubert's mistress, and one of the prototypes for his *Madame Bovary* (1856), poet Louise Colet was noted for her beauty but not her modesty. "The missing arms of the Venus de Milo have at last been discovered!" she once declared. "In the sleeves of my dress!"

∇ ∇ ∇

Colette (Sidonie-Gabrielle Colette; 1873–1954)

The French novelist began her writing career by ghosting stories for her author husband. He "taught" her the craft by locking her in a room until she finished each assignment.

As one would expect from her novel *La Chatte*, Colette was a great cat lover, perhaps the most ardent in all literary history. Claiming that she emulated the traits of felines—self-control, mental agility, etc.—the French author often kept up to two dozen in her house and was rarely without at least 10 pet cats.

Colette's last words are said to have been "Look, look!" as she pointed from her deathbed at the flashing lightning of the worst thunderstorm Paris had seen in over half a century. These were the words she once claimed were most responsible for her success as a writer. Throughout her childhood on the farm Colette's mother had exhorted her to "Look, look!" as she went about her daily chores, and this habit of curiosity and intense observation helped make her one of France's finest writers.

∇ ∇ ∇

Anna Comnena (1083–1148)

This Byzantine historian and poet plotted to overthrow her brother, Emperor John II, and install her husband, Nicephorus Bryennius, as emperor. When her husband refused to join in the conspiracy, the feisty lady turned to him and said, "Nature has mistaken our sexes, for *you* ought to be the woman!" In any case, her plot was discovered and Anna was sent to a convent, where she wrote a history, the *Alexiad*, studied medicine and became chief physician in a 10,000-bed hospital.

∇ ∇ ∇

Auguste Comte (1798–1857)

As a guide for the disciples who formed a kind of church around his positivist philosophy, the French philosopher fashioned and published the *Positivist Calendar* (1840), in which the names of those who had advanced civilization over the centuries replaced those of the saints. Gutenberg and Shakespeare were among the patrons of the 13 months in his new calendar.

Comte espoused an altruistic morality expressed in the motto "Live for others." But he was not one to undervalue himself. Told that he was dying of cancer, he cried, "What an irreparable loss!"

∇ ∇ ∇

Marquis de Condorcet (Marie-Jean-Antoine-Nicolas de Caritat; 1743–1794)

The French mathematician, writer and philosopher supported the Revolution, but was forced to flee Paris to escape the extremist Jacobins. When he stopped at a country inn to restore his strength, he made the mistake of ordering a 12-egg omelet. Reported by the innkeeper as a suspicious character, he was thrown into prison, where he died under mysterious circumstances, paying for his love of eggs with his life.

∇ ∇ ∇

Confucius (K'ung Fu-tzu; 551–479 B.C.)
Though Confucius left no writings but one poorly regarded book, his teachings, based on his golden rule ("What you do not like when done to yourself do not do to others"), shaped the character of China and her people. Confucius was venerated as a sage from the day he died, his burial place outside the city of K'iuh-fow (Kufow) still a place of homage. In this cemetery a number of disciples built huts; the site of one is now marked by a small house. A number of followers mourned their master's death in these huts for three years. His favorite disciple, Tze-kung, remained by his grave for twice that length of time. The Kung clan, which made its home in a nearby city, became a sacred caste after Confucius died and today numbers some 50,000 or more descendants.

∇ ∇ ∇

Hendrik Conscience (1812–1883)
When in 1837 Conscience told his proud French father, a follower of Napoleon, that he had written a book in Flemish, his father turned him out of the house and cut off his support. The Belgian writer, however, continued to write in his native tongue, and after a long period of poverty became one of his country's most celebrated authors.

∇ ∇ ∇

Henri-Benjamin Constant de Rebecque (1767–1830)
The French author and political philosopher, whose love affair with Madame de Staël is treated in his pschological masterwork *Adolphe* (1816), was a liberal with the courage of his convictions, which included staunch and heroic opposition to Napoleon, who forced him into exile. Constant fought many duels in his lifetime. During his later years he became a cripple when he slipped and fell while arguing in the Chamber of Deputies. This did not prevent him from accepting the challenge for a last duel, which he fought while sitting in a chair. (See also MADAME DE STAËL.)

∇ ∇ ∇

Nicolaus Copernicus (1473–1543)
Early in the 16th century the Copernican theory established that all the planets, including the earth, revolve in orbits around the sun, in opposition to the older Ptolemic theory that the sun and planets move around the earth. It immortalizes

Nicolaus Copernicus, the Latinized form of Mikolaj Kopernik, whose work revolutionized astronomy, changing man's entire outlook on the universe and influencing a profound change on the inner man as well. The great astronomer, born in Prussian Poland, made his living as a physician and canon of the cathedral of Frauenburg. He completed his theory as early as 1530, when he circulated in manuscript a brief, popular account of it, but *De Revolutionibus Orbium Coelestium* wasn't published until 13 years later, when he lay on his deathbed. Though the work was dedicated to Pope Paul III, it was placed on the church's index of forbidden books.

∇ ∇ ∇

Sergio Corazzini (1887–1907)
This precocious Italian poet never had time to fully develop as a craftsman. He used to tell people not to refer to him as a poet, explaining, "I am only an infant squealing." He died before he turned 20.

∇ ∇ ∇

Édouard-Joachim Corbière (1845–1875)
Other French poets have been madder than Corbière, but he had a unique, peculiar habit. He liked to spend his time painstakingly building scale-model ships, only to destroy them as soon as they were finished.

∇ ∇ ∇

Corinna (fl. 500 B.C.)
Called "the Fly" for some unknown reason, the Greek poet was reputedly a beautiful woman whose simple poems were chosen over those of the great Pindar's in five poetical contests. According to a traditional anecdote she once criticized Pindar for the absence of myths in his work. Pindar thereupon went to the opposite extreme. "One should sow by the handfuls, not with the whole sack," she told him.

∇ ∇ ∇

Luigi Cornaro (1467?–1566)
The noble Venetian author may have lived to well over 100. In middle age he gave up his profligate ways for the temperate life with a strict diet and no medicines, which he described in his *Discorsi della Vita Sobria* (1558). At 86 he wrote that he was "full of health and strength." "I constantly write," he testified, "and with my own hand, eight hours a day, and...in addition to this I walk and sing for many other hours...For I feel, when I leave the table, that I must

sing…Oh, how beautiful and sonorous my voice has become!" He continued writing and singing until his death.

∇ ∇ ∇

Pierre Corneille (1616–1684)

The creator of French classical tragedy was accorded what may be the highest praise ever given a dramatist. When Napoleon saw his play *Andromède*, he exclaimed, "If Corneille were alive I would make him king!"

Corneille began to fail in his later years nd his masterpieces were replaced by rather mediocre plays. When his *Agésilas* (1666) was followed by *Attila* the next year, the critic Boileau cruelly remarked, "After *Agésilas*, alas! But after *Attila*, stop!" (*"Après l'Agésilas, hélas! Mais après l'Attila, holà!"*)

∇ ∇ ∇

Lucius Annaeus Cornutus (fl. 1st century A.D.)

The Stoic Roman teacher, grammarian and tragic poet was exiled by Nero in 66 A.D. because he had the gall to say that the 400-volume history of Rome the emperor was contemplating was a little too long.

∇ ∇ ∇

Vincenzo Maria Coronelli (b. c. 1650)

As cosmographer to the republic of Venice in 1685 this Franciscan friar was assigned to write a general alphabetical encyclopedia in 45 volumes. Coronelli labored over the project for 30 years, but finished only seven volumes of the *Bibleoteca universale sacroprofana*. This despite the fact that one critic said there was never so quick a writer, one who "composed a folio volume as easily as others would a page."

∇ ∇ ∇

Matthias Corvinus (1440–1490)

Matthias I, the king of Hungary from 1458 to 1490, was called Corvinus, from the raven (Latin *corvus*) on his shield. Among the greatest of book collectors, he had a raven worked into the design of his books' gilt-tooled bindings, which are priceless treasures today.

The Hungarian king spent the equivalent of some $1 million a year on books and in 1497 founded one of the world's first literary societies, the Sodalitas Litteraria Danubia. Matthias Corvinus envied the writer's lot. "O authors," he once wrote to a scholar, "how happy you are! You strive not after blood-stained glory nor monarch's crowns, but for the laurels of poetry and virtue. You are even able to compel us to forget the tumult of war."

▽ ▽ ▽

Georges Courteline (c. 1860–1929)

The French playwright received a letter from a young writer challenging him to a duel. Replied Courteline to the poorly spelled and barely legible words: "My dear young sir. As I am the offended party, the choice of weapons is mine. We shall fight with orthography. You are already dead." (See SAINTE-BEUVE.)

▽ ▽ ▽

Prosper Jolyot de Crébillon (1674–1762)

Madame de Pompadour, a cultured woman whose library numbered some 3,500 volumes, saved the old playwright from starving to death in the attic where he lived with his 10 dogs, 15 cats and several ravens. When he went to Versailles to thank her for the pension she had awarded him, la Pompadour received him while in bed. Crébillon bent down to kiss her hand, but at this exact moment Louis XV entered the room. "Madame," the old man cried, "I am undone; the king has surprised us together!" Louis so admired his witticism that he helped him produce his last play, finished when he was 80.

▽ ▽ ▽

Claude Prosper de Crébillon (1707–1777)

The French novelist was known as *"Crébillon le tragique."* He loved the high life and his novels were notorious in his time, but this did not prevent him from being appointed French censor of literature. His dramatist father called him "the worst of my productions," but his did not prevent him from inheriting his father's pension when the old man died.

▽ ▽ ▽

Dictys Cretensis (created 4th century A.D.)

The idea for Chaucer's and Shakespeare's *Troilus and Cressida* came from a forged diary of "Dictys Cretensis," a supposed soldier in the Trojan War, that was actually written in the fourth century A.D.

▽ ▽ ▽

Marie Curie (1867–1934)

Autograph hunters were Madame Curie's *bête noire*, and she always refused to oblige them. One man, knowing this, sent her a check for $25 for her favorite charity, sure that the endorsed check bearing her signature would come back to him. But Madame Curie had her secretary send him the following note: "Madame Curie has asked me to thank you most kindly for your check, which, however, she is not going to cash. It so happens that she is an autograph collector and therefore will add you signature to her collection."

∇ ∇ ∇

Baron Cuvier (Georges-Léopold-Chrétien-Frédéric-Dagobert; 1769–1832)

In preparing the *Academy Dictionary*, a committee of the French Academy defined a crab as "a small red fish which walks backward." The great naturalist author came upon this description and told the committee: "You definition, gentlemen, would be perfect, but for three small exceptions: the crab is not a fish, it is not red, and it does not walk backward."

Several pranksters dressed in devil costumes stole into Cuvier's bedroom one night and woke the French zoologist and author from a sound sleep, stamping their hooved feet and crying, "Cuvier, we have come to eat you, we have come to eat you!"
Before he yawned, turned over, and went back to sleep, Cuvier said matter-of-factly, "All animals with horns and hooves are herbivorous. You won't eat me."

∇ ∇ ∇

Savinien de Cyrano de Bergerac (1619–1655)

Anyone with a prodigious nose is likely to be called a Cyrano de Bergerac after the eponymous hero of Edmond Rostand's play of the same name (1897). Rostand's hero was based on the very real Savinien Cyrano de Bergerac who had a nose every bit as long as his fictional counterpart's and whose exploits were even more remarkable. The historical Cyrano was a brave soldier, great lover and eloquently influential writer of comedies and tragedies whose works are said to have inspired Moliere, and Swift's *Gulliver's Travels*. This swaggering swordsman fought countless duels with those foolish enough to insult or even mention his nose, and his single-handed duel against 100 enemies while serving as an officer in the Guards is a well-documented fact. Cyrano's exploits became legend long before Rostand ficitionalized him. Surprisingly, he did not perish on the wrong end of a sword but far more prosaically. Cyrano died as a result of a wound caused by a falling beam or stone while staying at the home of a friend.

Henri-François Daguesseau (1668–1751)
Daguesseau, French chancellor as well as an author, noticed that his wife usually came down to dinner 10 minutes or so late every evening. He decided he would do something with the time. For little more than a year he wrote during those 10 minutes. While waiting for his wife he completed a work of three volumes, which became a best-seller when published.

∇ ∇ ∇

Saint Peter Damian (1007?–1072)
The ascetic Italian reformer, who wrote a terrible denunciation of the clergy called *Gomorrhianus* (c. 1050), confessed at the end of a saintly but difficult life "I, who am now an old man, may safely look upon the sered and wrinkled visage of a blear-eyed crone. Yet from sight of the more comely and adorned I guard my eyes like boys from fire. Alas, my wretched heart!— which cannot hold scriptural mysteries read through a hundred times, and will not lose the memory of a form seen but once."

∇ ∇ ∇

Gabriele D'Annunzio (1863–1938)
A possibly apocryphal story has the vain D'Annunzio refusing to accept a letter addressed "To Italy's Greatest Poet." He explained that he was the *world's* greatest poet.

A great hero in World War I, D'Annunzio served in the Italian cavalry, infantry, navy and air force. As a pilot he hoped for immortality even at the cost of his life. His plane was riddled with bullets in several engagements, he was wounded in the wrist during one dogfight and he lost his eye in another, yet he felt this was a small price to pay for the beautiful war poems he was writing.

Though he was a genuinely intrepid adventurer and probably the only writer who could ever call himself the dictator of a state (when he and his volunteer force occupied Fiume, now Rijeka, Yugoslavia, from 1919 to 1921), no one, including probably D'Annunzio himself, knew where reality ended and fantasy began for the Italian poet when it came to his sexual conquests. He bragged, however, that a thousand husbands hated him, and he would show visitors pillows that he said were filled with the soft locks of ladies who were virgins before he met them.

All the good publicity surrounding the poet as a great lover led one Parisian hostess to say: "The woman who had not slept with him became a laughingstock."

Megalomaniac almost to the point of insanity after his heroic acts and loss of an eye in World War I, D'Annunzio led over 12,000 "Ardite" proto-fascists into the port of Fiume in 1919 and annexed it. "Even if the citizens of Fiume do not desire annexation, I desire it against their wishes," he declared. Later, after declaring war on Italy and then returning home, he cried, "Citizens, Gabriele D'Annunzio is here. Say not a word. Continue to weep for joy."

∇ ∇ ∇

Dante Alighieri (1265–1321)

The immortal Italian poet's enemies reported him to the bishop for failing to kneel in church before the holy sacrament. Dante avoided punishment by telling the bishop, "If those who accuse me had had their eyes and minds on God, as I had, they too would have failed to notice events around them, and they most certainly would not have noticed what *I* was doing."

Dante met the girl he celebrated as Beatrice while attending mass, which is, oddly enough, the place where Petrarch met his Laura, and Boccaccio his Faimetta. "Beatrice" has since been identified as Bice Portinari and she is said to have married another man when very young. On her death in 1290, at the age of 25, Dante "lost the first delight of my soul," seeking consolation in philosophy and his poetry.

"I wonder, Signor Dante," Prince della Scala said, "why a man as learned as you should be hated by all my court, and that my court fool should be so beloved."

Replied a highly offended Dante, "Your Excellency would wonder less if he considered that we like those best who most resemble ourselves."

Dante, according to a traditional yarn, looked the unattractive Giotto in the eye and asked, "Why are your children so ugly when your frescoes are so beautiful?" More than his match at verbal sparring, the artist replied: "My frescoes I make by day, and my children by night."

∇ ∇ ∇

Georges-Jacques Danton (1759–1794)

The French revolutionary was annoyed with a fellow prisoner who kept stammering bad poetry while they both awaited the Terror's guillotine. Finally, he bitterly punned, "Plus de vers! Dans huit jours tu en feras assez. (No more verses! In a week you'll make enough of them)," *vers* meaning "worms" as well as "verse."

Darius the Great (c. 558–485? B.C.)

The limitations of "picture writing," the precursor of the alphabet, can be seen in the old story about Darius the Great, king of Persia, who received a hieroglyphic message from his enemies, the Scythians. The Scythians had sent him a live mouse, a frog, a bird, and arrows, instead of pictures of these things. Darius interpreted this to mean they would surrender come morning—the arrows, he thought, meant they would give up their arms; the mouse and frog represented surrender of the land and water; and the bird meant the Scythians would soon fly away from the field of battle. Accordingly, Darius went to bed without preparing his troops for attack, and the Scythians raided his camp that night and overwhelmed his armies. They then explained *their* intepretation of the live hieroglyphics: The bird meant the Persians would never escape the Scythians unless they could literally fly; the mouse and frog meant that the only other way they could escape would be to turn themselves into mice and burrow through the ground, or into frogs and hide out in the swamps; and the arrows meant they would never escape the infallible Scythian weapons.

∇ ∇ ∇

Alphonse Daudet (1840–1897)

A newspaper editor asked Daudet to write an article praising Emile Zola for finally finishing his 20-volume series about the Rougon-Macquart family. The French novelist and critic refused, telling him, "If I were to write that article, it would be to advise Zola, now that the family tree of the Rougon-Macquarts is complete, to go and hang himself from the highest branch."

∇ ∇ ∇

Leon Daudet (1867–1942)

When Daudet's son was found shot to death in a taxicab in the summer of 1925 the fiery French author and politician accused the driver of complicity in killing him. The driver sued and Daudet was sentenced to prison for his false accusation. After serving two years in a Paris jail cell he was freed by a prominent group of royalist friends who managed to trick the warden of the prison into believing that he had been pardoned. Daudet fled to Belgium where he lived the rest of his life.

∇ ∇ ∇

Dazai Osamu (Shuji Tsushima; 1909–1948)

The dissipated son of a rich family, Osamu attempted suicide many times in his short life and finally succeeded in drowning himself with his lover. Perhaps Japan's most important writer born in this century, he was in his short time a drug addict, alcoholic and an uncompromising opponent of Japan's militarists.

His book *The Setting Sun* (1947) gave a name, *Shayozaku*, to the aristocracy displaced by the war.

∇ ∇ ∇

Demosthenes (385?–322 B.C.)

Women, especially courtesans, were Demosthenes' chief distractions, and disastrous distractions they could be. "What can one do with Demosthenes?" his secretary once lamented. "Everything that he has thought of for a whole year is thrown into confusion by one woman in one night."

For months at a time Demosthenes practiced and perfected his oratory in a cave, patiently rehearsing his speeches. During these periods of self-enforced seclusion, he shaved only half of his face so that he wouldn't be tempted to go out into the streets.

Demosthenes' attack against his rival Aeschines in his *On the Crown* oration is one of the most famous pieces of invective in history. In it he called Aeschines' father a slave who "wore shackles on his legs and a timber collar round his neck" and charged that his mother "practiced daylight nuptials in an outhouse." Ending up by belittling Aeschines' acting career, he declared, "You were a third-rate actor, I a spectator at the play. You failed in your part, and I hissed you."

"The Athenians will kill you one day when they are in a rage," he told the Athenian statesman and orator Phocian, an advocate of peace. "And they will kill you," Phocian replied, "if they are one day in their senses."

When asked what was the first rule of oratory, he answered, "Action"; and which was the second, he replied, "Action"; and which was third, he still replied, "Action." (See VICENTE HUIDOBRO.)

When an Athenian crowd refused to hear him speak on an important matter, and hissed and booed, Demosthenes told them he wanted to tell a funny story and they listened. "A certain youth," he began, "hired an ass to go from his home to Megara. At noon, when the sun was very hot, both he who had hired the ass and the owner of the animal were desirous of sitting in the shade of the ass, and fell to wishing each other away. The owner insisted that he had hired out only the ass and not the shadow. The other insisted that as he had hired the ass, all that belonged to the ass was his." At this point in the story, Demosthenes turned to leave and the crowd clamored for him to finish the tale. "How is it you insist upon hearing the story of the shadow of an ass and will not give an ear to matters of great importance?" Demosthenes demanded, and the crowd finally permitted him to give the speech he had originally intended to make. But he never resolved the fine point in the story he had told.

There are legends that the great Greek orator was a stammerer, that he could not pronounce the letter *p*, and that he overcame his impediments by speaking with pebbles in his mouth against the sound of the surf, or by declaiming as he ran uphill. According to still another tradition, Demosthenes also mastered languages by copying Thucydides' direct and graphic *History of the Peloponnesian War* eight times.

Demosthenes committed suicide after the defeat of the confederate Greeks. The Macedonian general Antipater had demanded his surrender. Trapped by Antipater's emissaries in the sanctuary of the temple of Poseidon on Calauria, he drew his cloak over his head and sucked poison from a pen with which he was pretending to write a last letter. He stumbled from the temple, his last words: "But I, O gracious Poseidon, quit thy temple while I still live; Antipater and his Macedonians have done what they could to pollute it." An orator till the very end.

∇ ∇ ∇

Nicolas Deniker (1852–1918)

A follower of Apollinaire, this French poet, son of the librarian of the Museum of Natural History in the Jardin des Plantes, in Paris, was said to be "the only poet ever born in a menagerie."

∇ ∇ ∇

René Descartes (1596–1650)

Descartes's mother died shortly after giving birth to him. Descartes inherited the tuberculosis that killed her and as an infant was given virtually no chance to survive his coughing fits. But a midwife refused to give up on him and nursed him back to life. It is said that this is why he was named René—from Renatas, reborn.

Generally regarded as the founder of modern philosophy, the French philosopher may also be the inventor of roulette, a gambling game of French origin (though the game's name is first recorded in 1745).

In a letter to Jean-Louis de Balzac from Amsterdam, Descartes expressed one of the first defenses of city as opposed to rural living: "In this great city where I now am..." he wrote, "I take my walk every day amid the Babel of a great thoroughfare with as much freedom and repose as you could find in your garden walks; and I observe the people whom I see just as I should the trees that you find in your forests or the animals that graze there; even the noise of their bustle does not disturb my reveries more than would the murmuring of a stream. When I consider their activities I derive the same pleasures which you have in watching the peasants till your fields, for I see that all their toil helps to adorn the place of my abode, and supplies all my wants. If there be pleasure in seeing the fruit grow in your orchard…think you there is not as much in seeing the vessels arrive which bring an abundance of all the produce of the Indies and all that is rare in Europe?"

An old tale credits the French philosopher as the inventor of a robot constructed in the shape of a woman. Descartes had to ship the robot by sea; the curious captain of the vessel opened the crate it was packed in and examined the robot. Afraid that this lifelike thing capable of movement could only be the devil in disguise, he threw it overboard.

News reached Descartes in 1647 of Pascal's statement that "any vessel, however large, can be made empty of all matter," that is, made into a vacuum. "The only existing vacuum," Descartes replied, "is in Pascal's head."

When Descartes tried to convince Swedish Queen Christina that all animals are "mechanisms," she replied, "I have never seen my watch give birth to baby watches."

In September 1649, Sweden's Queen Christina sent a warship commanded by an admiral to fetch Descartes from Holland to teach her his philosophy. It was arranged that he would give her lessons three days a week at five in the morning, the only time the busy monarch could spare. Rising so early in the severe cold of the northern winter proved too much for him and he fell ill on February 1, 1650, and died 10 days later.

∇ ∇ ∇

Antoinette du Ligier de la Garde Deshoulières (1638–1694)

Married at 13, she followed her soldier-husband to the wars. One time, because she insisted that her husband be given his back pay, she was imprisoned in a rural chateau, and her husband, leading a small band of soldiers, rescued her. Studying and writing poetry on her own, she was later pronounced the best woman poet in France by Voltaire; some critics went so far as to call her "the French Calliope" and even "the tenth muse."

Diagorus the Atheist (fl. last half of 5th century B.C.)

A religious youth who spent much of his time writing religious hymns, Diagorus underwent a radical transformation and became a confirmed atheist. He claimed that some great wrong someone had done to him had gone unpunished by the gods and thus he refused to believe in them. In any event he went by the name Diagorus the Atheist and was sentenced to death at Athens for his blasphemous speeches and writing. He had to flee to Corinth, where he became lost to history.

∇ ∇ ∇

Denis Diderot (1713–1784)

In about 1770 Catherine II, Empress of Russia, allegedly wrote the French philosopher and man of letters as follows: "In all your plans of reform you forgot the difference between our positions. All your work is done on paper, which does not mind how you treat it...But I, poor Empress, must work upon human skin, which is much more ticklish and irritable."

Planning a short visit to see Catherine the Great in 1773, Diderot stayed five months. A man who forgot himself in the heat of discussions, he would usually speak to her two or three hours a day, dominating the conversation. Sitting close to Catherine, face to face, he was so carried away with his conversation that he continually pounded on her knees, leaving them so black and blue after a few days that the empress had to place a table between them for Diderot to pound on.

He had consistently criticized Boucher's paintings for their "simperings, affectations...frivolous women, libidinous satyrs [and] bastard infants..." But when the artist died at his palette, his conscience bothered him. "I have spoken too much evil of Boucher," he admitted. "I retract."

Diderot appears to have invented the phrase "staircase wit" (l'esprit de l'escalier), the smart remarks or ripostes one thinks of too late, on going down the stairs rather than at the party.

The famous French Encyclopédie edited by Diderot actually began as a 1745 translation by John Mills of Englishman Ephraim Chambers's Cyclopaedia. The vast revision made by Diderot of Mills's translation was mutilated by the king's printer, Lebreton. After Diderot had corrected the last proof sheet, Lebreton, fearing royal displeasure, secretly and hastily cut out anything that seemed daring or likely to give offense to the monarch. Diderot, beside himself with rage and grief, could no nothing.

While working on the *Encyclopédie* Diderot gave special attention to the machines he described in its pages. Spending days in workshops, he learned not only how to operate complicated machines such as stocking looms, but also how to take them apart and put them together again.

Arrested on the orders of the Comte d'Argenson in 1749, Diderot was cast in a cell of the fortress of Vincennes outside Paris. Even here the industrious encyclopedist kept busy. He read and annotated a copy of *Paradise Lost* he had in his pocket, using a toothpick for a pen and ink made from ground slate that he scraped from his prison walls and mixed with wine.

∇ ∇ ∇

Ludwig Dindorf (1805–1871)
This German writer, who worked prodigiously with his brother Karl (1802–1883) on important scholarly projects, was so quiet and unassuming, and lived so secluded a life, that his very existence was doubted. People argued that there was no Ludwig Dindorf, that Ludwig was a mere pseudonym that *Karl* Dindorf used because he wrote so much!

∇ ∇ ∇

Isak Dinesen (Karen Christence Dinesen, Baroness Blixen-Finecke; 1885–1962)
The Danish author's father, a writer and member of Parliament, committed suicide in 1895 when 50, mainly due to his lingering sorrow over the terrible death by typhoid of his niece, Countess Agnes Frijs in 1871. Wilhelm Dinesen had fallen in love with his young niece two years before her death and could never forget her. Isak Dinesen used her father as the basis for Ib Angel and her cousin as the model for Adelaide Von Galen in her story "Copenhagen Season."

∇ ∇ ∇

Diodorus Siculus (c. 40 B.C.)
A contemporary of Julius Caesar, this Sicilian author is one of the first writers on the legends and origins of mythology. He mentioned a Sicilian fountain called Acadia that had the magic power to determine if a manuscript were a true work of art. If writings floated when thrown in, they were genuine; if they sank to the

bottom of the fountain, they were false. Siculus makes no mention of *writers* being thrown in.

Siculus's history of the world, of which only 15 of 40 books survive, tells of one Greek city where politicians were required to propose all new laws with a noose around their necks. Should the law fail to pass, they were hanged.

∇ ∇ ∇

Diogenes (412?–323 B.C.)

The cynical Greek philosopher is said to have walked the streets of Athens with a lantern in broad daylight searching for an honest man, thus expressing his contempt for his generation. His house was a narrow, open earthenware tub which he trundled about with him. On seeing a child drinking from cupped hands, he threw away his only worldly possession, a wooden bowl. Yet the Greeks nicknamed him "dog" for what they considered his shameful ways; the word *cynic* itself comes from the Greek for "doglike" or "snarling."

Hearing that Plato defined man as "a two-legged animal without feathers," Diogenes delivered a plucked cock to the academy, remarking, "Here is Plato's man." Plato had to add to his definition: "with broad flat nails."

What is the proper time for supper, someone asked him. "If you are a rich man, whenever you please," he answered, "and if you are a poor man, whenever you can."

"What would you take to let a man hit you on the head?" he was asked. "A helmet," he replied.

Early in his life Mediterranean pirates captured Diogenes. When they told him he was destined for the slave market, he replied that he would like to be sold to a man who needed a master.

On being asked by Alexander the Great if he could oblige him in any way, Diogenes answered, "Yes, by standing out of my sunshine." To which Alexander admiringly replied, "If I were not Alexander, I would be Diogenes."

"What are you looking for?" Alexander asked Diogenes as he searched through a pile of human bones.

"I am searching for the bones of your father," the philosopher said, "but I cannot distinguish them from those of his slaves."

Aristippus of Cyrene, a pupil of Socrates, regarded pleasure as the only absolute good in life. His philosophy won him a place in the court of Dionysius, ruler of Syracuse, while Diogenes, who advocated a simple mode of life, lived in poverty. One day Aristippus came upon Diogenes in the street washing lentils for a soup he was making. "Oh, Diogenes," he said, "if you could but learn to do a small thing such as flattering Dionysius, you would not have the sad fate of living on lentils." Replied Diogenes, "O, Aristippus, if you could but learn to do a small thing such as living on lentils, you would not have the sad fate of having to flatter Dionysius."

A lawyer and a doctor are said to have asked the philosopher which one of them had precedence. Instructed Diogenes: "Let the thief go before and the executioner follow."

Shortly before he died he fell asleep and his physician awoke him, asking if anything ailed him. "Nothing, sir," he replied, "only one bother anticipates another—Sleep before Death."

Legend has it that Diogenes was so cynical that he asked to be buried upside down, believing the world would always be topsy-turvy. It is also said that he died on the same day as Alexander the Great. All that is known is that on his death the Corinthians erected to his memory a pillar atop of which rested a marble dog.

∇ ∇ ∇

Peter Gustav Lejeune Dirichlet (1805–1859)

The German mathematician and author, famous for his work on the theory of numbers, was a workaholic who literally wasted no words on personal correspondence. When his wife gave birth to their first child he telegraphed his father-in-law: "2 + 1 = 3."

∇ ∇ ∇

Etienne Dolet (1509–1546)

In his too brief life Dolet was a grammarian and historian and operated an important press. So fond was he of the works of Cicero that he declared, "I approve only of Christ and Tully." Dolet killed a painter during an argument but it was for heresy that he was later arrested and sentenced to death. In prison, before he was tortured and burned at the stake, he wrote *The Hell of Etienne Dolet*.

While walking to the stake he is said to have composed the punning pentameter: *Non dolet ipse Dolet, sed pia turba dolet.* ("Dolet himself is not sorry, but the devout throng grieves.")

▽ ▽ ▽

Domitian (51–96 A.D.)
Whatever one concludes about a Roman emperor who packed his brother, the Emperor Titus, in snow to hasten his end, there is no doubt that Domitian was a great patron of the arts. To inspire the writing of poetry, for example, he began the Capitoline games, which included contests in literature. Domitian was an author himself. Besides writing poetry, he authored a book entitled *On the Care of Hair.* His expertise, however, did him no good, for he became totally bald several years later.

▽ ▽ ▽

Fyodor Dostoyevsky (1821–1881)
So poor was the Russian author in his early years that he often had to pawn or sell his clothes. In fact, he once attested that he always pawned his overcoat five or six times each winter.

Dostoyevsky was generous to a fault when he had money. Late in his life beggars would station themselves along the route of his afternoon walk, knowing he would never refuse anyone if he had a ruble in his pocket. One afternoon his wife disguised herself as a beggar and, holding their daughter by the hand, approached him as he walked. "Kind sir, have pity on us!" she begged. "I am a sick woman with two children to look after." Dostoyevsky handed over a few rubles before recognizing her.

In 1849 Dostoyevsky was sentenced to be shot for political activities against the czar. On December 22nd he and 20 other prisoners were carted through the streets of Moscow to Semyonovsky Square, where an officer "allowed us to kiss the cross, broke a sword over each of our heads, and attired us for execution" in white shirts. "Present arms!" the commanding officer ordered the firing squad. The death sentence was read for each man and a priest preached to all the prisoners as perhaps 3,000 people watched. Hoods were placed over the prisoners' heads, they were tied to posts and the firing squad took aim. But after nearly a full minute—a minute that seemed forever—no shots were fired. Only then did an officer step forward to tell Dostoyevsky and the others that their lives were to be spared. The "execution" was only a cruel joke on the part of the czar and his advisers. Dostoyevsky's actual sentence was four years of hard labor in Omsk, Siberia, plus five more years of military service there.

While he was imprisoned in Siberia, reading became almost all of Dostoyevsky's life. One writer whose stories he read signed himself "L. T." and Dostoyevsky liked his work but thought it was ephemeral. "I believe he will write very little," Dostoyevsky said, "but perhaps I am mistaken." He certainly was— about Leo Tolstoy.

After his epileptic seizures Dostoyevsky would sometimes lose his memory: The names of the characters and the plot in novels he was writing (one reason for his detailed drafts), the names of friends, even his own name would escape him. The attacks were of a rare form now known as "Dostoyevsky epilepsy," during which he often had ecstatic visions and felt that he was at one with God in Paradise. But though he said he would not give up these moments for a cure, his attacks could be horrible, too, as his wife attests:

> Suddenly he broke off in the middle of a sentence, rose from the sofa and leaned over toward me. I surveyed his altered features with wonder, and at that very moment there came a fearful, inhuman shriek, and he began to sink farther and farther forward…An hour later there came a new attack, and this time it was so violent that he cried out with pain. Horrible! For several hours I sat listening to his cries and groans; his face was distorted with pain, his eyes stared crazily, his incoherent speech failed to make any sense. I was almost certain that my beloved husband was going insane….

Dostoyevsky wrote his two great novels, *The Gambler* and *Crime and Punishment*, simultaneously, working on one mornings and the other evenings over the time that it took to finish them.

In one of his novels he wrote a sentence reading, "Beside it stood a round table of oval form." Someone pointed out the obvious error, but he was a stubborn man, possibly with his own reasons for the sentence, even if he told no one what they were. "Leave it as it is," he said after a moment's reflection.

The writer's gambling addiction was a disease that plagued him and his family most of his adult life. When abroad in Germany he would lose every penny he had, including his train fare home, only to borrow money from friends and relatives and lose that as well. On many occasions he pawned and lost everything of value that he and his wife possessed. "It was dreadful to see how Fyodor Mikhailovich suffered during this gambling," wrote his understanding wife, Anna. "Pale and exhausted, he would return home and beg for more money. It was all he could do to stay on his feet. Then he would go back again, but after half an hour he would return even more depressed, and then it continued until he had gambled away all that we owned. When he had nothing left Fyodor

Mikhailovich would pass into a state of such despair that he would begin to weep, throw himself on his knees, and beg forgiveness for having tortured me in this fashion. Then I would always have to convince him that the situation was, in spite of everything, not entirely hopeless, that there was after all a way out."

Dostoyevsky's editor on the *Moscow Gazette* made a number of cuts and changes in the manuscript of *Crime and Punishment*, and the author was mostly grateful for them. "I do not regret *all* the deletions ..." he wrote to his editor. "Some of them actually improve the passage. I have been painfully aware for twenty years now of a fault in my writing— long-windedness—but I am quite unable to rid myself of it."

He received hundreds of letters about *The Brothers Karamazov*, which appeared in installments in a popular magazine. Most readers were concerned about who the murderer really was. To one of them the author wrote: "It is not merely the novel's action that is important. Every author must be allowed to expect that the reader has a certain insight into the human soul."

Dostoyevsky's first child was baptized on May 19, 1868, and died eight days afterward of pneumonia. A few days later the author wrote this moving letter to a friend: "Perhaps my love for my firstborn was quite ridiculous, perhaps I sounded ridiculous when I wrote about her [to you]...This little, three-month-old creature, so pathetic, so tiny, was already a person and an individual to me. She had begun to recognize me, to love me, and she smiled when I approached her. When I sang her songs in my funny voice, she liked to listen to them. She did not screw up her face or cry when I kissed her; indeed, she stopped crying when I came near her...I am not afraid to say it—I would willingly be crucified if I could bring her back to life." In another letter he had written that the child resembled him "right down to the wrinkles on my forehead—there she lies [in her cradle] as if she were working on a novel!"

When Dostoyevsky's third and last child, Aleksei, died of an epileptic fit in 1878, he visited the Optina Hermitage and spoke to the elder Father Amvrosi, a holy man famous for his asceticism and humility. The elder's words of consolation, according to Dostoyevsky's wife, later became the famous words that Zosima says to the bereaved mother in *The Brothers Karamazov*.

Few great novelists could claim to be actors, but in 1860 Dostoyevsky played the comic role of the postmaster in Gogol's *The Inspector General*. His theater director in St. Petersburg called him a fine actor "who knew how to evoke real Gogolian laughter."

Dostoyevsky's wife, Anna, tried to make her husband jealous as a means of curbing his roving eye for young women. Early in 1876, for instance, she sent him an anonymous letter warning that as soon as he left home his wife frolicked like a dove "beneath the free sky with no thought of returning to its nest." She added that if he doubted the warning, he should "just take a look at the medallion she wears around her neck, and there you will learn who it is she carries in her heart." When Dostoyevsky returned home he demanded to see the medallion. His wife later recalled the confrontation.

"'Let me see your medallion!' he shouted at the top of his voice. I realized I had pushed the joke too far and undid my collar in order to pacify him. But I did not manage to take my medallion off myself. Fyodor Mikhailovich was unable to control his rage any longer. With all his strength he tore from my neck the thin chain he had bought for me in Venice. When he found the medallion he went quickly over to the writing desk; bending over the medallion, he began to study it. I saw that his hands were shaking so badly that he almost dropped it.

"'It's all very well for you to laugh, Anna,' he said when he finally discovered that the medallion merely contained a picture of Lyubov [his daughter] and himself. 'But just think what a misfortune might have come of this! In my rage I might have strangled you by mistake!'"

The author had no patience with grammars and stylebooks. When he edited *The Citizen* he angrily instructed the newspaper's proofreaders: "Every author has his own style and consequently his own grammatical rules. I put commas where I deem them necessary, and where I deem them unnecessary others must not put them!...[And] remember that I never use superfluous commas: Never add or remove a single one!"

Cervantes's *Don Quixote* was Dostoyevsky's favorite book. In his diary he wrote: "If life on earth comes to an end and human beings in some othe world were asked whether they understood their life on earth and what conclusion they had come to about it, a man could just present the volume of *Don Quixote* and say: 'Here is my conclusion on life. Can you condemn me for it?'"

An ardent nationalist, Dostoyevsky could not abide his fellow Russian novelist Turgenev's views about their homeland. Turgenev always seemed to be out of the country, and Dostoyevsky claimed he once told him that "If Russia could be swallowed up by the earth, it would not be a great loss to mankind nor would it cause great concern." One time, when both authors were visiting Germany, Turgenev confided that he was writing a long article berating Russophiles and Slavophiles.

"I advise you, for the sake of convenience, to order a telescope from Paris," Dostoyevsky told him.

"What for?" Turgenev inquired.

"It's a long way from here," Dostoyevsky said, angering him. "You'll train the telescope on Russia and you'll be able to watch us. Otherwise it is difficult to make us out from here."

Dostoyevsky had strange reservations about Shakespeare. In a letter to his brother (May 31, 1858) he perhaps echoed Ben Jonson when he wrote: "A thing that has been written all at once cannot be ripe. They say there was not a blot on Shakespeare's manuscripts. That is why there are so many enormities and so much bad taste in him; he would have done much better if he had worked harder."

Fortified by cigarettes (which helped kill him) and tea thick and sweet, Dostoyevsky typically worked at his desk all through the night. In a letter to a friend he explained why:

> It is night now; the hands of the clock are approaching six. The town is waking up, but I have not gone to bed yet. And the doctors say that I must not overexert myself, that I must sleep at night and not sit for ten or twelve hours at a stretch huddled over my writing desk. Why do I write at night? Well, as soon as I wake up around one (P.M.), there is a ring at the door: someone has come to ask me for something, someone else wants something else, a third person comes with some request or other, a fourth demands that I shall resolve some request or other, a fifth demands that I shall resolve some quite unresolvable "accursed question" for him—otherwise I'll go shoot myself, he says. (And this is the first time I have seen him.)...When will I get the time to think, to work, to read, to live?

An aristocrat submitted samples of his 15-year-old son's work to the author and asked his opinion of it. Dostoyevsky told him the stories were weak and wretched. "In order to write well one must suffer much!" he added.

"Well, in that case it'll be better if he doesn't write at all," snapped the boy's father.

His lung disease, probably emphysema brought on by his chain-smoking, sent him from medical specialist to medical specialist, from St. Petersburg to Berlin. Being referred to one doctor after another, with no noticeable improvement, led to his famous satire on medical specialists in *The Brothers Karamazov*. "And this way you have of referring people to specialists!" the Devil exclaims in that novel. "If it's nose trouble you have, you're sent to Paris: there they have an important specialist in nasal disorders. You go to Paris and he examines your nose. 'I can only cure your *right* nostril,' he tells you, 'I don't want to have anything to do with your left nostril. It doesn't fall within my area of specialization. But after you've been treated by me, you can go to Vienna. There you will find another specialist who will be able to treat your left nostril.'"

Perhaps no literary speech in history was received as emotionally as Dostoyevsky's words in praise of Pushkin at the Moscow Pushkin Festival in 1880. The author spoke of the values of love and reconciliation, and was hailed as a prophet by the audience. Without any exaggeration he described the scene in a letter to his wife:

> At every page, sometimes at every sentence, I was interrupted by bursts of applause. I read in a loud voice, with fire…And when, at the end, I proclaimed the universal oneness of mankind, the hall seemed to go into hysterics, and when I finished, there was—I won't call it a roar—it was a howl of elation. People in the audience who had never met before, wept, sobbed, embraced each other, and swore to become better, not to hate each other any more but to love one another…Everyone rushes up to me on the stage; grandes dames, girl students, state secretaries, male students—they all hugged and kissed me…They kept calling me back for half an hour, waving their handkerchiefs…I hurried backstage, trying to escape, but they forced their way in behind me, all of them, especially the women. They kissed my hands, they wouldn't leave me alone. The students pushed forward. One of them in tears, fell down on the floor in front of me in hysterics and lost consciousness. It was a complete, total victory!…

Dostoyevsky had a morbid fear of being buried alive, a fear so prominent that when he stayed at a friend's house, he often left a note by his bed instructing his host not to bury him should he appear dead in the morning, but to call a doctor to thoroughly examine him.

The author actually dictated an account of his death, in the form of a letter to a friend. Dictating to his wife, Anna, on the morning of January 28, 1881, he described in the third person his dying of "an artery burst in the lungs"; the end of the letter read: "By 12:15 A.M. Fyod[or] Mikh[ailovich] was fully convinced that he was dying; he confessed and took communion. Little by little his breathing improved, the bleeding slowed down. But inasmuch as the burst blood vessel has not healed, the bleeding has not stopped."

In the margin of one of his last letters, a few months before his death, Dostoyevsky wrote: "The entire literary world, without exception, is hostile to me—only the readers of Russia love me."

No writer before or since had had a funeral procession as large as Dostoyevsky's. As pallbearers carried his coffin some three miles to the cemetery, over 100,000 people spontaneously lined the streets to pay their last respects. It was, in fact, the largest funeral procession ever held in Russia.

Numerous services were held in Dostoyevsky's poor apartment when he died. Visitors tramped up the crowded stairs, shook their heads at the dirt on the floors and held their noses at the vile smell of cats and boiled cabbage in the hallways. "So this is how our great writers live!" one visitor was heard to comment.

∇ ∇ ∇

Draco (fl. 620 B.C.)

There is a story that the Athenian lawmaker, a popular man despite the stern *Draconian* laws he imposed, was literally killed with kindness. While he was sitting in the theater at Aegina in about 590 B.C., other spectators hailed him by throwing their cloaks and caps in tribute. So many landed on Draco that he smothered to death.

∇ ∇ ∇

Dulot (fl. 1648)

Bouts-rimes ("rhymes without lines"), a versifying game that originated in 17th-century Paris and spread to England and other countries, was invented by this minor French poet in 1648. Dulot, about whom little is known (even his first name is a mystery), complained one day that all his valuable papers had been stolen, including over 300 sonnets. When someone remarked that this was a lot of sonnets for even a prolific poet to have written in such a short time, Dulot explained that they were all "blank sonnets"—he had just put down the rhymes at the end of each line, nothing else. What the poet had done in all seriousness seemed amusing to everyone else, and his method became the basis for the poetry game still popular today. Over two centuries later Alexandre Dumas père invited all the poets in France to compose poems using sets of rhymes made for the purpose by poet Joseph Méry. Some 350 poets made submissions, which were published in 1865.

∇ ∇ ∇

Alexandre Dumas père (1802–1870)

All his life Dumas was taunted about his black ancestry and his father, General Alexandre Dumas, a huge mulatto whom the enemy called "The Black Devil." One time even Balzac sarcastically called the author "That Negro," and French critics dubbed him Dumasnoir, which can mean "Dumas night" or "black," and is also the French for "ghostwriter," a stable of which the novelist was accused of using. Perhaps the cruelest trick played on Dumas was the time his enemies hired blacks working for a touring American circus to swarm around him crying, "Cousin! Dear Cousin!" as if they were at a family reunion.

The author's father was a huge man with the strength of tigers. When a boy, Dumas reportedly often saw him ride into the stable and chin himself on the crossbeam, while raising his horse between his knees.

Dumas's father died when the novelist was only four. Soon after, young Alexandre's mother saw him with great effort carrying two heavy pistols upstairs. "What are you doing with those guns?" she cried out. "I'm going up to kill God for killing my papa," the little boy replied.

A much printed, traditional anecdote goes as follows:
"You are a quadroon, Dumas?" a boorish acquaintance asked the French novelist.
"I am, sir," said Dumas.
"And your father."
"A mulatto, sir."
"And your grandfather."
"A Negro, sir."
"And may I inquire what your great-grandfather was?"
Finally Dumas could suffer the fool no longer.
"An ape, sir," he thundered. "My pedigree commences where yours terminates."

The novelist's romantic image was besmirched when he fought his first duel at the age of 23. In the midst of the fighting his trousers fell down and the duel had to be cancelled.

Dumas's first book *Nouvelles Contemporaines* (1826), a slim volume of army tales that he published himself, sold just *four* of the thousand copies printed.

In the phenomenal two years 1844 and 1845 he wrote *The Three Musketeers*, *The Count of Monte Cristo*, *Twenty Years After* and half a dozen other novels! Though he was aided by researchers, these books were not written by a committee, as their vitality today attests.

No one knows why he called his famous novel *The Three Musketeers* when there are clearly four valiant members of the king's musketeers—d'Artagnan, Athos, Porthos and Aramis— involved in the story.

Dumas, well-named père, claimed to have fathered 500 illegitimate children, one of whom is generally known as Alexandre Dumas fils, author of *La Dame aux Camélias*. (Dumas fils, incidentally, is only one of a number of authors who were illegitimate; others include Boccaccio, Erasmus, Alexander Hamilton, August Strindberg, Guillaume Apollinaire, Henry Stanley, Jack London and T. E. Lawrence.) In his later years Dumas père was reproached for holding a young actress on his lap while two others rumpled his hair. "Sixty is twenty times three," he replied, "which makes me twenty years old for each of these three young ladies."

The author had a menagerie of wild animals, including three monkeys he named after literary critics. He also owned a pet vulture. Dumas purchased Jurgatha, as he called her, in Tunis and brought her back to Paris, where he tamed her and tried to teach her to speak like Polly—never succeeding, of course, because vultures are silent birds without voice boxes.

In Dumas's huge cookbook, which runs to some 1,000 pages in several editions, there is a recipe that begins: "Take one or more feet of young elephants..."

Rarely, a famous author will be so kind as to lend his name to a work written by a needy unknown colleague. Dumas père did this for Paul Meurice in 1845, signing his name to a novel he wrote not a word of so that Meurice could get a 30,000-franc advance from a publisher—enough for him to "bring off a superb marriage." Meurice got married and the world got *Les Deux Dianes*. It was said at the time that "Everybody has read Dumas, but nobody has read everything of Dumas, not even Dumas himself." The obliging author was less obliging to the stable of ghostwriters he kept to churn out formula novels, paying them with little more than food and wine.

One evening Dumas sat with rival French playwright Alexandre Soumet at the final performance of Soumet's latest play. Dumas pointed Soumet's attention to a sleeping spectator, saying, "You see, my dear Soumet, why your play must close." The next evening, however, a Dumas drama was playing in the same theater and Soumet thought he had revenged himself when he drew Dumas's attention to a spectator sound asleep through the whole performance. "It seems, my dear Dumas," he said archly, "that one can be put asleep by your plays, too." But Dumas never blinked. "Why that's the same man who was asleep last night," he said. "He hasn't been able to wake up yet!"

Prince Metternich once asked Dumas to autograph his album. "I'd be delighted to," Dumas replied and forthwith wrote in the book: "Received from Prince Metternich 25 bottles of his oldest Johannesberg. Signed Alex. Dumas."
Prince Metternich laughed and the next day had the wine delivered to the writer.

He was asked how he had enjoyed a frightfully tedious party. "I should not have enjoyed it if *I* had not been there," he replied.

Dumas was bested when an inexperienced young novelist sent him a manuscript and requested that Dumas collaborate with him. "Sir," Dumas replied angrily, "how dare you yoke together a noble horse and a contemptible ass."

"Sir," the young man wrote back, "how dare you call me a horse?"

Though Dumas père led a fuller, busier life than any two average men, he nonetheless suffered from insomnia. Yet despite his restless nights the novelist invariably could be found eating an apple at seven o'clock every morning under the Arc de Triomphe. His doctor had ordered him to make this his regimen in the hope that it would help him form regular rising and sleeping habits. On finishing his apple, this man of strict habits would go home to write his novels on blue paper, his poetry on yellow paper and his nonfiction on rose-colored paper.

Dumas's prolific habits were known throughout Paris, where he was called the "uncrowned king" of the city and it was said that "when Dumas snores, all Paris turns in her sleep." An apocryphal story making the rounds at one time or another in his life told of an autumn leaf that blew in through the open window of his study, alighting on his desk. Dumas promptly signed it and sent it off to the printers.

In 1845 a friend bet Dumas that he could not write a book in three days. Dumas went home and began *Le Chevalier de Maison-Rouge*, the first volume of which he finished in just under 72 hours.

After writing for 20 years, Dumas sat down to compose a long, complicated tally sheet showing the economic results of his 73,000 hours of writing time. (It was actually directed to working men when he ran unsuccessfully for elective office.) Among numerous statistics, the novelist pointed out that his 400 books had paid the wages of 692 persons (compositors, printers etc.) for 20 years and that his 35 plays had given a livelihood to 1,041 persons for the 10 years he had been writing plays. "Adding rough work, coachmen, and the claque [paid applauders]," he pointed out, "[this worked] out to a GRAND TOTAL of 2,150 persons, who during an average of 15 years, earned their living directly through my writing activity." And he still had 22 years of writing left.

Toward the end of his life Dumas said: "I should have a fortune. I've earned millions. Any other man would have by this time 200,000 francs a year from investments alone, whereas I have 200,000 francs of debts."

Bailiffs, or process servers, were the bane of Dumas's life, constantly hounding him and serving him papers to appear in court, where he was continually being sued for his huge debts. One time the author was asked to give a donation to help bury a poor man, who he learned had been a bailiff.

"How much should I give?" Dumas asked.

"Five francs would be enough," he was told.

"Only five francs to bury a bailiff!" Dumas cried joyfully. "Here's ten. Bury two of them!"

As vain as he was vigorous and vital, he paid great attention to his appearance. "How do you grow old so gracefully?" an admirer once asked him. "Madame, I give all my time to it," he replied.

One of the greatest tributes ever made to a storyteller was paid when the great Dumas memorial in Paris was unveiled after his death. Said the main speaker: "If all who have ever had their lives lightened for a moment by the reading of one of your books would have contributed a penny toward your memory, we would have been able to cast your monument in gold."

∇ ∇ ∇

Alexandre Dumas fils (1824–1895)

The younger Dumas based his famous character Marguerite Gautier in *La Dame aux Camélias* (1848) on the Parisian courtesan Marie Duplessis, one of the novelist's many lovers. Marie Duplessis, who began her career as a streetwalker and was so beautiful that seven young men proposed a "one for each day of the week" syndicate to share her, died of tuberculosis when she was only 23.

Dumas fils received the present of a ring from the notoriously avaricious French actress Rachel. Bowing low, he immediately put it on her finger, explaining, "Mademoiselle, permit me to present it to you in my turn so as to save you the embarrassment of asking for it back."

The elder Dumas knew that he hadn't raised his son and namesake, author of *La Dame aux Camélias*, very well, once writing him: "When you too have a son, love him as I love you, but do not rear him as I have brought you up." Alexandre Dumas fils agreed, once commenting, "My father is a great big child whom I had when I was a boy." The son nursed the father in his final illness and later said that there was no gratitude: "He died as he lived...without noticing."

He was always sorry that his father acted so childishly, while the older Dumas regretted that his son had such an old head on young shoulders. One time a

Dumas père escapade drew a "What a great boy you are!" reproach from the son. "That's more than I was ever able to say about you," the father replied.

Off on a vacation together, Dumas and his son soon discovered that they had forgotten to take the keys to their trunks.
"What a pair of idiots we are!" Dumas cried.
"No need to couple the two of us in this," the younger Alexandre said.
"Very well then: What an idiot you are!" said his father.

Dumas was never angered by those spiteful critics who claimed that his son had the real talent in the family. On the contrary, hearing something to this effect one day, he held his son by the shoulders, looked into his eyes and said, "Yes, you're my best work. Someday I shall be known only as your father."

Attending a musical evening at the Paris salon of Madeleine Lemaire, where the walls were covered with some of the many popular flower paintings she had done, Dumas fils stepped back and examined the scene with a jaundiced eye. "Only God," he finally said, "has created more roses."

∇ ∇ ∇ ∇ ∇ ∇ ∇ ∇ ∇

Kurt Eisner (1867–1919)

The revolutionary Bavarian journalist's revelations regarding Germany's responsibility for World War I increased his already considerable unpopularity among German right-wingers. Shortly after he was elected president of Bavaria, when he was on his way to open the Bavarian assembly in 1919, he was shot to death in the street by the reactionary Count Arco-Vally.

∇ ∇ ∇

Filinto Elysio (Francisco Manoel de Nascimento; 1734–1819)

Though he had to flee Portugal because the Inquisition had ordered his arrest, Elysis remained the most esteemed Portuguese poet of his time. So many admirers imitated him at home that a whole school of poetry was named *Os Filintestas* after him. Filinto lived a long life and wrote his best poems between the ages of 70 and 85.

Empedocles (c. 484–424 B.C.)

Aristotle regarded this Greek philosopher, poet, scientist and statesman as the father of rhetoric, while others considered him the father of medicine. Empedocles discovered that air is a substance, and he is even thought to have conceived a crude "survival of the fittest" theory. The versatile genius was once offered the kingship of a city and refused it. Many legends have grown up about him, including tales that he could control the winds and raise the dead. Perhaps the most lasting is the story told by Lucian, and later by Milton, Lamb and Matthew Arnold, that when only about 40 years old he cast himself into the active crater of Mt. Etna to prove to people that he was immortal and was returning to the gods. Mt. Etna, however, destroyed the illusion by casting out his sandal.

∇ ∇ ∇

Quintus Ennius (239–169 B.C.)

"I grant you there are gods," the Roman poet once said, "but they don't care what men do, else it would go well with the good and ill with the bad—which rarely happens."

His contemporaries admired his genius while disliking his crude craftsmanship. Said Quintilian: "Let us revere Ennius as we revere the sacred groves, hallowed by antiquity, whose massive and venerable oak trees are not so remarkable for their beauty as for the religious awe they inspire."

The versatile poet bragged that the soul of Homer had passed through many bodies, including those of Pythagoras and a peacock, and now resided in his breast. Always sure of himself and his place in literary history, he composed the following epitaph for himself before dying of gout:

Pay me no tears, nor for my passing grieve;
I linger on the lips of men and live.

∇ ∇ ∇

Epimenides (6th century B.C.)

Many legends surround this semihistorical Cretan poet, the most famous being that he fell into a deep sleep in a cave and did not awake for 57 years. Epimenides is said to have been taken prisoner by the Spartans and put to death because he refused to prophesy favorably for them.

Desiderius Erasmus (1466–1536)

When in 1523, Ulrich Zwingli suggested that Erasmus should be made a citizen of Zurich, the Dutch humanist replied, "I wish to be a citizen of the world, not of a single city."

The illegitimate son of a priest, he became a monk only because his guardians, having embezzled his inheritance, cajoled him into it.

Erasmus once summed up his priorities to a friend. "When I get a little money, I buy books," he said, "and if any is left, I buy food and clothes."

In his early years as a scholar, Erasmus spent so much on books that he had little left to support himself. He once wrote to the bishop of Cambrai for help, imploring him: "My skin and my purse both need filling—the one with flesh, the other with coins. Act with your usual kindness."

Another time when pressed for money, Erasmus schemed to extract a gift of gold from a rich English lady. "Point out to her," he wrote a friend, "how much more credit I shall do her by my learning than the other divines whom she maintains. They preach ordinary sermons; I write what will live forever. They, with their silly rubbish, are heard in one or two churches; my works will be read by all who know Latin and Greek in every country in the world. Such unlearned ecclesiastics abound everywhere; men like me are scarcely found in many centuries. Repeat all this to her unless you are too superstitious to tell a few fibs for a friend." When this advertisement for himself failed, Erasmus wrote the lady directly, comparing her to all the great women of history and arousing her pity for lying that he was going blind. She sent him a large gift of money and his eyesight was miraculously restored. Erasmus, like many writers before and after him, "preferred to beg in freedom rather than decay in bonds" and turned down many church positions to continue his "free-lance" life.

Erasmus wrote his famous book *The Praise of Folly* in seven days while staying at Thomas More's home in England. Its Latinized Greek title, *Encomium Moriae* was conceived as a pun on More's name (*moros* the Greek for fool, *moria* for folly).

"My home," he once wrote to a friend, "is where I have my library."

At times his usually subtle and refined sense of humor could be crude and tasteless. On hearing that several heretics had been burned at the stake and their executioners had used a great deal of wood, Erasmus commented to a friend, "I would pity them less if they raise the price of fuel now that winter is coming on."

When he visited England, friends of Erasmus gave him gifts of money amounting to about $2,000 in today's money. Sir Thomas More mistakenly told him to take the money out of the country in French coins, believing that the English law prohibiting the export of gold or silver did not apply to foreign coins. It did and the coins were confiscated when Erasmus boarded his ship at Dover, leaving him almost a pauper. "I suffered shipwreck," he quipped, "before I went to sea."

▽ ▽ ▽

Sergei Esenin (1895–1925)
The Russian poet, who was married to the dancer Isadora Duncan, committed suicide by hanging himself. Before he did so, he cut his wrists and wrote a last poem in his own blood.

▽ ▽ ▽

Isabella d'Este (1474–1539)
"The first lady of the world," as poet Niccolò da Correggio called this Italian patron of the arts, was an intellectual prodigy who supported many artists and writers when she became duchess of Mantua, and whose letters are among the finest written during the Renaissance. One of her few strange indulgences was keeping dwarfs in her entourage (one of them was so short, said a court wit, that he would have drowned if caught in a one-inch rain). Isabella actually had six rooms and a chapel in her palace built to her dwarfs' measure.

▽ ▽ ▽

Euclid (fl. c. 300 B.C.)
The Greek mathematician and author, probably a pupil of Plato, was asked by Ptolemy I if there wasn't an easier way to learn geometry than the arduous way he taught it. "There is no royal road to geometry," Euclid replied.

▽ ▽ ▽

Euhemerus (c. 300 B.C.)
Writers have been known to exaggerate their sources but no one has exceeded the Greek author Euhemerus in this regard. It was this mythmaker's theory that the gods men popularly worshipped in the fourth century B.C. had all originally been kings and heroes (thus euhemeristic means interpreting primitive religious myths on a historical basis). In his philosophical romance *Sacred History* Euhemerus depicted the gods this way, insisting that they had merely been deified by their subjects or admirers. The writer claimed that he had found

documentary evidence confirming his theory inscribed on a gold pillar in a temple on the (unknown) island of Panchaea in the Indian Ocean.

∇ ∇ ∇

Leonhard Euler (1707–1783)

The Swiss mathematician and man of letters lived in a repressive Russia for many years, teaching at the St. Petersburg Academy, before he joined the staff of the Berlin Academy in 1741. Blind in one eye from too much study, he was considered abnormally quiet by Frederick the Great's mother. "Why don't you speak to me?" she asked him one time. "Madame," replied Euler, "I come from a country where if you speak you are hanged."

∇ ∇ ∇

Eupolis (c. 446–411 B.C.)

A bitter rival of his one-time collaborator Aristophanes—they accused each other of plagiarism—this Athenian comic poet may have died in the Peloponnesian War fighting for his homeland. One story, however, says that he attacked the Athenian leader Alcibiades once too often in his plays and an enraged Alcibiades drowned him.

∇ ∇ ∇

Euripides (c. 480–406 B.C.)

Legend has it that a group of Athenians held captive at Syracuse passed the time by enacting scenes from the great Attic dramatist's plays. So impressed were their hardened captors by these beautiful passages that they freed their prisoners and asked them to continue their playacting for a while as honored guests. When the former captives returned to Athens they honored the dramatist as a daring war hero who had liberated them.

So revered were Euripides' works in ancient Greece that prisoners were sometimes allowed to go free if they could recite passages from the poet. One time a vessel pursued by pirates wasn't allowed to enter a Sicilian harbor until some of the voyagers could recite a few lines from Euripides. And when Athens was conquered in 404 B.C. and about to be destroyed, the Spartan generals were moved to mercy by an Athenian singing the first chorus of Euripides' *Electra*.

One tradition holds that when the Athenian expedition to Syracuse failed in 415, the captured Athenians were chained and put to work in the stone quarries. All except those, Plutarch tells us, who could recite passages from the plays of Euripides.

Another ancient story, stemming perhaps from the fact that he lived alone with his books, hating society in general and women in particular, has it that a group of women at a secret festival plotted to murder Euripides because he had satirized them on the stage and had foiled their plans by sending his father-in-law to secretly spy upon them. This may not be true, but it is the plot of his play *Thesmophoriazusae*, which he wrote when 73.

Though his last years, in the words of a biographer, were spent staring out at the sea "all day long, thinking to himself and writing, for he simply despised anything that was not great and high," in his youth he had been a very active man. In addition to being a dramatist and accomplished painter he was an excellent athlete who won prizes at the games in Athens and Eleusis.

The Greek tragedian is said to have been "of a morose disposition," as might well be expected of a man who lost his wife, two sons and a daughter when they partook of a deadly but deceiving *Amanita* mushroom species. (*Amanita verna*, the destroying angel, is easily confused with several edible mushroom species.) Euripides himself possibly had an even more terrible death by natural forces: He is said to have been torn to death by the hunting dogs of King Archelaus of Macedonia, whom he served as court poet, or to have been ripped apart by a mob of women who objected to one of his plays.

∇ ∇ ∇

Johannes Ewald (1743–1781)
It wasn't until long after Shakespeare's *Hamlet* that Denmark had its first original native tragedy. This was Ewald's *Rolf Krage* (1770). The great lyric poet of the North also wrote the patriotic ballad "King Christian Stood by the Lofty Mast" (1770), long Denmark's favorite national song.

∇ ∇ ∇ ∇ ∇ ∇ ∇ ∇

Philippe-François Fabre d'Églantine (1750–1794)
This French poet and playwright is perhaps the only author in history to have named the months of the year. On the committee appointed to devise a new calendar during the French Revolution, he invented most of the picturesque names for its months.

Arrested on charges of treason during the Terror, d'Eglantine sang to the jury his pretty ballad "It is raining, it is raining, shepherd, bring in your white sheep." Deaf to his song, they sentenced him to death and he went to the guillotine, giving copies of his poems to people along the way.

∇ ∇ ∇

Gabriel-Urbain Fauré (1845–1924)
"What is the ideal tempo for a song?" the French poet, composer and songwriter was asked.

"If the singer is bad," he replied, "very fast."

∇ ∇ ∇

Abul Fazl (1551–1602)
Serving as historian of the great Mogul Emperor Akbar, Abul Fazl worked his way into the ruler's confidence and became his most trusted adviser, writing his chief history, the *Book of Akbar*, all the while. His influence grew so great, however, that he incurred the jealousy of a prince in Akbar's court, who hired an assassin to kill the author.

∇ ∇ ∇

Severino Ferrari (d. 1905)
This Italian poet had been declared insane and confined to a mental hospital in 1905. While there he was notified that he had been appointed professor of literature at the University of Bologna. The joy of at last winning this coveted post and the sorrow of being unable to accept it proved too much of a shock, and Ferrari dropped dead of a heart attack moments after hearing the news.

∇ ∇ ∇

Afanasy Fet (A. A. Shenshin; 1820–1892)
The Russian lyric poet and friend of Turgenev was reprimanded by some small-minded puritan for letting his poems be printed in an "improper" magazine. Replied Fet: "If Schmidt [the lowest St. Petersburg hack of the day] had been publishing a dirty sheet, bearing the title of a four-letter word, I would have let him publish my poems in it. Poetry purifies."

∇ ∇ ∇

Georges Feydeau (1862–1921)
The French playwright is apparently the originator of the old restaurant joke about the lobster with one claw. A waiter supposedly brought such a specimen

to his table, explaining that lobsters often fought in the tanks and were mutilated in this way. "Take this one away then," Feydeau said, "and bring me the winner."

One of Feydeau's early farces was almost booed off the stage on opening night, and a friend spotted the playwright himself standing in the aisle, joining in the hissing and catcalls. "Have you gone crazy?" his friend asked him. "No, this way I can't hear them," Feydeau replied, "and it doesn't hurt so much." (See also CHEKHOV.)

∇ ∇ ∇

Francisco de Figueroa (1536–1617?)
The Spanish pastoral poet wrote elegies, sonnets and songs in the Italian manner. He enjoyed great fame in his lifetime but his will ordered that all of his poems be burned on his death.

∇ ∇ ∇

Firdausi (Abul Qasim Mansur; fl. 999)
The longest poem composed by a single poet, and also the most profitable poem, was begun in A.D. 999 by the Persian author Abul Qasim Mansur, who used the pen name Firdausi. The *Shah-nama* or *Book of Shahs* was written for Sultan Mahmud, who promised Firdausi a gold dinar ($4.70) for every couplet he wrote of the 60,000-couplet epic that is a complete history of Persia's kings from 700 B.C. to A.D. 700. This would have come to $282,000 for the poem, but when Firdausi delivered it in the year 1010, the sultan reneged and gave him only 60,000 silver dirhams (about $30,000). Legend has it that the scornful poet gave half of the fee to a sherbet salesman and half to a bath attendant before leaving for another kingdom. Later, the story goes, Sultan Mahmud had a change of heart when a visiting troubadour quoted a beautiful couplet from the poem by Firdausi and ordered that 60,000 gold dinars' worth of indigo be sent to the poet along with his apologies. As the caravan pulled into Firdausi's village, however, it met a funeral procession carrying the poet's body to the grave. If Firdausi's family received the indigo, that would mean that over $312,000 was paid for the one poem, which is said to be the only poem written by a single author that became the national epic of a nation.

Another version of the poet's death has him wandering, old, broken and impoverished, in the streets of Tus, where he hears a child reciting a verse from the vicious satire he wrote of Sultan Mahmud, in which he taunts Mahmud's slave origins:

Had Mahmud's father been what he is now
A crown of gold had decked this aged brow.
Had Mahmud's mother been of gentle blood,
In heaps of silver knee-deep had I stood.

Knowing at last that all his country, even its children, grieved for his misfortunes, as would posterity, the poet, according to this story, went home, fell sick and died.

∇ ∇ ∇

Camille Flammarion (1842–1925)

The French astronomer and author once paid a young countess a compliment on her lovely skin. So grateful was she for this that she immediately remembered him in her will. When she died of tuberculosis a few years later, it was discovered that she had provided that a copy of his *Terres du Ciel* be bound with her skin. The book bears the inscription: Pious Fulfillment of an Anonymous Wish, Binding in Human Skin 1882. (See also EUGÈNE SUE and MAURICE HAMMONEAU.)

∇ ∇ ∇

Gustave Flaubert (1821–1880)

Flaubert and his publisher were charged with "immorality" when his novel *Madame Bovary* appeared in magazine form in 1856, but both were acquitted and the book was published a year later. The fictional Madame Bovary is based in part on Louise Colet (1810–1870), a French poet and novelist with whom Flaubert carried on an affair for some nine years, beginning in 1846. The real Madame Bovary lived in Paris with her husband, Hippolyte Colet, and her affair with Flaubert was the author's only serious liaison. It is hard to see where Flaubert could have gained his amazing insights into feminine psychology except by his intimate observations of this beautiful woman, who had obtained some notoriety by trying to stab a gossip columnist. However, the plot of *Madame Bovary*, and its heroine as well, to some extent, is also based on the life of Delphine Delamare. This woman, well known by a close friend of Flaubert's, was the wife of a colorless country doctor. Dreaming of a more romantic life, she took many lovers, spent everything she and her husband had saved, and finally committed suicide in 1848 when only 24 years old.

After reading his first novel, *The Temptation of St. Anthony*, to his friends Louis Bouilhet and Maxime Du Camp, Flaubert asked them for their frank opinion of it. Wishing to check what they regarded as his slide into romanticism, they were as frank as possible. "We think," said Bouilhet, speaking for the two of them, "you should throw it into the fire and never talk about it again."

Flaubert himself was once asked who Madame Bovary really was. "*I* am Madame Bovary," he replied.

Madame Bovary may have been his child, but the novelist certainly wanted no other children. "A son of my own!" he told a friend. "Oh, no no, no! Let my flesh perish with me, and let me not transmit to anyone the boredom and the ignominiousness of life."

When Flaubert was a boy, his physician father spilled hot barley water on his child's hand, causing partial paralysis and a permanent scar. Flaubert never forgot and used his father as the prototype for the fallible Dr. Larivière in *Madame Bovary* (1856).

His letters contain most of his famous literary dicta. In a letter written to a lady friend just after *Madame Bovary* was published came the most famous of all: "An author in his book must be like God in the universe, present everywhere and visible nowhere."

Flaubert knew the characters in his novels so well that he almost became them. While writing of Emma Bovary's suicide, he once confided, he could detect the taste of arsenic on his own tongue.

Despite several affairs, Flaubert remained a lifelong bachelor. It has been suggested, only somewhat facetiously, that he remained faithful to Madame Bovary, but more likely it was because of his mother, Anne-Justine-Caroline Fleuriot Flaubert, who lived with him until she died in 1872 and never freed him from her emotional apron strings. Flaubert once wrote to his mother: "I know very well that I shall never love another as I do you...Some will perhaps mount to the threshold of the temple, but none will enter."

The most discriminating and devoted of writers, he was invited to a weekend picnic by friends and declined because he had to work on a manuscript. His friends called early Monday morning to tell him what a good time they'd had and noticed that he was at the exact same place as on Friday—in the midst of writing a sentence divided by a comma. Lamenting his apparent lack of any progress at all, they were soon interrupted by Flaubert, who insisted that he had indeed made great progress. Why, he had changed the comma to semicolon on Saturday, and changed the semicolon back to a comma on Sunday!

He seems to have ended his long affair with Louise Colet mainly because she insisted on meeting his mother and he did not think her worthy of such an honor. He wrote a cruel last letter to her: "Madame: I was told that you took the trouble to come here to see me three times last evening. I was not in. And, fearing lest persistence expose you to humiliation, I am bound by the rules of politeness to warn you that *I shall never be in.*"

While traveling in the Orient he contracted a venereal disease in the brothels he visited. Despite picking up the malady that killed Maupassant and Baudelaire, among other French writers, he admired fallen women. "I like prostitution," he wrote to Louise Colet. "My heart has never failed to pound at the sight of one of those provocatively dressed women walking in the rain under the gas lamps…"

In an 1851 letter to his mother from Rome, Flaubert, who was lucky enough to have a small independent income, had this to say of what we call free-lancing today: "To practice art in order to earn money, flatter the public, spin facetious or dismal yarns for reputation or cash—that is the most ignoble of professions."

"Criticism occupies the lowest place in the literary hierarchy," he wrote to a friend. "As regards form, almost always; and as regards 'moral value,' incontestably. It comes after rhyming games and acrostics, which at least require a certain inventiveness."

"What a man Balzac would have been," he once said, "had he known how to write!"

"Writing is a dog's life," he admitted in a letter to a friend, "but the only life worth living."

"Do you know how many pages I have written this week?" he wrote to Louise Colet. "One, and I cannot even say a good one. What an atrociously delicious thing we are bound to say writing is—since we keep slaving this way, enduring such tortures and not wanting things otherwise."

"Prose was born yesterday," Flaubert once confided, "you have to keep that in mind. All possible prosodic [i.e., poetic] variations have been discovered; but that is far from being the case with prose."

Thomas Flournoy (fl. early 20th century)

This French "automatist," or practitioner of automatic writing (i.e., writing performed without the will of the writer), was one of several such authors who produced a book written in an "unknown tongue." In 1900 he published *Des indes à la planete Mars*, which he purported to have been written in "the Martian language."

∇ ∇ ∇

Bernard Le Bovier, Sieur de Fontenelle (1657–1757)

This French thinker, poet and man of letters, a nephew of Corneille, was told in his old age that he had to give up drinking coffee, for it was a slow poison that would ruin his system. "Doctor," he replied, "I am inclined to agree with you that it is a slow poison—very slow, for I have been drinking it for eighty years." He went on drinking coffee until he died, a month shy of his 100th birthday.

Even though he lived to be almost 100, dancing at a New Year's ball in the year of his death, he was in poor health all his life—a man who spit up blood at the slightest exertion.

"Death has forgotten us," an old friend said to him one evening. Replied Fontenelle, then well into his nineties: "Sh-shh!"

When he was approaching his 100th birthday, he abruptly entered the dressing room of Countess Anne Catherine de Ligniville d'Autricourt, a famous beauty of 32, and found her almost completely naked. Very politely he backed out of the room, bowing and saying, "Ah, Madame, if only I were but eighty years old."

∇ ∇ ∇

Girolamo Fracastoro (1483–1553)

A full-scale epidemic of venereal disease apparently first broke out in the Old World at the Siege of Naples during the Italian Wars (1495), although it had been noted in Europe long before Columbus. The plague became known under many names as it spread over the continent, but the word syphilis itself derives from the name of a character in a 1530 poem by Girolamo Fracastoro called *Syphilis sive Morbus Gallicus*, "Syphilis or the French Disease." In Fracastoro's New World fable Syphilis was a blasphemous shepherd who so enraged the sun god that he struck him with a new disease: "*He first wore buboes dreadful to the sight,/First felt strange pains and sleepless past the night;/From him the malady received its name.*" Fracastoro could have derived his character's name from the Italian for a native of *Sypheum* (now Montato) in Southern Italy, though the personal name more likely is from the Greek *suphilos*, "lover of pigs," or swineherd. In any case, the disease wasn't contracted among natives in the New World. In fact, the symptoms of syphilis may have been described by Thucydides as far back as 430 B.C. as "the plague of Piraeus." Over the ages its victims have included Herod, Julius Caesar, three popes, Henry VIII, Ivan the Terrible, Schubert, Goya, Keats and Goethe. Fracastoro, incidentally, escaped death by what many considered a miracle as an infant. While his mother cradled him in her arms, she was struck by lightning and killed, but the infant Girolamo escaped unharmed.

∇ ∇ ∇

Anatole France (Jacques Anatole Thibault; 1844–1924)
Although his fortunes would improve, the novelist was still a struggling author when the French government awarded him the Legion of Honor. A friend remarked that a cash award would have been better than the medal he received. "Oh, I wouldn't say that," France replied. "When I wear the sash, it will cover the stain on my jacket. That's useful."

His lifelong friend Mme. Arman de Caillavet both tirelessly promoted his career and urged him out of his inertia to write. In the dedication of *Crainquebille* (1904) he wrote: "To Madame de Caillavet, this book which I should not have written without her help, for without her help I should write no books."

"Never lend books," France advised a young author, "for no one returns them. The only books I have in my library are books that other folk have lent me."

∇ ∇ ∇

Frauenlob (Heinrich von Meissen; c. 1250–1318)
German poet Heinrich von Meissen became known forever by the name Frauenlob because in a famous debate with a rival poet he hotly defended the use of the word *Frau* for "lady" instead of the *Weib* that his opponent preferred.

∇ ∇ ∇

Fredegard (fl. 9th century)
This ancient poet of St. Riguier wrote a poem based on personal experience about a thrush "that sang so beautifully that he [the poet] lost his toothache."

Sigmund Freud (1856–1939)

His colleague Carl Jung was surprised to learn that the great enemy of repression was having disturbing, erotic dreams during his trip to America. "I continue to dream of prostitutes," he confided to Jung. "Then why don't you do something about it?" Jung replied. "But I'm a married man!" cried a shocked Freud.

One of Freud's students, knowing the cigar is often viewed as a phallic symbol by psychiatrists, asked the confirmed cigar smoker what he thought of this theory. Between puffs on his long Havana, Freud replied, "Sometimes...a cigar is just a cigar." (See also GEORGE SAND.)

"What progress we are making," he observed in a 1933 letter from Nazi Germany to his American disciple Ernest Jones. "In the Middle Ages they would have burned me. Now they are content with burning my books."

▽ ▽ ▽

Nikodemus Frischlin (1547–1590)

Wine in the poet was one of the ingredients of good poetry, claimed this German poet and scholar, who was charged with poisoning a young woman and whose enemies called him "a stinking, mangy poet...a lying, roguish abortion of the devil." Frischlin, possibly drunk, later tried to escape from prison, but the rope broke while he was lowering himself from his cell window and he fell to his death.

▽ ▽ ▽

Jean Froissart (1338–1410)

The great French chronicler, historian of 14th-century France, never won the security he deserved. Tradition holds that he died in such dire poverty that there was no money for his family to carve his name on his tombstone.

▽ ▽ ▽

Johann Fust (1400?–1466)

Very little is really known about the invention of printing. It is known that Johann Fust (or Faust), who died in 1466, is one of the pioneers of printing and advanced money to Gutenberg, later taking over his press and printing a Psalter in 1457. Fust was widely regarded as an infernal magician in his day. Isaac D'Israeli, the prime minister's father, tells this story about the printer in his *Curiosities of Literature* (1791):

When Fust had…printed off a considerable number of copies of the Bible to imitate those which were commonly sold as manuscripts, he undertook the sale of them at Paris. It was his interest to conceal this discovery, and to pass off his printed copies for manuscripts. But, enabled to sell his Bibles at sixty crowns, while the other scribes demanded five hundred, this raised universal astonishment; and still more when he produced copies as fast as they were wanted, and even lowered his price. The uniformity of the copies increased the wonder. Informations were given to the magistrates against him as a magician; and in searching his lodgings a great number of copies were found. The red ink, and Fust's red ink is peculiarly brilliant, which embellished his copies, was said to be his blood; and it was solemnly adjudged that he was in league with the Infernals. Fust at length was obliged, to save himself from a bonfire, to reveal his art to the Parliament of Paris, who discharged him from all prosecution…

∇ ∇ ∇ ∇ ∇ ∇ ∇ ∇ ∇

Galileo (Galileo Galilei; 1564–1642)

When Galileo was called before the Inquisition in Rome and forced to renounce the Copernican doctrine that the earth moves around the sun, which he had supported in his *Dialogue of the Two Chief World Systems* (1632), he was placed under house arrest for the remainder of his life and threatened with torture and death if he ever spoke such heresy again. Nevertheless, as he rose from his knees and shuffled toward the door, the old man was heard to mutter under his breath, "*Eppur si muove*—But still it moves."

∇ ∇ ∇

Federíco Garcia Lorca (1899–1936)

The gentle, perhaps best loved, Spanish poet of his day is said to have had a premonition of his death. Three months before the Spanish Civil War, Lorca was camping outside a remote village in Castile when at dawn a lamb appeared among the ruins of an old estate, "dropping like a gentle petal on the solitude of the place," as his friend the Chilean poet Pablo Neruda put it. But suddenly, to his great horror, a herd of wild pigs thundered into the clearing and tore the lamb to pieces, devouring it. Neruda always felt that García Lorca foresaw his death in this incident. Lorca was murdered by Nationalist partisans in July 1936 shortly after the outbreak of the Civil War.

Garcilaso de la Vega (Inca; 1540?–1616)

Remembered as the first South American in Spanish literature, the great Peruvian historian is also perhaps the only Incan writer whose work is known today. For Garcilaso de la Vega's mother "was of the Peruvian blood-royal" and he insisted that his illustrious heritage gave him the right to call himself "el Inca." This, in fact, was the name he used and the name he was known by.

∇ ∇ ∇

Pierre Gassendi (1592–1655)

This pious French philosopher, whose books preached the doctrines of Epicurus, was a vegetarian devoted to fasting for both religious and health reasons. He died one Lent of a fever from fasting too rigorously, although the 13 bloodlettings his doctors made also helped him along.

∇ ∇ ∇

Théophile Gautier (1811–1872)

The French architect Jules Vabre intended to publish a flawless French translation of Shakespeare and moved to London to perfect his English; even his close friends lost track of him because he spoke only English and even refused to open letters sent from France. One day in 1843 Gautier met him in the streets of London and was amazed to hear his strong English accent. "All you need to do, my dear Vabre, in order to translate Shakespeare," the poet joked, "is to learn French again!" But the monomaniac took him seriously. "You're quite right, I must start doing just that!" he exclaimed. Nevertheless, the translation never materialized.

∇ ∇ ∇

Aulus Gellius (c. 123–c. 165)

The Roman author of *Attic Nights*, "an ancient museum of curiosities" including anecdotes and literary history, is said to have invented the terms "classic" and "classical," by which he meant "art of the first class."

∇ ∇ ∇

Marie-Thérèse Geoffrin (1699–1777)

A power in literary society, Mme. Geoffrin gave weekly dinner parties attended by all the great French men and women of letters. In her later days she apparently grew more conservative, for as she lay on her deathbed she excluded all her friends from visiting her, "to defend my tomb from the infidels."

Comtesse de Genlis (Stéphanie-Felicité du Crest de Saint-Aubin; 1746–1830)

So genteel or prudish was this French society matron that she fired the bookseller who had supplied and arranged her library because he had placed books written by male and female authors on the same shelf.

∇ ∇ ∇

Étienne Saint-Hilaire Geoffroy (1772–1844)

In 1792 the great naturalist disguised himself as a commissioner of prisons and tried to free several Collège de France colleagues after they had been arrested by revolutionists and confined in St. Firmin prison. Failing to save his friends, largely because they refused to walk out of their cells behind him, Geoffroy returned to the prison the next day at four in the morning with a ladder that he propped up against a prison wall. His colleagues again refused to be rescued, but he managed to save 12 priests who had been condemned to death.

∇ ∇ ∇

Konrad von Gesner (1516–1565)

The Swiss scholar wrote important medical, natural history and philological works. In his *Bibliotheca Universalis* he strove to catalog all known Greek, Hebrew and Latin writings. He finished all but one volume of a proposed 21 and earned for posterity the title Father of Bibliography.

∇ ∇ ∇

André Gide (1869–1951)

While an editor at the *Nouvelle Revue Française*, Gide rejected Marcel Proust's *Remembrance of Things Past*, saying of the pages, "They're full of duchesses, not at all our style." Later he wrote an apologetic letter to Proust admitting that the rejection was "one of the most painful regrets and remorses in my life."

The Catholic mystic poet Paul Claudel had unsuccessfully tried to convert Gide. Several days after the author's death a telegram with Gide's signature appeared on a hallway bulletin board in the Sorbonne: "Hell doesn't exist. Better notify Claudel."

∇ ∇ ∇

Alberto Rojas Gimenez (d. 1927)

This bohemian poet from Chile originated the "Agu" school of poetry, the *agu* representing the first cry, or poem, of a newborn child. The generous Gimenez would often give away all the clothes on his body and when he had nothing left would quickly write a poem and leave it with those to whom he had given nothing else. One night this mysterious man was approached by a mysterious stranger who told him he wanted to "pay tribute" to him by leaping over his coffin when he died, and the man produced a notebook that recorded the names of others who had permitted this. Gimenez joyfully agreed and forgot all about the man. Years passed. The admirable poet, having given his jacket to someone in a bar, died of pneumonia contracted while he walked in his shirtsleeves across Santiago one bitter winter night. None of his poems had (nor has) ever been published. But at his wake his friends were amazed to see a mysterious stranger enter the room, brace himself, leap over the coffin and leave as suddenly as he had come.

∇ ∇ ∇

Paolo Giovio (1483–1552)

Giovio admitted that he had portrayed the people in his *Historiae Sui Temporis* according to how much money they paid him, but his book was nevertheless a major Renaissance history. For those who rewarded him, the pliable poet said, he wrote with his "pen of gold," while for the niggardly he used his "pen of iron."

∇ ∇ ∇

Joseph-Albert Glatigny (1839–1873)

While on tour in Corsica with a company of actors the French poet and dramatist was mistaken for a notorious criminal and arrested and put in irons for a week. It is said that this experience so weakened him that it caused his early death at the age of 34.

∇ ∇ ∇

Joseph Goebbels (1897–1945)

The term *book burner*, meaning "self-appointed censor" and worse, wasn't born until 1933, when thousands of pro-Nazi students ended a torchlight parade at the University of Berlin by burning a pile of 20,000 books while Nazi Propaganda Minister Joseph Goebbels proclaimed: "The soul of the German people can express itself. These flames...illuminate the...end of an old era and light up the new."

∇ ∇ ∇

Johann Wolfgang von Goethe (1749–1832)

As a young teenager he was so well known for his facile pen that a group of boys asked him to write a love letter to a friend in the style of a girl. When the young man received the trick letter, he was so taken with the way the "girl's" sentiments were expressed that he felt himself inadequate to answer and hired Goethe to write a reply.

In 1776 Goethe, incensed by criticism of his work, wrote the following doggerel, entitled "Reviewer":

> There was a fellow dropped in for lunch,
> Didn't bother me much, I just let him munch,
> Had the kind of meal I have every day;
> The fellow gorged himself mightily
> And for dessert ate up what I'd stored.
> But as soon as he'd left my larder cleared,
> The devil led him to my neighbor's, where
> After this fashion he discussed the fare:
> "The soup might have been more piquantly spiced,
> The roast more crisp, the wine better iced."
> A curse on that damnable knave, that evil-doer!
> Put the dog to sleep. He's a book reviewer.

Though Goethe is often painted as wise and austere, "the Wisest of Our Time," as Carlyle put it in *Sartor Resartus*, this consummate artist was a great lyric poet and all his early Sturm and Drang works were based on personal experience. Goethe did turn to classicism but not in his personal life. His wife Christiane, for example, was a lusty woman whose pet name for his penis was Herr Schönfuss, or "Mr. Nice-foot."

His romance, *The Sorrows of Young Werther* (1774), in which the hero Werthe kills himself, is said to have influenced many suicides, much to Goethe's despair. It is known that one young woman, a Fräulein von Lassling, took her life immediately afer reading it.

Goethe himself tried suicide after being rejected by a young woman in 1774. Keeping a sharp dagger near his bed, he attempted to stab himself in the heart on several occasions before retiring at night. He tried to "succeed in plunging the sharp point a couple inches deep into my breast," but could never make his hand perform the act and in time his broken heart mended.

At a dinner both men attended, the Reverend J. C. Hasenkampf called Goethe's *Werther* a "wicked piece of writing." Looking the author in the eye, he said, "May God improve your perverse heart!" Goethe simply replied, softly, "Remember me in your prayers."

To a neophyte poet who sent him a mediocre book of verse he wrote: "I have glanced through your little book. Since, however, in an epidemic of cholera, one must protect oneself against weakening influences, I have laid it aside."

An account that may be unreliable claims that Beethoven told the following story about Goethe at Teplitz in July 1812:

> Kings and princes can indeed bestow titles and orders, but they cannot make great men, who therefore must be held in respect. When two come together, such as Goethe and I, then these highborn gentlemen must observe what it is that counts for great with such as we. Yesterday we met the whole Imperial Family [of Austria], and Goethe disengaged himself from my arm in order to stand aside. I pressed my hat down on my head and went through the thickest of the crowd with my arms hanging at my sides. Princes and courtiers drew up in a double line; the Duke of Weimar took off his hat to me, and the Empress greeted me first. Much to my amusement I saw the procession file by Goethe, who stood at one side, bowing with his hat in his hand. I took him roundly to task for it afterward.

At about the same time in Teplitz, when Goethe and Beethoven would take walks together, people on the promenade often stepped to the side and saluted them. Said Goethe, quite annoyed: "What a nuisance! I can never avoid this sort of thing!" Replied Beethoven, smiling: "Don't let it bother Your Excellency; the homage is probably meant for me."

Looking on at the French Revolutionary army, which fought the professional troops of Prussia and Austria to a draw at the battle of Valmy in 1792, Goethe, on the staff of the Duke of Saxe-Weimar, uttered the prophetic words: "From today and from this place begins a new epoch in the history of the world."

Goethe is probably the only great poet ever to have an automobile named after him. In 1902 an admiring German manufacturer named the Goethemobile for the author.

"In our younger days," an aging Goethe wrote to a friend, "we were sure we could build palaces for mankind. With experience we learn that the most we can do is to clean up their dung hills."

∇ ∇ ∇

Nikolai Vasilievich Gogol (1809–1852)

The great Russian original *twice* burned the manuscript of the second part of his comic epic *Dead Souls* (1842). In 1845, during a spiritual crisis, he burned his drafts of part two, and seven years later, under the influence of a priest who encouraged him to renounce literature, he burned another version of part two after a period of prayer and fasting. He died 10 days later.

Carlo Goldoni (1707–1793)

The prolific Italian dramatist has been called one of the "most cheerful and lovable men in literary history." He himself explained his personality this way: "My mother brought me into the world with little pain, and this increased her love for me. My first appearance was not, as is usual, announced by cries; and this gentleness seemed then an indication of the pacific character which from that day forward I have preserved."

The founder of modern Italian comedy, he once bet a friend that he could write 16 comedies for the stage within a year. Not only did he win his bet, but the 16 plays included some of his best work. Yet, though this prolific author wrote some 250 plays over his long life, he died a pauper.

∇ ∇ ∇

Luis de Góngora y Argote (1561–1627)

This Spanish poet hardly deserves his fate in literary history. It is only fair to say that his arrows that were transferred into "flying asps" and his birds that became "feathered zithers" were part of a larger plan. Luis de Góngora y Argote wrote in a twisted, tortuous style in his later years, his syntax deliberately distorted in order to highlight words and create an unreal world. But he inspired many imitators, who inspired many critics, and unfortunately, his name is now a synonym for a deliberately obscure, meaningless and affected ornamental style. The Spanish poet after whom *gongorism* is named was essentially a lyric poet in his early years; his work was much admired by Cervantes, though no poem of his was published in his lifetime. Readers have discovered that his baroque *gongorisms*, a great influence on modern poetry, are far from meaningless, as difficult as the long poems like *Soledades* are to read.

∇ ∇ ∇

Gorgias (c. 485–375 B.C.)

One legend has it that the celebrated Sophist philosopher, whose fame is preserved in the dialogue of Plato bearing his name, was born during his mother's funeral. As his mother was being carried to the grave, cries were heard from the coffin and Gorgias was found inside, apparently having slipped out of his mother's womb after she died and was prepared for burial. In any case, the same legend has it that he lived a long life, and died when about 110.

Maxim Gorky (1868–1936)

The self-educated Russian author, who had to work for his living from the age of 8, grew so disgusted with his life of drudgery by the time he was 21 that he tried to commit suicide. Gorky wrote a note requesting that his body be dissected "to find out what sort of devil lived in me..." and shot himself in the chest. Luckily, the bullet only grazed a lung and he recovered from his wound.

∇ ∇ ∇

Jeremias Gotthelf (Albrecht Bitzius; 1797–1854)

Swiss pastor Albrecht Bitzius in 1837 published his humorous novel *Bauernspiegel*, which purported to be the life of a Jeremias Gotthelf narrated by himself. The novel proved so popular that the author retained his character's name for his nom de plume on all his many novels and short stories.

∇ ∇ ∇

Comte de Gramont (Philibert; 1620–1707)

The expression *a Gramont's memory*, a convenient one, derives from a tale told about the count and Lady Elizabeth Hamilton. While visiting England in 1663, the sharp-tongued Gramont is said to have grossly insulted and refused to apologize to La Belle Hamilton, whose brothers followed him as he prepared to leave the country, drew their swords, and asked if he hadn't forgotten something. "True, true," he replied, unruffled. "I promised to marry your sister." This he did. In fact, it would be expected, judging from the French courtier's life. Only the year before his marriage, Philibert, Comte de Gramont, had been exiled from Paris for attempting to rival King Louis XIV in a love affair. The French diplomat's memoirs, a masterpiece of the genre, vividly describe the licentious court of England's Charles II. They were written by Gramont's brother-in-law, Anthony Hamilton, from materials supplied by the count. So sharp-tongued was Philibert that one writer describes the immense feeling of relief expressed by the French court when, in 1707, it was announced that he had died. Even at 87 he was still a threat to anyone who crossed him.

At table Charles II bragged to Gramont that his English servants waited on him on bended knee as a form of respect. "I thank Your Majesty for the explanation," Gramont replied. "I thought they were begging your pardon for serving you so bad a dinner."

Bernard Grasset (fl. early 20th century)

The French publisher fought a duel with a newspaper critic who had savaged one of the books on his list. Wounded on the forearm, he was, according to a biographer, "happy he had shed blood in defense of one of his authors."

∇ ∇ ∇

Friedrich Melchior von Grimm (1723–1807)

Baron von Grimm was the foremost literary historian of his day through his newsletter *Correspondance Littéraire*. But "the most French of Germans" was a proud, vain man who spent a good part of the day staring into mirrors. He drenched himself in so much perfume that he was known as "the musk bear." When an actress spurned his love he lay on his bed for almost a week "with his eyes open...without speaking, eating, or stirring."

Grimm was adept at unctuously praising the prominent, but some of them saw through him. Frederick the Great would subscribe to his *Correspondance Littéraire* only if he would agree to "spare me his compliments."

"What is the use of this new invention?" the German man of letters was asked. "What is the use of a newborn child?" Baron von Grimm replied. (The anecdote is also told of Benjamin Franklin.)

∇ ∇ ∇

Jacob Grimm (1785–1863) and
Wilhelm Grimm (1786–1859)

The brothers Grimm, immortal for their fairy tales, started their German diction- ary, *Deutsches Wörterbuch*, in 1854. Scholars did not complete it until 1971—the world's longest literary gestation with 33 volumes and 34,519 pages and a price of $3,000.

∇ ∇ ∇

Jean Grolier de Servières (Vicomte d'Aguisy; 1479–1565)

Rich, ornate bookbindings are called Grolier bindings, after Jean Grolier, who was not a bookbinder or printer but a prominent French bibliophile. Grolier collected books and had them bound by the best artisans of his day, with each book bearing the inscription *J. Grolerii et amicorum*. All the books in his library, sold in 1675, are world-famous collector's items. Some 350 of the 3,000 volumes are known to be still in existence.

Hugo Grotius (1583–1645)

The Dutch statesman and author, whose *Adamus Exul* (1601) provided some inspiration for Milton's *Paradise Lost*, was in 1619 condemned to life imprisonment for conspiracy against the state and jailed in the fortress of Louvestein. His wife obtained permission to stay with him and she soon conceived an ingenious escape plan. She sent Grotius's books out of the prison concealed in a chest of linen. After a few times the guards let the chest pass without checking the contents. Then, when she had sent out all the books, she persuaded her husband to conceal himself in the chest and be smuggled out. "This chest is so heavy, there must be an Armenian in it," the soldiers complained, and she laughed, "There are indeed Armenian books in it!" The chest was carried to the house of a friend, and Grotius, dressed like a mason, with hod and trowel, crossed over the border.

∇ ∇ ∇

Francesco Guicciardini (1483–1540)

Guicciardini was called the greatest historian of the 16th century for his masterpiece, the 10-volume *Storia d'Italia*. Once Charles V kept his noblemen and generals waiting for hours in an anteroom while he talked with Guicciardini. "I can create a hundred nobles in an hour," he said, "but I cannot produce such a historian in twenty years."

∇ ∇ ∇

Carlo Guidi (1650–1712)

This Italian lyric poet is said to have "died of shock" after he had translated a religious work into Latin and presented a copy to Pope Clement XI, and it was brought to his attention that the Latin word *sine* (without) had been printed as *sin* throughout the book.

∇ ∇ ∇

Lucien Guitry (1860–1925)

A young author sent the French actor a play he had written, with a covering note saying, "I bet you a louis that you don't read this script." Guitry returned the manuscript unopened along with an envelope containing a louis and a note reading, "You win."

∇ ∇ ∇

Sacha Guitry (1885–1957)

The French playwright, son of actor and author Lucien Guitry, lay on his deathbed when a young reporter called on him. "I know, sir, that your moments are precious," the reporter apologized. "No, my friend," said Guitry. "It isn't that they're precious— it's that they're numbered."

∇ ∇ ∇

Johann Christian Günther (1695–1723)

Günther, his poetry much admired by Goethe, drank so heavily that his family broke with him, refusing him any more help. He sank even lower, wandering through Europe until he reached Leipizig, where the author J. B. Mencke tried to befriend him. Mencke recommended Günther to Frederick Augustus II, King of Poland, but the dissolute poet appeared at the audience completely drunk, much to the king's displeasure, and was thrown out of the room. He died drunk several years later, when only 28 years old.

∇ ∇ ∇

Gustavus III (1746–1792)

The brilliant, handsome Swedish king wrote the first Swedish drama, *Gustavus Adolphus' Magnanimity* (1782). Before this the only plays seen in Sweden were foreign plays acted by foreign actors. Gustavus, in fact, composed a series of plays and encouraged other native authors to write more.

Gustavus refused to beware the ides of March when a letter warned him not to attend a masquerade ball on March 15, 1792. Though he wore a mask to the ball, an assassin involved in a conspiracy of nobles to overthrow the monarchy recognized him by the medals he wore and shot him. "I feel like the Pope borne in procession through Rome," he joked as he was carried back to the palace, but 10 days later he was dead of his wounds, at the age of 45.

∇ ∇ ∇

Johann Gutenberg (c. 1398–1468)

Few great men of relatively modern times have left such meager records of their lives as Gutenberg, the German printer generally believed to be the inventor of movable type. No likeness exists of him and his life is veiled in obscurity. Gutenberg may have adopted his mother's maiden name, for his father's surname appears to have been Gensfleisch. It is known that the goldsmith Johann Fust loaned the printer money to establish a press at Mainz, which Gutenberg lost to him in 1455 when he failed to repay the loan. But no book extant bears Gutenberg's name as its printer, and though he is still regarded as a likely candidate, he may not have invented printing in the West or even printed the *Gutenberg Bible* (1450). The Bible is certainly not the first book to be printed in Europe. Gutenberg himself had printed several small books before it. As for movable type, it had been used in Korea before its uncertain European invention.

Whoever printed the Gutenberg Bible produced a beautiful work complete with colored initials and illumination by hand. It is often called the Mazarin Bible because the first copy to come to attention was found in the library of Cardinal Mazarin in 1760.

A traditional story has Gutenberg saying to a friend: "With my 22 soldiers of lead I shall conquer the world."

∇ ∇ ∇ ∇ ∇ ∇ ∇ ∇ ∇

Al-Hadram (c. 1000)
The Moorish scholar attended a rare book auction in Cordova and found himself outbid for a volume he wanted. The rich, successful bidder explained that he bought the volume because it was the exact size he needed to fit a vacant niche in his library. "I was so vexed," Al-Hadram recalled, "that I could not help saying to him, 'He gets the nut who has no teeth.'"

∇ ∇ ∇

Hadrian (A.D. 76–138)
Among the most capable of Roman emperors, Hadrian was also one of the few rulers in history who could claim to be a poet, and wrote an autobiography and many speeches in addition to his poems. With the exception of several epigrams his poetry was generally regarded as rather mediocre. He saved his most inspired and best poem until the very end, writing it on his deathbed. This celebrated dying address to his soul begins, roughly:

> O carefree little soul, thou, darting away,
> Guest and comrade of this my clay,
> Where will you go, to what place
> Bare and ghostly and without grace?

∇ ∇ ∇

Hafiz (Shams-ud-din Mohammed; c. 1300–1390)
Hafiz means "one who remembers," and was a title given to anyone who learned all 114 chapters or *suras* of the Koran by heart. The Persian poet Hafiz, however, hardly led an ascetic life; he loved wine, women and song, much to the displeasure of his monastic colleagues, and his poems and drinking songs sing of

love, nature and good times. Not fully appreciated in his rigid conventional world, he managed to live an apparently happy and long life, not dying until he was about 90. He is buried at Shiraz, near the grave of Sa'di, another great lyric Persian poet. The greatest Persian poet of his time, in a country where poets were honored like generals, a future generation enshrined the melodious poet's remains in a garden called the Hafiziyya in Shiviaz, Iran, which, ablaze with roses, is one of the most beautiful monuments to a poet in the world.

According to legend, when the Tatar scourge Timur (Marlowe's Tamburlaine), who had once compacted 2,000 men with bricks and clay and built a minaret with them, invaded Shiraz, he reproached the impoverished poet for writing lines declaring that he would give all of Bokhara and Samarkand for the mole on a pretty woman's cheek. "I have subjugated most of the habitable globe...to embellish Samarkand and Bokhara, the seats of my government," he cried, "and you, miserable wretch, would sell them both for the black mole of a Turk of Shiraz!" "Alas, O Prince," the poet replied, "it is this prodigality which is the cause of the misery in which you find me," and Timur was so pleased with the answer that he spared his life and rewarded him with a valuable gift.

∇ ∇ ∇

Hakam II (913?–976)
Few rulers surpassed this caliph of Spain in his love of literature. A poet himself, he aided hundreds of poets and artists. A contemporary historian wrote: "He would...send gifts of money to the celebrated authors in the East, to encourage the publication of works, or to obtain the first copies of them. In this way, knowing the Abu'l Faraj of Isfahan had written a work entitled *Kitab al-Aghani*, he sent him 1,000 dinars of pure gold [about $50,000 today], upon which the author forwarded him a copy of this work, even before it had appeared in Iraq."

∇ ∇ ∇

Max Halbe (1865–1945)
Early in his career the German playwright often hadn't enough money to eat or pay his rent. "Herr Halbe, if you don't pay up now," his exasperated landlady told him one time, "I'm afraid I'll have to take you to court." "My dear lady, please don't," Halbe begged. "Let me make another suggestion—raise my rent."

∇ ∇ ∇

al-Hamadhani (Badi al-Zaman; 969–1007)
al-Hamadhani, renowned for his fluency, his fabulous memory and the poetical puzzles he constructed, enjoyed a fame in his lifetime equalled by few poets

anywhere. The Arab poet was widely known as *Badi' al-Zaman*, "the wonder of the age."

∇ ∇ ∇

Hammad (c. 743)

The Caliph Hisham, a patron of the arts who amassed a great library, could not recall a poem he had read many years before and summoned the poet Hammad. The poet remembered all of the poem, recited it and Hisham rewarded him with two slave girls and 50,000 dinars, more than $250,000. So the story goes. In any case, Hisham's great library was ruined by his son Hisham II, a weakling who allowed the clergy to weed out from the royal library all books that they thought impugned the Sunni creed in any way.

∇ ∇ ∇

Maurice Hammoneau (fl. 19th century)

Sold at auction in New York in early 1978 was a 21-volume series about animals by French author Marucie Hammoneau. The author had hunted down each animal described and used the appropriate animal skin to bind each volume. Included was a book on human beings; no explanation was given about the source of the cover. Earlier in France a publisher with a weird sense of humor had produced an edition of Rousseau's *Social Contract* bound in the skins of aristocrats guillotined during the French Revolution. (See also CAMILLE FLAMMARION and EUGÈNE SUE.)

∇ ∇ ∇

Knut Hamsun (1859–1952)

The Norwegian author, born Knut Pedersen, suffered the semistarvation described in his first novel *Hunger* (1890) while he tried to make a living working as a laborer and streetcar conductor in his own country and the United States. Hamsun's life was a hard one before he won the Nobel Prize for literature in 1920, but he managed to travel extensively despite his lack of money. Largely a self-educated man, he did not know much French when he visited France for the first time during the winter of 1894–95. "At the beginning, didn't you have trouble with your French?" a friend asked him when he returned. "No," he replied, "but the French did."

When the Nobel Prize-winning author supported the collaborators called Quislings after the Nazis invaded Norway in World War II, his countrymen mailed back thousands of his books to him, including a morocco-bound complete set of his works that had been publicly auctioned off for the equivalent of 25 cents. So many books were received by his hometown post office that additional workers had to be hired to deliver them.

$$\triangledown\ \triangledown\ \triangledown$$

Han-shan (fl. late 8th century)

Little is known of the life of the untutored Buddhist "poet-recluse" of China, who lived on Cold Mountain in Chekiang province all his adult life. Supposedly, the provincial governor there made a collection of all Han-shan's 300-odd poems, copying them from the trees and rocks where Han-shan had written all of them. (It spoils a good story to relate that the provincial governor, one Lu-ch'iu Yin, may have written the poems himself and invented a spurious author, Han-shan, for them.)

$$\triangledown\ \triangledown\ \triangledown$$

James A. Harden-Hickey (1854–1898)

Euthanasia: The Aesthetics of Suicide (1894) by James A. Harden-Hickey, self-styled King of Trinidad, no doubt influenced many people to kill themselves, describing as it does some 90 poisons and 50 instruments to use to commit suicide, and illustrating many methods with line drawings. Harden-Hickey, true to form, used one of them himself. He committed suicide by taking an overdose of morphine.

$$\triangledown\ \triangledown\ \triangledown$$

Alexandre Hardy (1569–1631)

Among the most prolific of playwrights, the French dramatist claimed to have written over 600 plays, though only 34 survive. All his plays were written for the same troupe of actors, with whom he toured the country.

$$\triangledown\ \triangledown\ \triangledown$$

Otto Erich Hartleben (1864–1905)

This German poet, playwright and short-story writer, who followed Nietzsche in rejecting morality and led a bohemian life, has been compared to de Maupassant for his storytelling genius, but he wrote only intermittently between drinking bouts and died before he fulfilled his great promise. Hartleben never lost his sense of humor even at the end. One time a doctor gave him a complete examination and advised him to stop drinking. "My advice, Herr Hartleben, will cost you three marks," he said. "But I'm not taking it," said Hartleben, and walked out the door without paying.

Jaroslav Hashek (1884–1923)

The Czech novelist and short-story writer died an alcoholic when only 39. He left his projected six-volume novel *The Good Soldier Schweik* unfinished, having completed only four volumes. Few people realized that the ending was written by his good friend Karel Vanek, whose philosophy was much like his own.

∇ ∇ ∇

Wilhelm Hauff (1802–1827)

This German poet and novelist had a promising career until he wrote a parody of the novels of H. Clauren (the pseudonym of K. G. S. Heun). This would have been fine but Hauff went too far; he published the parody, *Der Mann in Monde* (1825), under Clauren's name! After he was sued for damages, his life became increasingly difficult, and though he continued writing, he died two years later when not yet 25.

∇ ∇ ∇

Jabir ibn-Hayyan (fl. 8th century)

Geber, or more properly, Jabir ibn-Hayyan (*Jabir* is the Arabic for *Geber*) was an eighth-century Arabian alchemist who wrote his formulas in seemingly unintelligible jargon and anagrams in order to avoid the death penalty for sorcery. For this reason Dr. Johnson, Grose and other prominent word detectives believed that *gibberish*, "nonsense or words without meaning," derives from his name. Geber could not have written all the 2,000 books attributed to him, but he was a prolific writer, respected enough for many medieval scientists to cite him as an authority, and for one 14th-century Spanish alchemist to go so far as to adopt his name. Today many authorities speculate that *gibberish* is imitative of the sound of nonsense, an echoic word like "jabber," "gabble," "giggle" and "gurgle," and that its derivation, at most, was only influenced by Geber's name.

∇ ∇ ∇

Georg Wilhelm Friedrich Hegel (1770–1831)

When the great German philosopher received his theological certificate at Tubingen University in 1793, it noted that he was especially deficient in philosophy. It is said that Hegel never looked young. Even as a student at Tubingen his prematurely elderly appearance earned him the nickname "Old Man." Later as a teacher he was not popular among his students: His abstruse lectures were difficult to follow and interrupted by his constant coughing; every sentence came out with a struggle.

Hegel never believed anyone fully comprehended his work. "Only one man ever understood me," he said as he lay dying. Then he added, as his last words, "...and even he didn't understand me."

∇ ∇ ∇

Gunnar Heiberg (1857–1929)

Heiberg, a brilliant dramatist who had the misfortune to follow too closely behind the footsteps of Ibsen, was even unluckier in the looks nature willed him. He was among the ugliest of authors ever born. In fact, his repulsive physical appearance led to his becoming a writer. He wanted to be an actor but no one in Germany nor all of Europe would even give him a audition, and he turned to writing plays instead.

∇ ∇ ∇

Herman Heijermans (1864–1924)

The Dutch writer wrote realistic sketches of Jewish family life under the pseudonym Samuel Falkland. He also wrote many novels and dramas, including the unusual *A Case of Arson* (1904). In this one-act play an actor named Henri de Vries played all of the seven witnesses who appeared as characters.

∇ ∇ ∇

Heinrich Heine (1797–1856)

"The last Romantic," as the German poet called himself, was alienated from his family because he converted from Judaism to Christianity, and from his country because of his liberal politics. Heine died in exile and the last eight years of his life were years of suffering with a terrible spinal disease. Though he wrote some of his best work in this period, he was confined to bed so long, in so much pain, that he told a friend he was condemned to a "mattress grave."

Strange as it seems for a poet who wrote so well in both German and French, Heine's worst subjects in school were languages. But then he failed in German grammar, too. His overall school record was so poor that his mother despaired for his future. (See also ÉMILE ZOLA.)

"Ordinarily he is insane," he observed of Savoie, who had been appointed ambassador to Frankfurt by Lamartine in 1848, "but he has lucid moments when he is only stupid."

A friend asked Heine why he was so despondent one day. "Well, I just met ——— in the street," Heine explained. "I stopped for a moment to exchange ideas, and now I feel like a complete idiot."

Heine sat in the library trying to work while two old women across from him gossiped loudly for over an hour. Heine, a true gentleman, sought a way to quiet but not offend them and finally leaned over to ask: "Pardon me, ladies, but does my reading interfere with your conversation?"

He would not have enjoyed this age of unauthorized biographies and letter collections, believing as he did that "To publish even one line of an author which he himself has not intended for the public at large—especially letters which are addressed to private persons—is to commit a despicable act of felony."

"Mademoiselle," Heine said to a beautiful young actress, "you would surely want to be escorted home by a talented, wealthy, handsome young aristocrat."

The ingenue brushed past him shaking her head. "I would definitely prefer not to be escorted," she said.

But Heine blocked her way again. "Then obviously I am the one to escort you," he said. "For I am neither handsome, wealthy, nor aristocratic, and you can see for yourself that I am no longer young. The fact is, I am poor, a bit weather-beaten, and a poet."

The beautiful actress took his arm.

"If one has no heart," he wrote to his friend Julius Campe in 1840, "one cannot write for the masses."

Because Heine was born a Jew and was a revolutionary in spirit, all of his works were outlawed and burned by the Nazis in 1933—all except his great master-work *Die Lorelei*. So beloved was this poem that the people would not give it up. The Nazis had to list it as the work of "Anonymous" and spare it from the flames.

"Whenever they burn books," he once said, "they will also, in the end, burn human beings."

The German poet's last will and testament read: "I leave my entire estate to my wife on the condition that she remarry; then there shall be at least one man to regret my death."

Heine, "who united so much wit with so much pathos," according to a contemporary critic, died in a filthy Parisian garret, deserted by all the literary world save his friend, composer Hector Berlioz. As he lay dying, he turned to his old friend and commented bitterly, "I always knew you were an original, Berlioz."

On his deathbed he said, in French: "God will pardon me. It is His trade."

His last words were: "Write...write...pencil...paper..."

∇ ∇ ∇

Heliodorus of Emesa (fl. 4th? century A.D.)
The world's first romance novel, in which the heroine's virginity is preserved through a series of narrow escapes, was the *Aethiopica*, or *Egyptian Tales*, of Heliodorus. Tradition has it that the author of this great-grandfather of all romance novels was the Christian bishop of Thessalonica.

∇ ∇ ∇

Charles Jean François Hénault (1685–1770)
Voltaire grew so angry at criticisms made of his *La Henriade* after he had read it at a party that he threw the only copy of the poem into the fire. Luckily Charles Hénault rescued it from the flames. "You owe me an epic and a nice pair of sleeve ruffles," the French man of letters told him.

∇ ∇ ∇

Henry III (1551–1589)
The Macabre style of book bindings is, strictly speaking, that of the bindings made for France's Henry III after the death of his mistress, the Princess of Cleves. Tears, skulls and bones tooled in silver were used to express the king's grief. A hard-luck king indeed, Henry III was assassinated—while suppressing a rebellion—by a Dominican friar before he turned 38.

∇ ∇ ∇

Heraclitus the Obscure (c. 535–c. 475 B.C.)
He may have died trying to prove a riddle (though of the life of the Greek philosopher Heraclitus the Obscure much is obscure). In any case, Diogenes Laertius tells the following story of his death:

> And at last becoming a complete misanthrope, he used to spend his time walking about the mountains, feeding on grasses and plants; and in consequence of these habits he was attacked by the dropsy, and so he returned to the city, and asked the physicians, in a riddle, whether they were able to produce a drought after wet weather. And as they did not understand him, he shut himself up in a stable for oxen, and covered himself with cow dung, hoping to cause the wet to evaporate from him by the warmth that this produced. And as he did himself no good in this way, he died, having lived seventy years.

Hermippus (c. 431–404 B.C.)

Hermippus, the only writer known in history as "The One-Eyed," lost an eye in an accident early in life. The Athenian writer of Old Comedy was a bitter opponent of Pericles and accused him of being a bully and coward. He wrote some 40 plays, of which the fragments of nine are preserved.

∇ ∇ ∇

Miguel Hernández (1910–1942)

When a young man, the Spanish poet asked Pablo Neruda to help him find work near Madrid. Neruda admired the younger poet, "a peasant with an aura of earthiness about him," he once recalled, "who told me earthy stories...[who told me] how exciting it was to put your ear against the belly of a sleeping goat...[to] hear the milk coursing down to the udders, a secret sound no one but that poet of goats has been able to listen to." The older Chilean poet tried to get Hernández work and finally interested a viscount high up in Spain's Ministry of Foreign Relations, who shared Neruda's enthusiasm for the young man's poems. "Miguel Hernández," Neruda told him, "your future is all set, at last. The viscount has a job for you. You'll be a high-ranking employee. Tell me what kind of work you want, and your appointment will go through." Hernández thought about his answer for hours and finally, "with the radiant look of someone who has found the solution to his whole life," said to Neruda: "Could the viscount put me in charge of a flock of goats somewhere near Madrid?"

∇ ∇ ∇

Herodotus (c. 480–425 B.C.)

"The father of history," as Cicero called him, wrote the first masterpiece of Greek prose. It is said that when he read his *History* publicly at Athens he so pleased the Athenians with his account of the Persian War that they voted him 12 talents (the equivalent of perhaps half a million dollars today). He quips in his book: "I am under obligation to tell what is reported, but I am not obliged to believe it..."

∇ ∇ ∇

Hesiod (c. 846–c. 777 B.C.)

The Greek poet, author of the *Theogony*, had been a shepherd as a boy. He became a poet after he fell asleep on the slopes of Helicon and dreamed that the Muses breathed into his body the soul of poetry. So legend says, just as it says that Hesiod beat even Homer in a poetry contest. Legend also tells how Hesiod at an advanced age read his love poems to and seduced the maiden Clymene, whose brother killed him and threw his body into the sea. Clymene gave birth to his son, the lyric poet Stesichorus.

George Heym (1887–1912)

This German poet and short-story writer was a death-obsessed man who wrote of a "God of the City" with "slaughterer's fist" and kept a skull decorated with vine leaves on his desk. Yet he was a giant physically and a superb athlete, though he explained his love of sports in his diary as resulting from "shame" of his emotional delicacy. He drowned when not yet 25 after trying to save a friend who fell through the ice while they were skating on the River Havel.

∇ ∇ ∇

Nazim Hikmet (fl. 19th century)

Accused of trying to incite the Turkish navy to rebellion, the poet was tried aboard a warship and imprisoned for several days in the section of the ship's latrines where human wastes were stored. Sitting in excrement about 1 1/2 feet high (he was too weak to stand), Hikmet kept his sanity by reciting all the poems and singing all the songs he knew until he was finally removed to a permanent prison, where he served 18 years.

∇ ∇ ∇

Hipponax (fl. c. 540 B.C.)

Hipponax of Ephesus was a short, ugly, crippled man with a disagreeable temper and vicious wit. The Greek poet is said to have ruthlessly lampooned every notable in Ephesus, "from the lowest criminal to the highest priest of the temple." Once he said that woman brought two days of happiness to a man, "one when he marries her, the other when he buries her."

The sculptors Bupalus and Athenis are said to have exhibited a statue ridiculing the deformed, ugly poet. Hipponax's pen, however, proved sharper than their chisels. He counterattacked with such corrosive wit that his bitter verses drove each sculptor to hang himself in despair.

∇ ∇ ∇

Adolf Hitler (1889–1945)

Hitler's original title for *Mein Kampf* was *Four-and-a-Half Years of Struggle Against Lies, Stupidity, and Cowardice.* (Much later this inspired *Time* magazine critic Timothy Foote to observe, "Everyone needs an editor.")

During World War II, when America was at war with Germany, U.S. courts determined that Hitler was entitled to international copyright for *Mein Kampf,* even though he was a "stateless German" when the book was published. Ironically, Hitler's case established a precedent for refugee European authors to secure international rights on their books and thus collect their royalties. (Before the ruling an author had to be a citizen of a country to be entitled to international copyright.) Hitler's book had accumulated $22,666 in royalties in the U.S., but when he failed to appear to collect it, the money was seized by the government.

∇ ∇ ∇

Hokusai Katsuhika (1760–1849)

The Japanese artist—ranked by Whistler as the greatest painter since Velásquez—was also a poet who wrote when his house burned down: *It has burned down;/How serene the flowers in their falling*. The poem is typical of his reaction to the poverty he suffered over a long life in which he created five hundred volumes of 30,000 drawings. Hokusai called himself "The Old Man Mad With Painting" and described his life this way: "From my sixth year onwards a peculiar mania for drawing took possession of me. At my fiftieth year I had published quite a number of works of every possible description, but none were to my satisfaction. Real work began with me only in my seventieth year. Now at seventy-five the real appreciation of nature awakens within me. I therefore hope that at eighty I may have arrived at a certain power of intuition which will develop further to my ninetieth year, so that at the age of a hundred I can probably assert that my intuition is thoroughly artistic. And, should it be granted to me to live a hundred and ten years, I hope that a vital and true comprehension of nature may radiate from every one of my lines and dots…I invite those who are going to live as long as I to convince themselves whether I shall keep my word. Written at the age of seventy-five years by me, formerly Hokusai, now called the Old Man Mad With Painting." He finally died 14 years later at age 89. On his deathbed he lamented, "If the gods had given me only ten years more I could have become a really great painter."

∇ ∇ ∇

Ludwig Holberg (1684–1754)

Baron Holberg has been called by a Swedish critic "the founder of Danish literature…[he] found Denmark without books and wrote a library for it." Before him the Danish language was rarely heard in a gentleman's house and it was said that a gentleman "wrote Latin to his friends, talked French to the ladies, called his dogs in German and only used Danish to swear at his servants." Though he was second only to Voltaire in his day, Holberg is not well known outside his country today.

∇ ∇ ∇

Johann Christian Friedrich Hölderlin (1770–1843)

While serving as tutor to the family of a Frankfurt banker in 1796, the German poet fell in love with the banker's wife, the beautiful Suzette Gontard, who returned his love. Her jealous husband discovered them and forced Hölderlin to leave Frankfurt. The poet then began to slip into the mental illness that grew into an advanced state of schizophrenia after Suzette tragically died five years later. Though he wrote beautiful poetry in his lucid moments he never recovered from his illness.

▽ ▽ ▽

Arthur Holitscher (1869–1941)
When Thomas Mann's *Tristan* was published in 1900, his character Detlov Spinell reminded many readers of the German novelist and musician Arthur Holitscher. Holitscher himself charged Mann with spying on him with opera glasses to obtain the book's detailed physical description. Mann denied this.

▽ ▽ ▽

Karl Eduard von Holtei (1798–1880)
Another author-actor, like Shakespeare, Molière, Samuel Foote and many more, the German poet wrote novels as well as plays and is remembered for having introduced vaudeville into Germany. The poet-actor was also very popular in his time for his unrivaled, brilliant recitations of Shakespeare.

▽ ▽ ▽

Homer (? 9th century B.C.)
Nothing is known about the Greek poet called Homer, if there was indeed just one author of the *Iliad* and the *Odyssey*. At least 11 Greek cities, for example— Smyrna, Chios, Colophon, Salamis, Rhodes, Argos, Athens, Kyme, Ithaca, Ios and Pylos—have been suggested as the poet's birthplace, not to mention foreign countries like Egypt and Babylonia.

▽ ▽ ▽

Horace (Quintus Horatius Flaccus; 65–8 B.C.)
While it is unwise to take Horace literally in this case—if only because he was a satirist who constantly mocked himself and his talent—the great Roman poet records that he fought in the battle of Philippi (42 B.C.) threw down his shield and ran away to be rescued, trembling, by the god Mercury, "who wrapped him in a mist."

The poet held that all purple patches (*purpureus pannus*), ornate, overexaggerated passages, should be deleted from literary works, which should then be put away for eight years before being reedited and published.

Hortensius (Quintus Hortensius Hortalus; 114–50 B.C.)

Because he polished and published his speeches, the flamboyant rhetoric of Hortensius greatly influenced Roman style. Only Cicero eclipsed him as a speaker, and great actors like Roscius attended his law trials to learn from his eloquent delivery. He became one of Rome's richest men, as can be seen by the 10,000 casks of wine he bequeathed to his heirs.

∇ ∇ ∇

Huchbald (fl. 9th century)

The author of *Eclogue on Baldness* (*Ecloga de Calvis*) appropriately dedicated his book to Charles the Bald. The 146-line poem has been called "a reductio ad absurdum of alliteration," *every* word beginning with the letter *c*.

∇ ∇ ∇

Victor Hugo (1802–1885)

When his mother died in 1821 Hugo refused to accept any money from his hated father, whom he called "the brigand of the Loire," and for a whole year lived and wrote on 700 francs in an attic in Paris's Rue du Dragon. Years later he would use this experience in writing about Marius in *Les Misérables*.

The French novelist had an ego second to none. So constantly did the word *I* appear in his conversation that one of his friends called him "a walking personal pronoun."

The inscription over his study door read:

To rise at six, to dine at ten,
To sup at six, to sleep at ten,
Makes a man live for ten times ten.

British author Richard Monckton Milnes told of calling on Hugo in Paris and finding him seated like a king at the head of the room, his disciples like a court around him. As he entered he heard Hugo intone, "As for me, I believe in God!" After a short reflective silence, one of the novelist's followers replied in all seriousness, "How sublime! A God who believes in God!"

As active sexually as he was intellectually and politically, Hugo was a master of love as well as poetry. Truly indefatigable, he was carrying on two or three affairs at a time into his seventies, possibly including one with Sarah Bernhardt. Only death inhibited Hugo; his diary for the year of his death, at 83, recorded numerous sexual acts.

Juliet Drouet, a well-known courtesan, played the part of Princess Negroni in Hugo's *Lucrèce Borgia* (1833), using her real name, Juliette Gauvain. Hugo decided to reform this woman and for several years confined her in a little apartment only he was allowed to visit. She remained his mistress for over 50 years and is the subject of his loveliest lyrics.

French police found Hugo and Léonie Biard in bed together when they raided a Paris love nest at the request of Léonie's husband, artist Auguste Biard—adultery then being a criminal offense in France. Hugo claimed immunity as a lord, but poor Léonie went to prison. As for Hugo's wife Adèle, she was very understanding, even visiting Léonie in jail, which was more than Hugo ever did. Adèle, however, later took her own lover for revenge.

Hugo's wife tried with great patience for over 20 years to make him faithful, but his myriad love affairs finally so angered her that after the birth of their fifth child she refused him all sexual relations. When this didn't work, the beautiful Adèle added insult to injury by becoming the mistress of his arch-rival, the critic Sainte-Beuve, which didn't work either.

An editor described Hugo's almost illegible manuscripts as "a sort of battlefield on paper, in which the killed words were well stamped out and the new recruits pushed forth in anything but good order."

When the French inspector general of theaters censored passages in Hugo's *Hernani* that were disrespectful of the monarchy, a literary war ensued in which romanticists supporting Hugo took sides against the classicists, and there were actual pitched battles for weeks inside and out of the theater. Professional claques were hired by the classicists and Théophile Gautier led romanticist volunteers, urging them to take their stand "upon the rugged mount of Romanticism, and to valiantly defend its passes against the assault of the Classics." It was a costly victory for the romanticists, with many injured and at least one young man dead in a duel.

When Hugo wanted to know how his publishers liked *Les Misérables*, he wrote them simply: "?" His publishers shortly responded "!"—completing the briefest correspondence in literary history.

One morning Rodin invited a group of art critics to view a sculpture he had done of Hugo standing on the edge of a cliff with the Muses and ocean deities surrounding him. But the sculptor had left the window open the evening before and a fierce storm had reduced the surrounding figures to a sea of mud in which Hugo lay face up. Yet as soon as Rodin opened the door to his studio the critics began to applaud. "Wonderful! Marvelous!" one man cried. "Victor Hugo rising from the bed of slime, what a symbol! You have represented the ignominy of an epoch in which the inspiration of the bard alone survived, noble and pure. How beautiful!"

Read an autographed prophecy on the wall of the room in the Place des Vosges, Paris, in which Hugo died:

I represent a party which does not
yet exist: the party of revolution, civilization.
This party will make the twentieth century.
There will issue from it first the United
States of Europe, then the United States of the World.

The great actor to the end, Hugo's last request was to be buried in a pauper's coffin. When his body lay in state for a night under the Arc de Triomphe, it was in the plain pine box of a pauper, in which he was buried at the Pantheon.

∇ ∇ ∇

Vicente Huidobro (1893–1948)

The Chilean poet and diplomat, who crowned himself "The God of Poetry," had written a pamphlet entitled *Finis Britanniae* (1919) in which he predicted the immediate collapse of the British Empire. No one took him seriously but then Huidobro disappeared. French newspapers headlined "Chilean Diplomat Mysteriously Kidnapped" and the search began for the poet. He was found alive a week later outside the door of his Paris home, a package under his arm. "English Boy Scouts kidnapped me," he told the police. "They tied me to a column in a basement and forced me to shout a thousand times: 'Long live the British Empire!'" Huidobro then passed out, or pretended to. When the police opened his package and found a new pair of pajamas bought by the poet himself three days ago in a posh Paris shop, they concluded that his story was a hoax perpetrated by Huidobro to bring attention to his pamphlet. The poet's good friend, painter Juan Gris, who had believed the story, never spoke to him again. As for Huidobro, he went on living his maxim, "The poet's first duty is to create; his second duty, to create; his third duty, to create!" (See DEMOSTHENES.)

∇ ∇ ∇

Sah Husain (1539–1593)

This Punjabi poet was noted in his lifetime for his love of singing and dancing. After four centuries his songs are still as popular as ever. His tomb on the outskirts of Lahore has become the center of that city's spring musical fair.

Ahmad ibn Husein (fl. 12th century)

> I am known to the horse-troop, the night and the desert's expanse
> Not more to paper and pen than the sword and the lance.

Not long after the ancient Persian poet Ahmad ibn Husein wrote this couplet, he was attacked by robbers. When he tried to escape, his slave reminded him of his words. He fought and was killed.

∇ ∇ ∇

John Huss (1369?–1415)

The Czech religious reformer and author refused to recant his beliefs and was burned at the stake as a heretic after his writings were destroyed. Legend has it that on seeing an old woman adding wood to his pyre, he exclaimed, "Sancta simplicitas!" (Pure simplicity!) In any case, he chanted hymns as the fire consumed him.

∇ ∇ ∇

Hypatia (d. 415)

Legend says that the pagan philosopher and mathematician, who drew huge audiences to her philosophy lectures at the Alexandrian Museum and wrote an unknown number of books, remained a virgin despite the fact that she married. According to another story, a young man propositioned the beautiful Hypatia and she hiked her dress, telling him, "This symbol of unclean generation is what you are in love with, and not anything beautiful." She met her end when a band of Christian fanatics "pulled her from the carriage, dragged her into a church, stripped her of her garments, battered her to death with tiles, tore her corpse to pieces, and burned the remains in a savage orgy."

∇ ∇ ∇

Hyperides (389–322 B.C.)

The distinguished Greek orator was celebrated as a politician, lawyer, jester and a writer of forensic speeches. He was also a lover of Phryne, the famous Athenian courtesan who lived and loved memorably in the fourth century B.C. There was a gold statue of Phryne at Delphi dedicated by her admirers. Her real name was Mnesarite, but the courtesan was commonly called Phryne, "toad," because of her smooth complexion. Born in Boeotia, the country girl made good at her trade in Athens, where her beauty earned her a fortune so great that she once offered to rebuild the walls of Thebes if the words "Destroyed by Alexander, restored by Phryne the courtesan" were inscribed upon them. (There were no takers.) That her body was the most beautiful of her time, or perhaps any other, is illustrated by Praxiteles' statue called Aphrodite of Cnidus, which she is said to have posed for. During a festival of Poseidon at Eleusis, Phryne took off her clothes, let down her hair, and in full view of the crowd stepped into the sea, inspiring Apelles to paint his great Aphrodite Cenadyomene, for which she modeled. But there is no better story about Phryne than that of her trial for impurity. Her lover Hyperides defended her. Just when it seemed that she would lose her case—and her life was at stake—Hyperides pulled the courtroom stunt of all time. Ripping open her robe, he exposed her breasts to the jury, who agreed with him that something so good could not be all bad and let Phryne go free.

▽ ▽ ▽ ▽ ▽ ▽ ▽ ▽

Henrik Ibsen (1828–1906)

A friend asked the Norwegian playwright why he had hung a picture of his rival August Strindberg over his desk. "He is my mortal enemy and shall hang there and watch while I write," Ibsen replied.

When author John Paulson protested that he had meant no harm by portraying the Norwegian playwright as Pehrsen in *The Pehrsen Family* (1882), Ibsen sent him a card with one word written on it: "Scoundrel."

It was Ibsen's habit to get himself writing every morning by first feeding a pet scorpion that he kept in a jar on his desk.

The eponymous heroine of Ibsen's *Hedda Gabler* (1890) was suggested to him by the beautiful Emilie Bardach, a Viennese woman he fell in love with in 1889, when he was 61 and she only 17. Although her bold, loose ways frightened him and he never met her again after that summer, he thought of her as the "May-day of my September life" and wrote to her years later that the few months he spent with her were the happiest and most beautiful in his life.

When Ibsen and Dostoyevsky stayed in Dresden in 1869, both authors were accustomed to taking a stroll early in the evening before returning home to work all night long. The two literary giants walked through the same park, visited the same cafés and went home to houses nearby. They could not have helped but notice one another, but never made any known contact in all the time they were there.

"You seem to be improving," his attending nurse told Ibsen during his final illness.

"On the contrary," Ibsen countered.

These were his last words, winning him his last argument.

∇ ∇ ∇

Ibycus (fl. 6th century B.C.)

Legend has it that the Greek lyric poet was attacked and killed by robbers. As he lay dying Ibycus saw a flock of cranes overhead and said, "Those cranes will avenge me." Not long after in the theater at Corinth one of the robbers, seeing a flock of cranes fly overhead, turned to his companion and said, "There go the avengers of Ibycus." He was overheard, and the murderers were brought to justice.

∇ ∇ ∇

Ihara Saikaku (Hirayama Togo; 1642–1693)

The Japanese poet, also considered one of Japan's finest prose writers, did not like the slow rule-bound poetic style common in Japan in his day, quipping that "It makes mold in the bottom of the ears, and moss in the mouth." Nothing moldy about him, though. Saikaku still holds the Japanese (and probably world) record for the most verses written in 24 hours. Sometime in 1684 he composed, in one day and a night, an incredible 23,500 consecutive verses.

∇ ∇ ∇

Ikhnaton (Amenhotep IV; 1380–1326 B.C.)

The poet-king of Egypt changed his name to Ikhnaton because he despised the corrupt religion of Amen and his name Amenhotep contained the name of Amen. Ikhnaton wrote a long passionate poem to Aton, which is regarded as the first outstanding expression of monotheism and one of the great poems of history. But after finding his truth of universal unity, he tragically decided that all other creeds were illegal. He ordered all old temples closed and even went so far as to have the word Amen hacked out from hundreds of monuments honoring his father Amenhotep III. Though he otherwise lived like a saint, the people secretly hated him and his saintliness, which extended to his diplomatic relations and encouraged other countries to take advantage of him. Under the poet-king Egypt shrank from a vast empire to a small state. Ikhnaton died when only 30, fully aware of his failure as a ruler, and soon after his death his name and the name of Aton were being chiseled off all the monuments *he* had had effaced. All was as before, except that it was now forbidden to even speak Ikhnaton's name and the people referred to him as "The Great Criminal."

∇ ∇ ∇

Ikku Jippensha (d. 1831)

Ikku was the most delightful of impoverished authors. Poor and owning no furniture, he hung his walls with pictures of the furniture he would have had if he could afford to buy it; he made offerings to the gods in the same way. When his publisher came to call on him one day, Ikku prepared a bath for him, donned the man's clothes—he had no good clothes of his own—and then went out properly attired to make social calls. As a last wish the Japanese novelist requested that certain packets be placed on his corpse when he was cremated. After the pyre was lighed, it developed that the packets contained firecrackers. (See also BALZAC.)

∇ ∇ ∇

Cosmos Indicopleustes (c. 547)

The name of the Roman author of *Topographia Christiana* eternally reflects his great mission in life. He earned his sobriquet by sailing to India in an effort to prove that the world was flat.

∇ ∇ ∇

Innocent X (Giambattista Pamfili; 1574–1655)

Before he became Pope, Innocent X was an infamous book theif who was caught red-handed stealing a rare copy of *L'Histoire du Concile de Trente* from a French painter's studio while visiting with a religious party. The future pope was evicted bodily by the painter, and some historians believe that this action contributed to the ill feeling toward France that marked the pontifical reign of Innocent X from 1644 to 1655.

∇ ∇ ∇

Hunain ibn Ishaq (809–873)

One Islamic ruler jailed the eminent physician and translator for a year, threatening him with death, because Hunain refused to concoct a poison to use on an enemy of the king. Hunain was the translator into Arabic and Syrian of 140 treatises of Galen, in addition to the works of Hippocrates nd many other scientific authors. He wrote so much that the ruler Al-Mamun nearly bankrupted the state by paying Hunain in gold the total weight of the books he had translated.

Isidore of Seville (c. 560–636)

Isidore is said to have run away from home when his teachers called him stupid. Sitting down by a well he noticed a deep furrow in a stone at the edge of it. A maiden come to fetch water explained to him that the furrow was made over the years by the rope that lowered and raised the basket. Said Isidore to himself, "If by daily use the soft rope could penetrate the stone, surely perseverance could overcome the dullness of my brain," and he returned home to study hard and later become the learned biship of Seville. The legend, however, does not advise that Isidore's major work, an encyclopedia of sorts called *Twenty Books of Etymologies or Origins*, is now regarded as what one modern critic calls "a lasting monument to the ignorance of his time."

∇ ∇ ∇

Nazrul Islam (b. 1899)

This Bengali writer earned the title "The Rebel Poet" because of his anti-British activities (he was twice jailed for sedition) and his long poem "The Rebel." Much of his powerful poetry and prose was banned in India by the British, but he remained a prolific author until mental illness silenced him toward the beginning of World War II. One time the poet went on a hunger strike in prison, coming close to death, and Rabindranath Tagore sent the following telegram to him, ending his fasting: "Give up hunger strike, our literature claims you."

∇ ∇ ∇

Abdul Kassem Ismail (938–995)

The strangest of libraries belonged to Abdul Kassem Ismail, the grand vizier of Persia. It consisted of 117,000 books arranged alphabetically on the backs of 400 camels, which walked in a fixed order wherever the grand vizier traveled.

∇ ∇ ∇

Isocrates (436–338 B.C.)

The "old man eloquent," as Milton called the great Athenian orator and author, created a style of balanced clauses and long sentences that Cicero, Milton, Massillon and Emund Burke, to name but a few, based their prose styles upon. Isocrates starved himself to death at the age of 98 when King Philip of Macedonia defeated his native Athens.

Giles Jacob   See EMPEROR SIGISMUND.

∇ ∇ ∇

Jami (1414–1492)

A poetaster brought the Persian poet a poem he had written without using the letter *alif*. Jami read the poem, pondering it for a moment, and finally said, "It would be better if you had left out the other letters, too." (An anecdote that has been told of several authors.)

Some say that the classic poet and mystic took his pen name from the town of Jam, where he was born. Others, however, hold that he is so named because in his poems he often compares the town's name with the same word (Jam), meaning "winecup."

∇ ∇ ∇

Jules Janin (1804–1874)

This French novelist and drama critic had handwriting so bad that he literally couldn't read his own manuscripts. He once rewrote an entire story, dictating it, rather than try to decipher the original for the printer.

∇ ∇ ∇

Alfred Jarry (1873–1907)

The dramatist of the theater of the absurd has been called "the supreme buffoon" and is said to have pointed his revolver at a man who presumed to stop him on a corner in Paris and ask for street directions. The poet Apollinaire was an admirer of his satirical *Ubu Roi* and once described a visit he made to the absurdist's weird apartment in the Rue Casette:

> "Monsieur Alfred Jarry?"
> "Second floor and a half."
> I was somewhat puzzled by that answer from the concierge. I climbed up to where Alfred Jarry lived—second and a half turned out to be correct. The stories of the house had seemed too high-ceilinged to the owner, so he had cut each of them in two. In this way the house, which still exists, has 15 stories, but since it is actually no higher than the houses around it, it is but a reduction of a skyscraper. For that matter, reductions abounded in Alfred Jarry's abode. His second and a half was but the reduction of a story: Jarry was quite comfortable standing up, but I was taller than he, and had to bend. The bed was but a reduction of a bed—a pallet: Low beds were the fashion, Jarry told me. The writing table was but the reduction of a table: Jarry wrote on the floor, stretched out on his stomach. The furnishing was but the reduction of furnishing, consisting solely of a bed. On the wall hung the reduction of a picture. It was a portrait of Jarry, most of which he had burned, leaving only the head… The library was but the reduction of a library, to put it mildly. It consisted of

a cheap edition of Rabelais and two or three volumes of the *Bibliothèque Rose*. On the mantelpiece stood a large stone phallus, made in Japan, a gift to Jarry from Felicien Rops. This virile member, larger than life, Jarry had kept covered with a purple velvet sheath ever since the day when the exotic monolith had frightened a literary lady. She had arrived breathless from climbing up to this second floor and a half, and bewildered at finding herself in this furnitureless "Great Chamber." "Is it a cast?" she inquired. "No," answered Jarry. "It's a reduction."

"My child is playing here—you might have killed him!" a woman shouted after Jarry fired a pistol into a hedge surrounding a yard. "Madam, I would have given you another!" the deranged playwright gallantly replied.

∇ ∇ ∇

Jinsai Ito (1670–1705)

A Japanese historian told the following story about the improverished philosopher, who had put aside all material ambition:

> Jinsai was very poor, so poor that at the end of the year he could not make New Year's rice cakes; but he was very calm about it. His wife came and, kneeling down before him, said: "I will do the housework under any circumstances; but there is one thing that is unbearable—our boy Genso does not understand the meaning of our poverty; he envies the neighbor's children their rice cakes. I scold him, but my heart is torn in two." Jinsai continued to pore over his books without making any reply. Then, taking off his garnet ring, he handed it to his wife, as much as to say, "Sell this, and buy some rice cakes."

∇ ∇ ∇

Étienne Jodelle (1532–1573)

Jodelle's play *Cleopâtre captive* (1552) tried to establish classical drama on the French stage. Jodelle himself played the role of Cleopatra. After the play's first performance his friends celebrated its success by organizing a procession in which a goat garlanded with flowers was presented to the author. His opponents, however, charged that the "pagan ceremony" was proof that the playwright intended to introduce the rites of Bacchus into France. Jodelle never equalled the success of his first play and died in poverty when only 41.

∇ ∇ ∇

Frantz Jourdain (fl. early 20th century)

In 1911 Apollinaire was arrested in connection with the theft of the Mona Lisa from the Louvre. Although the charges were dropped and he was released after several days (the thief turned out to be a mad Italian housepainter with "a mission" to return the painting to its native land), petitions had been circulated through Paris protesting the arrest and demanding the poet's release. However, when Jourdain was asked to sign, the French architect and author remembered how Apollinaire had lambasted his work in a piece of art criticism. "What? My signature to get Apollinaire released?" he cried. "Never! To get him hanged, any time you like!"

▽ ▽ ▽

Said ibn Judi (d. 897)

The son of the prefect of Cordova was as great a poet as he was a warrior and a greater lover than both. "I traverse the circle of pleasures as a frenzied war horse that has taken the bit in its teeth," he once wrote. "I leave no desire unsatisfied!" Unfortunately, the circle of his pleasures included the wives of fellow officers. Once caught him *in media res* with his wife and ran them through with a sword.

▽ ▽ ▽

Julian the Apostate (331?–363)

The pagan Roman emperor considered himself a philosopher and wrote so much that, as he put it in a letter, "my fingers are nearly always black with ink." Anyone who thought there was anything more important than philosophy, he wrote to Eumenius, "is a deluded man trying to delude you." Julian carried a library with him on his military campaigns. "Some men," he observed, "have a passion for horses, others for birds, others for wild beasts; but I from childhood have been possessed by a passionate longing to acquire books." His reign, however, lasted only two brief years, until he was killed in a skirmish.

▽ ▽ ▽

Juvenal (Decimus Junius Juvenalis; c. 60–c. 136 A.D.)

The Roman satirical poet bought a farm at Tibur in his prosperous years, at a time when poetry was a great fad in Rome and everyone "from fool to philosopher" wrote it. When asked why he would want to live in the country, he said that his compelling reason was to escape the poets infesting Rome.

Franz Kafka (1883–1924)

Kafka's fiancée, Felice Bauer, told him that she would like to sit beside him while he wrote. In a letter to her he explained that he could not write if she were there. "One can never be alone enough when one writes," he told her, "why there can never be enough silence around one when one writes, why even night is not night enough…I have often thought that the best mode of life for me would be to sit in the innermost room of a spacious locked cellar with my writing things and a lamp. Food would be brought and always put down far away from my room, outside the cellar's outermost door. The walk to my food, in my dressing gown, through the vaulted cellars, would be my only exercise. I would then return to my table, eat slowly and with deliberation, then start writing again at once. And how I would write! From what depths I would drag it up!"

Believing that he had failed at his life's work, the Austrian author's last request was for his friend Max Brod to burn all his papers and unpublished manuscripts. Brod refused to do this, rationalizing that Kafka did not really want it done or he would not have asked someone he must have known would never do such a thing. Instead Brod himself published Kafka's three immensely influential novels, *The Trial* (1925), *The Castle* (1926), and the unfinished *Amerika* (1927).

∇ ∇ ∇

Gustave Kahn (1859–1936)

In the preface to his *Premiers poèmes* (1897) the French author claimed to be the first poet to write free verse (vers libre), though Milton clearly had experimented with it long before, as had Walt Whitman, among others.

∇ ∇ ∇

Kaibara Ekken (1630–1714)

This great and humble scholar once sailed on a ship where a fellow passenger presumed to lecture on Confucius. The audience found the man a pretentious bore and soon only one listener remained, listening with such intense concentration that when the lecturer finished he asked his name. "Kaibara Ekken," the scholar replied. The lecturer was abashed to learn that for several hours he had been trying to teach Confucianism to Japan's greatest Confucian master.

Georg Kaiser (1878–1945)

The prolific German dramatist, the author of some 70 plays, decided in his first years as a writer to let the world support his art. After being supported for a while by his family, he married a rich woman in 1908, lived comfortably for a time, and when her money ran out a decade or so later, sold her estate without her permission. Not stopping there, he rented a villa and proceeded to sell all the furniture in it. Tried for theft, he made a notorious, impassioned speech before the court claiming that the artist had the privilege of immunity from the common laws of life, was above the law in this respect. Unfortunately for Kaiser the court thought otherwise and he was sentenced to six months in jail.

∇ ∇ ∇

Emperor K'ang-hsi (d. 1721)

The Chinese emperor ordered a huge encyclopedia prepared for him by his royal scholars. The *Ku chin t'u shu chi ch'eng*, as it was called, filled 5,020 volumes. Today a copy of the work, bound in 700 volumes, can be seen in the British Museum.

∇ ∇ ∇

Immanuel Kant (1724–1804)

The German philosopher was a man of strict habits, his life arranged with mechanical regularity. A little man barely five feet tall with a weak constitution, he avoided serious illness by his strict regimen. It is said that he never traveled more than 40 miles from his home in Königsberg, that although he earned his living as a professor of geography he never saw a mountain or the sea, that his daily walk in all kinds of weather always began exactly at 3:30 and that not once in 30 years did he fail to rise at 5 o'clock in the morning after his faithful servant Lempe called him.

As a teacher Kant was far from the rigid lecturer one would expect. He is said to have talked extemporaneously from a few notes and livened his lectures with anecdotes. He tried to exert most of his energies on students of intermediate talent, believing that the geniuses would help themselves, and that the dunces were beyond help.

Kant was a faithful friend but he could not bear to visit friends in sickness and after their death he repressed all memories of them. When his servant Lempe left him, he made this entry in his diary: "Remember, from now on the name of Lempe must be completely forgotten."

Vuk Stefanovitch Karafich (1787–1864)

Karafich is known as "the father of Serbian literature" because of his reform of the Serbian alphabet. His simplified alphabet was based on the principle "Write as you speak, and read as it is written!" One authority says, "Hardly any other language in the civilized world has such a simple, logical, scientific spelling system and orthography as the Serbian has in Karafich's system." (See also IVAR ANDREAS AASEN.)

∇ ∇ ∇

Nikolai Mikhailovich Karamzin (1766–1826)

In his *Poor Lisa* (1792) the Russian novelist, who also wrote the first real history of Russia, told of a seduced peasant girl who drowned herself in a pond when her lover deserted her. The novel became so popular that Russian women long made pilgrimages to the spot.

∇ ∇ ∇

Erik Axel Karlfeldt (1864–1931)

This Swedish lyrical poet is another author (see JEAN-PAUL SARTRE) who declined the Nobel Prize for literature. Karlfeldt was on the prize committee for many years but turned down the award in 1918. The committee prevailed, eventually, awarding him the prize posthumously, 13 years later.

∇ ∇ ∇

Khagani (1106–1185)

The Persian poet was an arrogant satirist who had no respect for anyone no matter what his or her age. This led his elderly tutor to send him the following note:

> My dear Khagani, skillful though you be
> In verse, one little hint I give you free:
> Mock not with satire any older poet;
> Perhaps he's your sire, though you don't know it.

∇ ∇ ∇

Abu'l-Fath Umar al-Khayyami ibn Ibrahim (b. 1038)

This Persian astronomer, who wrote several mathematical works, invented a calendar more accurate than our own. His expertise as an early weather forecaster is seen in this anecdote related by his friend Nizami-i-Arudi:

In the winter…the King sent a messenger to Merv bidding its governor tell Umar al-Khayyami to select a favorable time for him to go hunting…Umar looked into the matter for two days, made a careful choice of the desirable time, and himself went to superintend the mounting of the King. When the King had gone a short distance the sky became overcast, a wind rose, and snow and mist supervened. All present fell to laughing, and the King wished to turn back. But Umar said, "Have no anxiety, for this very hour the clouds will clear away, and during these five days there will be no drop of moisture." So the King rode on, and the clouds opened, and during those five days there was no wet and no cloud was seen.

∇ ∇ ∇

Sören Kierkegaard (1813–1855)
The Danish philosopher and theologian led a short, tortured life, but his own satirical gifts might have made him smile at Hans Christian Andersen's use of him in the story "The Galoshes of Fortune." In what is certainly among the most unusual fictional transformations of real-life prototypes, Kierkegaard appears in the fairy tale as a parrot.

∇ ∇ ∇

Kino Tsurayaki (fl. 935)
In his *Tosa nikki* the Japanese author assumed the character of a woman, for at that time fiction writing in Japan was largely the province of women. Some critics claim that as a result Japanese literature is probably the only national literature in the world in which the most renowned works are by women.

∇ ∇ ∇

Heinrich Wilhelm von Kleist (1777–1811)
The romantic German dramatist and prose stylist, his physical health deteriorating, fell in love with an incurably ill woman, Henrietta Vogel. In a letter he called her: "My Jette, my all, my castle, meadows, sum of my life, my wedding, baptism of my children, my tragedy, my fame, my guardian angel, my cherub and seraph!" You will kill me if you love me, she told him, and he shot her fatally on November 21, 1811, as they walked along the Wannsee River near Potsdam, and then turned the gun on himself.

Friedrich Gottlieb Klopstock (1724–1803)

Late in his life admirers of the German poet journeyed from Gottingen to Hamburg seeking an explanation for a difficult passage in his *Messias* (1748). After reading the passage aloud, Klopstock replied: "I cannot recollect what I meant when I wrote it, but I remember it was the finest thing I ever wrote, and you cannot do better than devote the rest of your lives to the discovery of its meaning." James Joyce later made a similar comment to an admirer.

∇ ∇ ∇

Arthur Koestler (1905–1983)

Koestler, born in Budapest, did not begin writing in English until he was almost 35. His novels and nonfiction were often directly concerned with issues of the day and he frequently expressed his belief in the right to euthanasia. Late in life he suffered from Parkinson's disease, and he and his wife committed suicide together.

Said Koestler to an adoring fan who wanted to meet him: "Liking a writer [i.e., his work] and then meeting the writer is like liking pâte de fois gras and then meeting the goose."

When Koestler saw the first newspaper headlines reporting the use of the atomic bomb on Hiroshima, he remarked to a friend "That's the end of the world war, and it's also the beginning of the end of the world."

∇ ∇ ∇

Karl Theodor Körner (1791–1813)

Considered to be one of Germany's greatest war poets and patriots, Körner was severely wounded near Leipzig in the German war of liberation in 1813. Rejoining his outfit a month or so later he was mortally wounded at Gadebusch. His famous war song *Das Schwertlied* is said to have been finished only moments before his death.

∇ ∇ ∇

August von Kotzebue (1761–1819)

The German writer was luckier with his plays, some of them famous in their time, than he was with his politics. In Russia, where he served as a minor official, he fell from grace and spent a few months in Siberia as a convict. Soon afterwards he was restored to favor, only to see his patron, Czar Paul, assassinated. After wandering between Russia and his own country, he finally returned to Germany in 1817 as a secret political informant for Czar Alexander I. Liberal Germans suspected his activities, and he was stabbed to death by Karl Ludwig Sand, a zealous nationalist who became a martyr after being executed for the assassination.

∇ ∇ ∇

Józef Ignacy Kraszewski (1812–1887)

One of the busiest authors in world literary history, the Polish novelist, poet, critic, dramatist, historian and journalist also found time to work as a farmer and social worker, and was imprisoned several times for various political activities. His output includes a series of novels, 29 in all, covering the whole of Polish history from prehistoric times. Despite his crowded life his works, those published in book form alone, fill 641 volumes.

∇ ∇ ∇

Karl Kraus (1874–1936)

The Viennese satirist and critic published his famous radical magazine *Die Fackel* (*The Torch*) from 1899 until his death, writing the whole of it from 1911 on. On the back cover was the warning: "It is requested that no books, periodicals, invitations, clippings, leaflets, manuscripts or written information of any sort be sent in. No such material will ever be returned, nor will any letters be answered. Any return postage that may be enclosed will be turned over to charity."

Kraus had his rules like any editor, but they weren't usually like the rules of most editors. Once he confided: "I have decided many a stylistic problem first by head, then by heads or tails."

∇ ∇ ∇

Ivan Andreevich Krylov (1769–1844)

This Russian fabulist put his stories in the mouths of animals, like Aesop and La Fontaine before him. Rather ironically, he died of eating too many partridges.

∇ ∇ ∇

Prince André Kurbsky (1528–1583)

To Kurbsky belongs the distinction of being the first émigré Russian writer. Kurbsky left Russia in 1564 after a bitter quarrel with Ivan the Terrible. Settling in Lithuania, he exchanged written insults with the czar for almost 20 years before he died. Ironically, the letters of the two men show Ivan to be a far better writer than the nobleman poet. Ivan lived a year longer, when he died in a fit of anger after losing a chess game. However, Prince Kurbsky's first letter to Czar Ivan is, according to a Russian historian, "the first surviving document of Russian dissent and Russian émigré prose."

Pierre-Francine Lacenaire (1800–1836)

A poet and a criminal imprisoned for theft, among other crimes, Lacenaire is said to have been partly the inspiration for Hugo's Jean Valjean, though the author must have used no more than a pinch of him. Lacenaire was finally sentenced to death for murdering an elderly couple for their money. The jaded poet expressed relief that he had been tried in Paris. "It would have been very disagreeable," he sighed, "to have been executed by a provincial executioner."

∇ ∇ ∇

Jean de La Fontaine (1621–1695)

The French poet and author of the *Fables* married a girl of 16, and their marriage was an unhappy one despite the birth of a son. When the boy was four years old the couple separated and La Fontaine began his literary career. Many years later, he met his son in Paris. On being told that La Fontaine was his father, the young man replied, "Ah, yes, I thought I had seen him somewhere!"

La Fontaine's forgetfulness was the basis of numerous stories. On many occasions, for example, he wore his stockings wrong side out. Also famous was his childlike nature. He is said to have fought a duel with an admirer of his wife. When the duel ended, neither contestant hurt, he invited his opponent to dine at his house.

La Fontaine once defined fables in a poem:

Fables in sooth are not what they appear;
Our moralists are mice, and such small deer.
We yawn at sermons, but we gladly turn
To moral tales, and so amused we learn.

Along with Molière, Racine and Boileau, La Fontaine was part of the quartet of the Rue du Vieux Colombier so famous in French literary history. The group met regularly to discuss literary matters. Whenever one of them said something that offended the others, he was required as a punishment to read aloud passages from Jean Chapelain's epic *La Pucelle* (1656), which Boileau had savagely satirized (delaying the publication of its remaining cantos for over two centuries).

The great fabulist, who said, "I use animals to instruct men," was very absentminded as he grew old. One time he gave this excuse for being late for dinner: "I have just come from the funeral of an ant; I followed the procession to the cemetery, and I escorted the family home."

In his old age La Fontaine said that he divided his time into two parts—"one for sleep, the other for doing nothing."

"He shall find eternal salvation," said his nurse of La Fontaine when he took his last breath. "He was so simple that God would not have the heart to damn him."

∇ ∇ ∇

Selma Lagerlöf (1858–1940)

As a child the Swedish Nobel Prize-winner was sent to Stockholm in the hope that an eminent physician there could cure her lameness. While she stayed in the city she entered in her diary the following story about a schoolboy she observed playing in a graveyard:

> I feel a little afraid of those schoolboys, but...there is one boy in particular. He is poorly clad like the others, but he is not quite so wild. I have often noticed that he stands looking on while his comrades are fighting their hardest. He has beautiful blue eyes and perhaps, when he is full grown...
>
> One day I saw the quiet boy sitting with head bowed, all alone on the largest of the stone coffins...I stopped in front of him, as I wished to say something comforting—for I felt so well acquainted with that boy! I was waiting until I could think of something really nice to say, when he suddenly raised his head, pulled a wry face and, with a savage look, roared at me: "Why do you stand there glaring at me, you limping devil's spawn!"
>
> I made no retort, but went on my way. But I wished that the elegant couple who lay in the big stone coffin would raise the lid a trifle and tweak his nose...

Not everyone agreed with the selection of Lagerlöf for the Nobel Prize for literature in 1909. Shortly after the award she became a judge on the prize committee. Observed fellow judge, former Prime Minister Hjalmar Hammarskjöld, "She writes idiotically but she votes intelligently."

∇ ∇ ∇

Comte de Lagrange (Joseph-Louis; 1736–1813)

Exhausted from his labors while revising his *Mécanique Analytique*, the French mathematician collapsed, hitting his head on his desk. This began a protracted illness from which he never recovered. But he accepted his fate without much regret. "I was very ill yesterday, my friends," he told visitors to his bedside one afternoon. "I felt I was going to die. My body grew weaker little by little; my intellectual and physical faculties were extinguished insensibly. I observed the well-graduated progression of the diminution of my strength, and I came to the end without sorrow, without regrets, and by a very gentle decline. Death is not to be dreaded, and when it comes without pain it is a last function which is not unpleasant...Death is the absolute repose of the body."

∇ ∇ ∇

Dionysius Lambinus (Denis Lambin; 1520–1572)

The great French scholar and author provided a mine of information in his commentaries on classical authors, but his example prompted critics to coin from his name the word *lambiner* to express trifling, dawdling and diffuseness. Lambinus is said to have died of a heart attack brought on by his fear that he would die as his friend Petrus Ramus had in the massacre of St. Bartholomew's Day.

∇ ∇ ∇

Lao-Tzu (b. c. 604 B.C.)

It is uncertain whether the Chinese philosopher, reputedly the founder of Taoism, is an historical figure. Lao-Tzu is said to have been born Li Erh and to have written the *Tao-teh-keng*, which is central to Taoism. Legend has it that after a supernatural conception he was carried in his mother's womb for 62 (or 81) years so that his hair was all snow white at birth, and that he lived to be over 200 years old.

∇ ∇ ∇

Marquis de Laplace (Pierre Simon; 1749–1827)

When Napoleon asked the confirmed atheist why his five-volume masterpiece of astronomy *Mécanique Céleste* (1799–1825) made no mention of God, Laplace reputedly replied, "I had no need of that hypothesis."

Life made him less sure of everything. "That which we know is but a little thing; that which we do not know is immense," were his last words.

∇ ∇ ∇

Comte de Lautréamont (Isadore-Lucien Ducasse; 1846–1870)

Little is known of the life of Lautréamont. The young Uruguayan poet, whose violent, anguished work was so important to the surrealists, died in Paris shortly before his 24th birthday. It is known that he is probably the only writer to have taken his pen name from the title of a novel. Wanting to fall as low as possible, to in fact be a fallen archangel, he chose his pseudonym from the title of Eugène Sue's novel *Lautréamont* (1837), a tale of the Parisian underworld whose eponymous hero was a criminal.

Paul Léautaud (1872–1956)
"I was never lucky with women," wrote the French critic, the illegitimate son of a young actress. "I was three days old when my mother dumped me." Throughout his childhood Léautaud was forced to wear cast-off costumes from the Comédie Française wardrobe, which, one writer says, "gave him a defiant taste for looking peculiar." Often he would attend opening nights dressed in two shabby jackets, as he did not own an overcoat, and he always slept in his street clothes.

∇ ∇ ∇

Antoine-Marin Lemierre (1733–1793)
This dramatist and poet always felt that his production of *William Tell*, which inculcated revolutionary principles, somehow shared responsbility for the excesses he witnessed during the French Revolution. His sorrow over this is said to have been a major cause of his death.

∇ ∇ ∇

Ninon de Lenclos (1620–1705)
Molière and other great French literary figures were regulars at the French courtesan's famous salon. Literary legends abound about this apostle of free love and her myriad affairs, including the true story that in her will she left a thousand francs to her attorney M. Arouet's young son—that is, Voltaire. Legend has it that when Louis XIV's mother had her confined in a monastery for her indiscretions she seduced all 439 monks there. Another tale claims that in her later years her own son, separated from her since infancy, fell in love with her and killed himself on learning that she was his mother.

∇ ∇ ∇

Vladimir Ilyich Lenin (V. I. Ulyanov; 1870–1924)
Jean Cocteau once told an interviewer that he remembered the Russian revolutionary from his early days in Paris. Lenin, already wearing the goatee he became famous for, frequently vowed that he would overthrow the Russian monarchy. Cocteau claimed that Lenin supported himself by working for the painter Domergue as a "housemaid," making beds and filling coal scuttles.

According to the Russian poet Maxim Gorky, Lenin listened to a Beethoven sonata one evening with a feeling approaching guilt. "It affects your nerves," he told Gorky, "makes you want to say stupid, nice things and stroke the heads of people who could create such beauty while living in this vile hell."

Pope Leo X (1475–1521)

Whatever his competency as a pope, Leo was a good improvisational poet and one of history's great patrons of literature. Probably more books were dedicated to him—some 5,000—than to any other person in history. One of these books was the translation of a fifth-century poet who had advocated the abolishment of "poisonous" Christianity, apparently a book that Leo did not read after accepting the dedication.

∇ ∇ ∇

Leonardo da Vinci (1452–1519)

Leonardo—painter, sculptor, musician, scientist, inventor and thinker—is not generally thought of as a writer, but he holds the distinction of having written a 36-page manuscript on cosmology that holds the record for the most expensive manuscript ever sold at auction. Leonardo's manuscript brought $2.2 million in 1980, more than the $2 million auction record for a rare book—a Gutenberg Bible.

In 1980 Leonardo's notebook "Of the Nature, Weight and Movement of Water" sold for $5,126,000 at auction, the highest price ever paid for a manuscript.

If his works were judged by their number, Leonardo was more author than artist. He claimed to have written 120 manuscripts, 50 of which remain, compared to his few completed paintings, although so far as is known none of his 5,000 or so pages was published in his lifetime—or had any of the genius of his art. His library contained only 37 books.

Pope Leo X might have become Leonardo's patron, but he came upon him in his studio mixing varnish to preserve a painting before he had ever painted it. "This man will never do anything," he commented, "for he begins to think of the last stage before the first."

When his young companion Francesco Melzi wrote to Leonardo's brothers telling them of his death in France, he added as a postscript: "It would be impossible for me to express the anguish that I have suffered from this death; and while my body holds together I shall live in perpetual unhappiness. And for good reason. The loss of such a man is mourned by all, for it is not in the power of nature to create another..."

Before he died Leonardo had written, "As a day well spent makes it sweet to sleep, so a life well used makes it sweet to die."

Mikhail Lermontov (1814–1841)

The Russian poet was horrified to learn of fellow poet Alexander Pushkin's death in a duel in 1837 and wrote his poem "On the Death of a Poet" about Pushkin's tragic passing. Three years later Lermontov himself was killed in a duel.

∇ ∇ ∇

Alain-René Lesage (1668–1747)

Lesage's comedy *Turcaret* satirized French financiers so scathingly that several moneylenders are said to have offered him 100,000 francs if he would refuse to let the play go on the stage.

Lesage arrived an hour late for his appointment to read his play *Turcaret* at the salon of the Duchesse de Bouillon. "You have made us lose an hour!" the duchess angrily reproved him. "I will make you gain twice that time," Lesage replied and he walked out of the house.

So popular was the French novelist and dramatist's *Le Diable Boiteux* (1707), a comedy about the private lives of Parisians, that a journal of the day reported that "two seigneurs of the court fought, sword in hand, in Barbin's shop, to get the last copy of the second edition."

∇ ∇ ∇

Gotthold Ephraim Lessing (1729–1781)

Toward the end of his life the German dramatist grew very absentminded. One night he came home and found his house locked. As he had forgotten his key, he knocked on the door, but the servant called out, "The professor is not at home."

"Very well," Lessing replied, "Tell him I'll call another time."

"The first critic in Europe," according to Macaulay, Lessing resented religious dogma of every kind and kept his belief to the end. A few days before his death he told friends, "When you see me about to die, call a notary; I will declare before him that I die in none of the prevailing religions."

∇ ∇ ∇

Li Po or Li Tai-Po (c. 701–762)

China's greatest poet was the descendant of emperors. His mother named him Po or "The Bright" because at his birth she had a dream in which she saw the shining planet Venus and considered this an omen. A precocious child, Li Po was an accomplished poet by the time he was 20 and improvised poems for the emperor even while drunk. He was so valued that the emperor himself seasoned his soup and held the inkstone while he composed. Wine, love and song were his themes, while religion or philosophy had no place in his work. But as brilliant and popular as Li Po was, the emperor never rewarded him with high rank, only because the emperor's concubine Yang Kue-fei thought that some of Po's verses slandered her and she poisoned the emperor against him. Actually, the court eunuch Kao-Li-shih had lied to Yang Kue-fei about the poems, because the eunuch had lost face one night when the emperor ordered him to kneel down and pull off a drunken Li Po's muddy boots. The emperor did give Po money to leave the court and issued an imperial edict that enabled him to obtain wine free of charge wherever he should go. A happy Li Po left, joining up with eight other poets and forming a new coterie called The Eight Immortals of the Wine Cup. From Li Po to Edgar Allan Poe it has often been the same.

"The Keats of China" first came to the attention of the emperor T'ang Ming Huang when no one in his court could translate an important message from Korea written in an obscure dialect. A minister advised Ming to order Li Po to present himself at court immediately, "for there is nothing of which he is not capable." Li Po, however, refused to come, explaining that he could not possibly be worthy of the task requested of him, since he had been rejected by the mandarins at the last examination for public office. Emperor T'ang Ming Huang promptly gave him the title of "doctor of the first rank" and Li Po then translated the message, but not before first making his examiners among the ministers take off their boots in his presence.

Most scholars say that there is no evidence to refute the legend that the lighthearted winebibber rowed out onto a lake on a lovely summer evening and fell from his boat, drowning when he tried to kiss or embrace the moon's reflection—even if it does seem too perfect an end for a moon-obsessed poet who wrote in one of his thousand poems of "the moon in the water you can never grasp."

∇ ∇ ∇

Georg Christoph Lichtenberg (1742–1799)

An acquaintance made fun of the German satirist's rather conspicuous ears without reckoning on his sharp tongue. "Well, just think of it," Lichtenberg replied. "With my ears and your brains we'd make a perfectly splendid jackass."

∇ ∇ ∇

Ulrich von Lichtenstein (c. 1200–c. 1276)

This romantic German poet, a Styrian knight, carried chivalry to an extreme seldom exceeded. The minnesinger had his harelip sewn up to please his lady.

He thrilled to drink the water in which she washed and waited among the lepers at her gate to get a look at her. Once he fought for her in a tournament, and she made it known that she was surprised that he still had a finger which she thought he had lost in her honor. Ulrich promptly cut off the offending finger and sent it to her as a tribute.

∇ ∇ ∇

Detlev von Liliencron (1844–1909)
The German lyric poet and novelist, who lived in America for a time, listened to a nobleman bragging about his aristocratic forebears, who it seemed could be traced back at least to Noah's ark and had fought in every war since the Crusades. Finally, he could take it no longer. "You remind me of a potato," he told the nobleman. "Why?" the man asked. "Because the best part of you is underground."

∇ ∇ ∇

Lin Yutang (1895–1976)
The Chinese author rarely answered his mail promptly. "If you keep most letters in your drawer for three months," he held, "and then read them, you realize what a waste of time it would have been to reply."

∇ ∇ ∇

Carolus Linnaeus (Carl von Linne; 1707–1778)
Linnaeus, the most famous of all naturalists, not only dubbed us (perhaps *unwisely*) *Homo sapiens* but chose far more names for things than any other person in history, classifying literally thousands of plants, animals and minerals. The great Swedish name caller did have a sense of humor. The name of the plant genus *Quisqualis* is one joke played by Linnaeus. When he examined the plant, he did not know how to classify it or for whom he could name it. He therefore called the genus *Quisqualis*, which in Latin means, literally, "who or what for." *Quisqualis* (pronounced kwis-kwal-is) clearly shows that the naming process is not always so serious a matter; it might even be called an anonymous eponymous word, or a word in want of an eponym.

The botanist wanted no fuss made over him when he died and ordered in his will that no wake be held after his death. His wife also ignored instructions that she should: "Lay me in a coffin unshaven, unwashed, unclothed, wrapped only in a sheet. Nail down the coffin forthwith, that none may see my wretchedness…"

Liu Ling (c. 720)

One of those Chinese poets called "The Eight Immortals of the Wine Cup," Liu Ling drank to wash his soul, in the words of his fellow immortal Li Po, of "the sorrow of ten thousand ages." Liu believed that "the affairs of this world are no more than duckweed in the river." It was his wish to always be followed by two servants, "one with wine, the other with a spade to bury him where he fell."

∇ ∇ ∇

Liu Yung (c.987-c. 1053)

Though he came from a prominent family, the Chinese poet never settled down to the important official job he could have had for the asking. He preferred to wander all his life, associating mainly with courtesans, singers and artists. Tradition has it that when he died in poverty, courtesans and singing girls took up a collection to bury him and feasted on his grave on the day of the Feast of the Dead.

∇ ∇ ∇

Mikhail Vasilievich Lomonósov (c. 1711–1765)

Both his poetry and his *Russian Grammar* played a large part in reforming the Russian language. He became so celebrated that the name of his native village of Denisovka was changed to Lomonósov.

∇ ∇ ∇

Cassius Longinus (c. 220–273)

This political adviser to Queen Zenobia probably wasn't the Longinus who wrote the famous literary critical work called *Longinus on the Sublime*, but he was certainly capable of producing it. Cassius Longinus was ranked the first of Greek critics of his time. Few in any period of history could match his learning. He was, in fact, so well read that he was called "the living library," and "walking encyclopedia."

∇ ∇ ∇

Félix Lope de Vega Carpio (1562–1635)

The Spanish author wrote more than 2,200 plays in his lifetime, far more than any other author in history. Several of his plays were written overnight and 100 of them in a day each—these records no author has come close to equaling.

The playwright did not print his plays, for fear that fewer people would then come to the theter. But publishers regularly sent men with amazing memories to his performances. After sitting through two or three hearings, these men committed the plays to memory and dictated them to the publisher's printers. Though known "memorizers" were sometimes barred from the theater—at one performance Lope's cast refused to go on until one such man was ejected—the publishers were always quick to find replacements.

Lope de Vega's life was as passionate and prolific as his literary productions. His many love poems are dedicted to several of his many mistresses. The Spaniard was married twice and fathered at least four children out of wedlock, including three born to Spanish actress Micaela de Lujan, who starred in several of his plays.

The author and his great contemporary Cervantes were enemies, probably because Lope de Vega smarted under the satire of himself and his works in *Don Quixote*, which he probably read in manuscript. A former friend of Cervantes, he wrote in a letter to a prominent physician on August 4, 1604, that his own plays were odious to Cervantes and that "no poet is as bad as Cervantes, nor so foolish as to praise *Don Quixote*." This is the first recorded mention of Cervantes' masterpiece.

Cervantes began his career trying to keep up with Lope's output, but he gave up when he learned that the playwright had in one week written 10 plays, one of them tossed off before breakfast. "There is no competing with 'a monster of nature,'" he remarked.

The idol of Spain, he was so beloved that one reviewer who dared criticize him lived in fear of assassination. Wherever Lope went he was engulfed by crowds of admirers. No other playwright in history has known such adulation. In his own day his name indeed came to mean anything superlative of a kind, such as Lope cigars, Lope melons and Lope horses.

Lope de Vega's last days were sad ones, especially because of the death of his son Lope and the elopement of his daughter Antonia, both of which events are said to have "wounded him to the soul." A contemporary wrote that every Friday he "scourged himself so severely that the walls of his room were sprinkled with his blood."

An old story claims that on his deathbed Vega asked how much time he had remaining. His death was imminent, he was told. "All right then, I'll say it," he declared. "Dante makes me sick."

In reality Lope de Vega did not die on the same day as Shakespeare, as the traditional story holds. When Shakespeare died, England was still using the

Julian calendar; Spain had already adopted the Gregorian calendar, by which
Shakespeare died on May 3, 1616.

▽ ▽ ▽

Pierre Loti (1850–1923)

So shy was the French novelist, born Louis-Marie-Julien Viaud, that his friends
named him *le Loti*, after an Indian flower that grows in lonely, secluded areas.
When he began writing he took the nickname as his pseudonym.

▽ ▽ ▽

Louis XIII (1601–1643)

The French king took an active interest in France's first newspaper, the *Gazette*
(later *the Gazette de France*) and was a frequent contributor from its inception in
1631, often taking his paragraphs to the printers and watching them set into type.

▽ ▽ ▽

Pierre Loüys (1870–1925)

This French poet and novelist, who was related to Victor Hugo, came from a rich
family and inherited 300,000 francs on turning 21. He spent all of it within just
three years after a doctor mistakenly told him he had only that long to live.

Like Prosper Mérimée (*q.v.*), Loüys pretended to be a woman when he wrote
Chansons de Bilitis (1894), a celebration of lesbian love purportedly written by a
Greek woman poet. Though Bilitis did not exist, one critic claimed that he had
read the poems in the original Greek text.

▽ ▽ ▽

Lucan (Marcus Annaeus Lucanus; 39–65 A.D.)

Some critics of his day thought the precocious Lucan too rhetorical, "a model
rather for the orator than for the poet," said Quintilian. When Lucan heard this,
he probably assumed the attitude many bestselling authors have had through
the ages. In any case, Martial has him quip: "There are those who say I am not a
poet; but the bookseller who sells me thinks I am."

The Emperor Nero, who alone considered himself a great poet, was jealous of
Lucan's literary brilliance and forbade him to write any more poems or recite his
poems in public. An indignant Lucan joined in a conspiracy against the emperor.
When the conspiracy was uncovered, Nero would listen to no eloquent argu-
ments or abject pleas, or even Lucan's craven attempt to gain immunity by
denouncing his own mother. Nero commanded the precocious poet to commit

suicide and Lucan opened a vein and ended his life at the age of 26. "As his blood flowed," the Roman historian Tacitus writes, "when he perceived that his feet and hands were growing cold and life ebbing gradually from his extremities, while his breast was still warm and retained intelligence, [he remembered] a poem composed by himself in which he had told of a wounded soldier dying by the same form of death [and] then repeated the lines, and that was his last utterance."

∇ ∇ ∇

Lucian of Samosata (c. 125–c. 190)

The Greek satirist, whose *The True History*, the story of a visit to the moon, inspired *Gulliver's Travels*, among many other works, wrote ironic true tales of life in Athens. In one he wrote of a musician's simultaneous debut and swan song: "Harmonides, a young flute player and scholar...at his first public performance began his solo with so violent a blast that he breathed his last breath into his flute, and died upon the spot."

His work, including two mock tragedies with gout as the theme, is often remembered as among the most curious of his day. In his "The Trial of the Vowels," a legal action is brought by the letter sigma against the letter tau for the encroachments of the latter: The vowels form the jury.

Lucian was called "the Blasphemer" because he attacked both the gods and Christianity. In one of his works he described himself as "a terrible dog who bit while he laughed." He may have been ripped to death by mad dogs for his impiety. According to the *Suidas*, the great 10th-century Greek encyclopedia based upon ancient Greek lexicons, Lucian "is said to have been killed by [rabid] dogs, he having been rabid against the truth."

∇ ∇ ∇

Lucretius (Titus Lucretius Carus; c. 99–c. 55 B.C.)

Little is known of the life of the greatest of philosophical poets. According to St. Jerome he was driven mad by a love philter, wrote several books while suffering from insanity, and finally died by his own hand in his 43rd year (probably it was his 44th). Tradition holds that the love potion was administered by his wife, tradition not explaining why.

Lucius Licinus Lucullus (c. 119–57 B.C.)

Lucullus, a celebrated Roman general and consul who drove Mithridates' fleet from the Mediterranean, among other military successes, had been relieved of his office by Pompey in 67 B.C. But he had amassed a fortune and retired into the elegant leisure for which he has become famous, spending huge sums on public displays and on his estates. His library, among the largest and most famous in Rome, became a literary center and helped him write his account of the Marsian War in Greek. Horace tells us he lavishly entertained the artists, poets and philosophers with whom he surrounded himself, and that his feasts were famous throughout Rome. The gourmand even had files of menus listed according to cost, serving the most expensive ones to his most important guests, and it is said that on one occasion an unparalleled dinner cost him the equivalent of more than $8,000. Another time, Plutarch says, he ordered his cook to prepare a particularly magnificent meal and was reminded that he was dining alone that night. "Lucullus will sup tonight with Lucullus," he replied, or, "Today Lucullus is host to Lucullus." These sayings are now used to indicate a luxurious meal enjoyed by a gourmet who dines alone.

∇ ∇ ∇

St. Lucy (d. c. 303)

St. Lucy or Lucia, whose feast day is celebrated on December 13, was a Sicilian virgin martyr said to have lived in Syracuse in the reign of Diocletian. Though she was threatened with outrage, no force was able to move her from the spot on which she stood—neither boiling oil nor burning pitch had the power to move or hurt her, until she was slain with the sword. This would be a good reason for her to be the patron saint of writers that she is, but more likely the designation has something to do with her being the patron saint of those afflicted with eye problems (writers often having such trouble). One legend says a nobleman wanted to marry her for the beauty of her eyes. She tore them out and gave them to him, saying, "Now let me live to God." She is represented in art as carrying a palm branch on a platter with two eyes on it.

∇ ∇ ∇

Martin Luther (1483–1546)

The first recorded use of the word that was to give Luther's rebellion against the Church its historic name came in a 1518 letter Luther himself wrote to Duke George advising that "a common *reformation* should be undertaken of the spiritual and temporal estates."

There is no record in the transcript of the diet of Worms that Luther made the immortal reply *"Hier stehe Ich, Ich kann nicht anders"* ("Here I stand, I can do no other") when he was asked in his appearance there on April 18, 1521, if "you do not repudiate your books and the errors which they contain." The famous words have only been traced thus far to the earliest *printed* version of his reply.

Luther claimed to "know Satan very well," a Satan who was very real to him. Once he claimed to have scared off the devil by throwing an inkpot at him, another time by calling him filthy names, still again by playing the flute. So used to the devil was he that when a noise woke him at night, he would often assume that it was just Satan and go right back to sleep again.

He loved children and brought up eleven orphaned nephews and nieces as well as his own six offspring. His favorite daughter Magdalena died when only 14. As she was buried he spoke aloud to her: *"Du liebes Lenichen,* you will rise and shine like the stars and the sun..." Then he added, "How strange it is to know that she is at peace and all is well, and yet be so sorrowful!"

Luther was always under intense scrutiny. "My enemies examine all that I do," he once complained. "If I break wind in Wittenberg they smell it in Rome."

He could sound as full-blooded and lusty as Rabelais. "Women wear veils because of the angels," he explained one time. "I wear trousers because of the women."

To Protestant preachers who wanted to outlaw plays, Luther replied, "Christians must not altogether shun plays because there are sometimes coarseness and adulteries therein; for such reasons they would have to give up the Bible too."

∇ ∇ ∇

Rosa Luxemburg (1870–1919)

The Polish-born German revolutionary author and editor, known as "Rote Rosa," was arrested in 1919 for inciting a riot during the Spartacist uprising. The little crippled woman was brutally attacked and kicked to death by army officers while being brought to prison. Her body was thrown into a canal and only recovered several days later.

Niccolo Machiavelli (1469–1527)

Machiavelli's stage comedy *Mandragola* has a prologue that warns all critics: "Should anyone seek to cow the author by evil-speaking, I warn you that he, too, knows how to speak evil, and indeed excels in the act; and that he has no respect for anyone in Italy, though he bows and scrapes to those better dressed than himself."

It took Machiavelli only a few months to write his famous *Il Principe* (*The Prince*) in 1513. But the book wasn't printed until 1532, almost 20 years later and five years after the author had died. *Il Principe* did, however, circulate in manuscript up until this time and unauthorized copies were made of it.

∇ ∇ ∇

Macrobius (fl. c. 400)

Among the Latin author's works was the *Saturnalia,* or *Feast of Saturn,* an ancient *Curiosities of Literature* that has been quoted for over 15 centuries now. In it, among numerous quotations and *bon mots* and anecdotes is the first mention of the old puzzle "Which came first, the chicken or the egg?" (*Ovumme prius fuerit aut gallina?*)

∇ ∇ ∇

Maurice Maeterlinck (1862–1949)

"I know you don't understand picture technique," Samuel Goldwyn told the Belgian author. "You don't have to. Just go home and write your greatest book over in the form of a scenario." Several weeks passed and Maeterlinck returned with a script of his earlier *Vie des Abeilles* (1901). "Now we'll see something," Goldwyn crooned, taking the scenario into his office. Not long after he came rushing out, highly agitated. "My God," he cried, "the hero is a bee!"

∇ ∇ ∇

Jean de Magnon (fl. 1663)

Biographer to the king of France, Magnon boasted that he would write an encyclopedia in heroic verse so all-encompassing that it would make all libraries "useless ornaments." He did produce some 10 books of his projected work (published as *La Science universelle,* 1663) but did not live to finish it, robbers killing him one night on a lonely Paris street. Perhaps it was just as well that he left his project unfinished, for critics called what he had done among the most incorrect, obscene and flat verses in French poetry.

Jón Magnússon (c. 1610–1696)

This Icelandic author wrote a lurid work called the *Pislar Saga* in which he described how he had been persecuted by witches or magicians. His superstitious tale led to the burning at the stake of two innocent people.

∇ ∇ ∇

François de Malherbe (1555–1628)

Because France's Henry the Great gave him "more compliments than money," Malherbe was forced to sell his poems to the highest bidder. The poems were classic in their simplicity and clarity; they had to "breathe well" and be "welcome to the ear," and he always recited them to his butler before committing them to their final form.

A perfectionist until the very end, the French poet, critic and translator squirmed impatiently on his deathbed listening to his confessor describing all the joys of paradise. "Please stop," Malherbe finally told him. "Your ungrammatical style is giving me a distaste for them."

∇ ∇ ∇

Bronislaw Malinowski (1884–1942)

The great anthropologist and author told of speaking to "an old cannibal, who, hearing of the Great War raging in Europe, was most curious to know how we Europeans managed to eat such enormous quantities of human flesh." When Malinowski told him that Europeans didn't eat their slain enemies, "he looked at me in shocked horror and asked what sort of barbarians we were, to kill without any real object."

∇ ∇ ∇

Stéphane Mallarmé (1842–1898)

A professor of English at a small college, the French symbolist poet led a quiet, uneventful life "pursuing perfection through renunciation of the actual." This he did in many ways, including typographical experiments, the abandonment of punctuation in poetry, and the invention of a new punctuation and construction in prose. One morning two friends of the poet came upon him cleaning a littered area in a woods outside Paris. They asked him just what he was doing. "I have invited some Parisians to come to tea tomorrow," he explained, "so I am cleaning up the banquet hall."

He hated his early years in the provinces. "Ah," he wrote to a friend, "I'll tell you that here one sinks into the very depths of despondency. Nothing happens:

you turn around and around in a narrow circle like the brainless horses of fairground circuses, accompanied by the most god-awful music!"

∇ ∇ ∇

Bertil Malmberg (1889–1950)
When late in his career the Swedish poet switched from a traditional to a modernistic style, he was asked why he had made the change. "I attribute it to the effects of a brain hemorrhage," he explained.

∇ ∇ ∇

Frederick Edward Maning (1812–1883)
This strong, 6-foot-3-inch tall New Zealander can be called the only Maori author of any renown. The writer became a favorite of the wild Ngapuhi of New Zealand, who adopted him into their tribe. After he married the chief's daughter he was christened "Pakeha-Maori" (foreigner turned Maori).

∇ ∇ ∇

Thomas Mann (1875–1955)
Mann left Germany in 1933 with the advent of Hitler, and four years later he received a letter from the dean of the philosophical faculty at Bonn University advising him that because of his actions against the German (Nazi) state his name had been deleted from the university list of honorary doctors. The novelist wrote in reply: "In the Word is involved the unity of humanity, the wholeness of the human problem, which permits nobody to separate the intellectual and artistic from the political and social, and to isolate himself within the ivory tower of the 'cultural' proper."

On an early visit to America he prepared a speech in English praising his publisher, Alfred Knopf. "He is not only a publisher," Mann said to guests gathered at a testimonial dinner, "he is a creature, too." (He had meant to say "creator.")

He didn't get along with playwright Bertold Brecht. One time he read a play of Brecht's and commented, "Just imagine, the monster has talent." When Brecht heard this backhanded compliment, he replied, in pointed reference to Mann's famous long novels, "As a matter of fact, I always found his short stories quite good."

Mann took a healthy view of bad reviews, writing:

We all bear wounds; praise is a soothing if not necessarily healing balm for them. Nevertheless, if I may judge by my own experience, our receptivity for praise stands in no relationship to our vulnerability to mean disdain and spiteful abuse. No matter how stupid such abuse is, no matter how plainly impelled by private rancors, as an expression of hostility it occupies us far more deeply and lastingly than the opposite. Which is very foolish, since enemies are, of course, the necessary concomitant of any robust life, the very proof of its strength.

A Hollywood screenwriter, cornering Mann at a party, continually put himself down in comparison to the Nobel Prize–winning German writer. He was nothing compared to Mann, he went on, his scripts were feeble, he was a mere hack, a zero, a nonentity. Mann, the epitome of politeness, listened until the writer left and then turned to his host. "That man has no right to make himself so small," he said. "He is not that big."

∇ ∇ ∇

Aldus Manutius (Teobaldo Mannucci; 1450–1515)
The noted Italian printer Aldus Manutius, the Latin name of Teobaldo Mannucci, invented *italic type*, in which the preceding two words are printed, and established the custom of the publisher's colophon (his was a dolphin, symbolizing speed, and an anchor, symbolizing stability). A compulsive worker, he hung this inscription over the door of his study: "Whoever thou art, thou art earnestly requested by Aldus to state thy business briefly, and to take thy departure promptly…For this is a place of work."

∇ ∇ ∇

Mao Tse-tung (1893–1976)
Whatever one might think of his politics, Mao was an accomplished poet, and certainly the only poet in modern times to head one of the great powers. Mao's 37 traditional poems were widely circulated. His *Selected Works*, however, achieved a far wider audience, having been compulsory reading for everyone in China.

∇ ∇ ∇

Jean-Paul Marat (1743–1793)
An extreme skin disease forced the Swiss-born French Revolutionary author to do most of his writing in a bath of warm water, which alleviated his condition. If any writer could be called a workaholic it was Marat. He allotted only two hours for sleep every night and once wrote, "I have not had fifteen minutes' play in over three years." It was in his bath, of course, pen in hand and paper on the

board spanning the tub, that his political enemy Charlotte Corday stabbed him to death.

∇ ∇ ∇

Cristoforo Marcello (fl. 16th century)

During the sack of Rome in 1527 the destruction of libraries and art was immense and many authors and scholars suffered terribly, several of them committing suicide rather than bear their tortures. Baldus watched as the only copy of his new, unpublished commentary on Pliny was used to start a bonfire, all the poems of Marone were similarly burned, another scholar's house was burned to the ground and the poet Paolo Bombasi was murdered. The scholar Cristoforo Marcello suffered perhaps the worst torture; all of his nails were pulled out of his fingers by the invaders.

∇ ∇ ∇

Marguerite, Queen of Navarre (1492–1549)

The queen of Navarre, to whom Rabelais dedicated *Gargantua*, and who wrote or collected the tales of the *Heptameron*, was much loved by all who knew her. One charming legend claimed that "she was born smiling, and held out her little hand to each comer."

∇ ∇ ∇

F. T. Marinetti (Filippo Tommaso Marinetti; 1876–1944)

This Italian futurist poet, who became one of the first members of the Fascist party, wrote rather banal poems when all the propaganda was said and done, but no one ever *read* poetry with such animation. At his readings the little Dali-mustached man who advocated burning all libraries and flooding the world's museums, "adorned with diamond rings, gold chains, and hundreds of white flashing teeth," not to mention his inevitable spats, wing collar and bow tie, would wave his arms violently, mix Italian with the French he wrote in and imitate the sound of machine guns, cannon, diving airplanes, even the loud puffing noises of a locomotive—anything to illustrate his poetry, which was said to be supported by his father's string of Egyptian brothels.

∇ ∇ ∇

Giambattista Marini (1569–1625)

Cavalier Marini, as the pompous Neapolitan poet Giambattista Marini was called, headed the *seicento* school of Italian literature, which became noted for its flamboyance and bad taste. Poems like his 45,000-line *Adone* show brilliant mastery of technique but were intended to dazzle the reader at any cost, and their extravagance led to his name becoming a word (Marinismo) for any florid, bombastic style characterized by pages full of sound but signifying nothing. Marini, or Marino, had his troubles with censors, too. His satirical works were not appreciated by his satirized patrons and he was forced to leave Italy and take refuge in Paris.

After Marini ridiculed his verses, rival Italian poet Gasparo Murtola decided to kill him. Murtola hid behind some bushes and shot at Marini. Instead of hitting him, however, he succeeded in wounding a servant of the Duke of Savoy, who had him sentenced to death. Marini, good heart that he was, intervened and persuaded the duke to pardon him.

Few poets have made a more triumphal return to their homeland than Marini did when he ended his exile in 1624. It is said that noblemen escorted him into Naples, women and children threw kisses to him from their balconies and even highwaymen threw roses at his coach.

∇ ∇ ∇

Pierre Carlet de Chamblain de Marivaux (1688–1763)

Few writers would want to share the undeserved fate of this French writer, though he made important advances in the development of the novel. His name, in the form of "marivaudage," means an affected, overstrained style, as exemplified by the witty bantering of lovers in his two unfinished novels and thirty plays. Marivaux's subtle, graceful works, mostly excellent studies of middle-class psychology, led a contemporary to remark that his characters not only tell each other and the reader everything they had thought, but everything that they would like to persuade themselves that they have thought. Marivaudage has also been described as "the metaphysics of love-making." The author was much admired in his own time, though not by Voltaire, whose work he criticized, and it is said that Madame Pompadour secretly provided him with a large pension.

∇ ∇ ∇

Martial (Marcus Valerius Martialis; c. 40–104 A.D.)

The Roman epigrammatist of Spanish birth wrote what is perhaps literature's most unflattering portrait of an author's mistress, writing of one of his lovers: "Your tresses, Galla, are manufactured far away; you lay aside your teeth at night as you do your silk dresses; you lie stored away in a hundred caskets, and your face does not lie with you; you wink with an eyebrow brought to you in the morning. No respect moves you for your outworn carcass, which you may now count as one of your ancestors."

Many of his brilliant epigrams were impromptu compositions delivered on the spur of the moment and not at all prepared beforehand.

When he came to Rome from Spain, the poet lived in a cramped third-floor apartment and depended on the favor of rich patrons for a living, but he always bit the hand that fed him. To one of his patrons, he wrote: "I don't know whether Phoebus fled from the dinner table of Thyestes. At any rate, Ligurinus, we flee from yours. Splendid, indeed, it is, and magnificently supplied with good things, but when you recite you spoil it all. I don't want you to set before me a turbot or a two-pound mullet. I don't want your mushrooms or your oysters. I want you to keep your mouth shut!"

∇ ∇ ∇

Karl Marx (1818–1883)

Marx's book that changed the world was very nearly a victim of piles. The author suffered badly from hemorrhoids while working on *Das Kapital* (1867) in London. As he complained in a letter to his friend and collaborator Friedrich Engels: "To finish I must at least be able to sit down…I hope the bourgeoisie will remember my carbuncles."

According to the Russian journal *Sputnik*, Marx received this letter from his German publisher while living in London and researching his seminal work in the British Museum:

Dear Herr Doktor:

You are already 18 months behind time with the manuscript of *Kas Kapital* which you have agreed to write for us. If we do not receive the manuscript within six months, we shall be obliged to commission another author to do the work.

When the exiled German revolutionary was buried in London on March 17, 1883, only eight friends followed his coffin in the rain to Highgate Cemetery. One was his friend and collaborator Friedrich Engels, who later completed *Das Kapital*, the major text of socialism. "On the afternoon of the fourteenth of March," he began in his funeral speech, "at a quarter to three, the greatest living thinker ceased to think. Left alone for less than two minutes, when we entered we found him sleeping peacefully in his chair—but forever." He went on to say that though Marx had more enemies than any man on earth "I make bold to say that…he had hardly a personal enemy."

Margaret Maultasch (1318–1369)

The "Ugly Duchess," as she was also known, was nicknamed Margaret Maultasch, the name by which history remembers her, because her big mouth resembled a pocket (the German *maultach* means "pocket mouth"). Legend depicts the Countess of Tyrol as a woman of great power and greater evil. Her connection with literature is an interesting one. A well-known portrait of her served Tenniel as the model for the duchess in his famous illustrations for Lewis Carroll's *Alice in Wonderland*.

∇ ∇ ∇

Guy de Maupassant (1850–1893)

The French short-story writer and novelist, who died of syphilis when only 43, suffered for many years from the effects of the disease and the myriad cures he took to alleviate it, which ranged from sunbathing to large doses of morphine. His pain was so great that he often "longed to stick a bullet" in his head and he in fact did attempt suicide at least once. De Maupassant had always been an athletic man, an especially excellent rower, and literary friends like Flaubert at first found him little more than "a simple young athlete." During the final stages of his illness, excessive physical exercise in fact so weakened his constitution that it hastened his death.

Maupassant was a protégé of Flaubert, who admonished him in a letter early in his career: "You must—do you hear me, young man?—you *must* work more than you are doing."

Early in his career de Maupassant was promoted to the Cabinet de l'Instruction Publique in the French Ministry of Marine. Yet it is said his chief had reservations about his promotion. A report he wrote criticized de Maupassant as "not having reached the standard of the department in the matter of [prose] style."

Dining with Henry James in London, Maupassant pointed to a pretty woman across the room. "Go and get her for me," he said, and James replied that since he didn't know the woman he certainly couldn't properly introduce her. "Surely you know *her*?" Maupassant said, pointing to another pretty woman. "Ah, if I only spoke English!" But James refused again. He, in fact, refused Maupassant five times, and the French writer finally remarked irritably, "Really, you don't seem to know anyone in London."

A year before he died of syphilis de Maupassant tried to commit suicide. Already suffering from delusions caused by the disease—seeing ghosts and imagining that his brain was seeping out his nostrils—he cut his throat late one night while staying in Cannes. He was saved only because a servant heard him cry out and summoned a doctor who sewed up the huge wound.

∇ ∇ ∇

Vladimir Vladimirovich Mayakovsky (1893–1930)

The great Russian futurist poet wasn't appreciated by Lenin, who found his *150,000,000* (about a boxing match between the 150 million Russian Ivans and President Woodrow Wilson) "incomprehensible rubbish." After he shot himself, the poet's reputation fell even lower, until his beloved Lili Brik wrote to Stalin pointing out the shameful attacks being made against him. Wrote the all-powerful Stalin on the margin of her letter: "Mayakovsky was and remains the best and most talented poet of our Soviet Epoch." On the basis of this one hastily scrawled sentence, Mayakovksy was resurrected and became in effect Russia's official laureate, with monuments and museums to him springing up throughout the country.

∇ ∇ ∇

Jules Mazarin (1602–1661)

Mazarin, the papal legate to Paris, was made a cardinal in 1641. Entering the French service, he became prime minister and later founded the famous library, the Bibliothèque Mazarine. Cardinal Mazarin was a resourceful man. When, for example, Louis XIV proved difficult to teach in conventional ways, he taught the Sun King history, geography and other subjects by printing instructive text on "educational" playing cards.

∇ ∇ ∇

Meir of Rothenburg (c. 1215–93)

In 1286 this German rabbi and poet was arrested and thrown into prison in Alsace on some trumped-up anti-Semitic charge. His friends offered to have him released by paying the ransom on his head, but he refused, fearing that he would set a precedent for extortion involving other Jews. He died in prison seven years later.

∇ ∇ ∇

Menander (c. 342–292 B.C.)

The Greek poet is now considered the greatest master of comedy of his era but wasn't a very successful writer in his lifetime. He was successful at love. A rich, handsome man, he loved the beautiful courtesan Glycera. When Ptolemy I invited Menander to his court at Alexandria, the poet sent the playwright Philemon in his place, explaining, "Philemon has no Glycera."

An ancient writer tells us how Demetrius, governor of Athens, came to meet the poet: "Menander, famous for his comedies—whom Demetrius had not known personally though he had read him and admired his genius—came, perfumed and in flowing robe, with languid step and slow. Seeing him at the end of the line the tyrant asked, 'What effeminate is that who dares enter my presence?' Those nearest replied, 'This is Menander the writer!'"

Said Aristophanes of Byzantium, "O Menander, O Life, which of you imitated the other?" Menander originated many popular proverbial sayings, including "Conscience makes cowards of us all" ("Conscience makes cowards of the bravest men"), "Evil communications corrupt good manners" and, perhaps, "I am a man and consider nothing human alien to me." Possibly the most famous of these proverbs is "the good die young"—in his original words: "Whom the gods love, die young; that man is blest/Who, having viewed at ease this solemn show/Of sun, star, ocean, fire, doth quickly go/Back to his home with calm uninjured breast." Menander died young himself, at the age of 50, drowning after a seizure of cramps while swimming in the harbor at Piraeus.

▽ ▽ ▽

Catulle Mendès (1841–1909)
Two years or so before his death Baudelaire impulsively asked the French poet Catulle Mendès, "Guess how much I have earned in the whole of my working life?" He proceeded to answer his own question by enumerating everything he had written over his career and what he had been paid for each effort and came up with a total of 15,892 francs 60 centimes (about five times that amount, or under $20,000, in today's world). This comes to some 600 francs a year over 25 years.

▽ ▽ ▽

Antonio Escobar y Mendoza (1589–1669)
This Jesuit churchman and author wrote and preached such interesting sermons that he became famous throughout Spain. His sermons were so popular that he preached at least once a day for 50 years.

▽ ▽ ▽

Emperor Menelik II (1844–1913)
Supported by the Italians, the former king of Shoa (central Abyssinia) conquered all of Abyssinia and became its first modern ruler in 1868. But though he was modern in outlook, Menelik, who claimed to be a direct decendant of the Biblical Solomon by Sheba, had some rather primitive beliefs. The most harmful of these proved to be his habit of eating pages from the Bible whenever he felt ill. This

did indeed seem to improve his health over many years, until he suffered a major stroke. Trying to recover from it, Menelik ate the entire *Book of Kings*, which proved the end of him.

∇ ∇ ∇

Prosper Mérimée (1803–1870)
The French author wrote six plays before he turned 21, attributing them all to "Spanish actress Clara Gazul" under the title *Le Théâtre de Clara Gazul* (1825) because he thought his first published work would be more successful if people believed a celebrity had written it. Mérimée actually posed for the book's faked frontispiece portrait of "Clara Gazul," wearing a silk mantilla. Before his hoax was exposed, "Clara's" book was widely acclaimed. Another time Mérimée published supposed translations of Spanish poetry that were really his own original poems.

∇ ∇ ∇

Merwan (c. 790)
Harun al-Rashid of *Thousand and One Nights* fame was a cultured monarch, so fond of good stories, it is said, that he "rewarded excellent lady raconteurs by taking them to bed," this considered a great honor. Himself a poet, there was nothing he loved so much as good poetry. In fact, the Arab ruler once gave the court poet Merwan, for one brief laudatory ode, 5,000 gold pieces (worth perhaps $250,000 today), 10 Greek slave girls, a robe of honor and his favorite horse.

∇ ∇ ∇

Pietro Metastasio (1698–1782)
The Italian poet, born Pietro Trapassi, was an urchin singing in the streets when the wealthy drama critic Gian Vincenzo heard him and adopted him, changing his name to Metastasio (Greek for Trapassi). Vincenzo reared and educated him, leaving him a fortune, but the poet spent his inheritance in a few years and was forced to apprentice himself to a lawyer. Forbidden to write under the terms of his contract, he had to publish his first poems under a pseudonym.

∇ ∇ ∇

Julien Offoy de La Metbrie (1709–1751)
In one of his books the French physician and philosopher described death as the last act of a farce. He himself died at a dinner given for him by a patient he had saved from death—after stuffing himself with a pheasant pâté and coming down with a raging fever. "For once," Voltaire quipped on hearing the news, "the patient has killed the doctor."

Cardinal Giuseppe Caspar Mezzofanti (1774–1849)

Lord Byron called the chief keeper of the Vatican library "a walking polyglot; a monster of languages; a Briareus of parts of speech." (Briareus was a mythical giant with 59 heads and 100 hands.) The cardinal could speak 60 languages and 72 dialects fluently and could translate 114 languages, such exotics as Geez and Chippewa among them. Byron had good reason to speak so highly of him. It was Mezzofanti who taught the British poet to speak Cockney, of all things!

▽ ▽ ▽

Michelangelo Buonarroti (1475–1564)

> The night thou seest here, posed gracefully
> In an act of slumber, was by an angel wrought
> Out of this stone. Sleeping, with life she's fraught.
> Wake her, incredulous wight; she'll speak to thee.

With these words Italian poet Gianbattista Strozzi gave his intepretation of Michelangelo's statue of Night. Michelangelo, a poet as well as a sculptor, liked the pun on his name but didn't agree with the interpretation, writing a poem that gave his own explanation (and a key to his personality):

> Dear is my sleep, but more to be mere stone,
> So long as ruin and dishonor reign.
> To see naught, to feel naught, is my great gain;
> Then wake me not; speak in an undertone.

A priest once regretted that Michelangelo had not married and begotten children, the artist and poet explaining: "I have too much of a wife in my art, and she has given me trouble enough. As to my children, they are the works that I shall leave; and if they are not worth much, they shall at least live for some time."

A jealous man with a sharp tongue, Michelangelo was noted for his rude criticism of rivals. "Your father," he once told Francia's handsome son, "makes better forms by night than day."

Michelangelo preserved his creative genius even in extreme old age. There is a device said to have been invented by him: an old man in a go-cart, with an hourglass upon it, bearing the inscription *Ancora imparo*—YET I AM LEARNING!

The artist disliked Leonardo da Vinci and had a celebrated quarrel with him. One day several Florentines were discussing Dante's *The Divine Comedy* when they saw da Vinci passing by and asked him his interpretation of several verses.

Michelangelo, a devoted student of Dante's work, happened to appear at that moment. "Here is Michelangelo," da Vinci said. "He will explain the lines." "Explain them yourself!" Michelangelo retorted, thinking the older artist was making fun of him. "You who made the model of a horse to be cast in bronze and could not cast it, and left it unfinished, to your shame! And those Milanese capons thought you could do it!" With that he stalked off fuming, leaving a scarlet-faced da Vinci behind.

▽ ▽ ▽

Comte Honoré-Gabriel Riquetti de Mirabeau (1749–1791)

Despite the French revolutionary and propagandist's sonorous oratory, many, unjustly or not, distrusted his motives, especially those who learned of his secret alliance with the king, by whom he was paid in his last years. "He is capable of anything for money," a contemporary said of him, "even of a good action."

▽ ▽ ▽

Mishima Yukio (1925–1970)

In his *Patriotism* (1960) Mishima describes the suicide of a young army officer and his wife. This was the first indication of the novelist's absorption with those who died in a 1936 attempt to wrest power from Japanese politicians and give it to the emperor. On November 25, 1970, he emulated these "patriots." Mishima had delivered the final installment of his last novel to his publisher that day. Soon afterward he and his private "army" forcibly entered the eastern headquarters of the Japanese Self-Defense Force, where he committed seppuku, hoping to convince the Japanese to reflect on how much they had lost of their cultural history.

▽ ▽ ▽

Mithridates (132–63 B.C.)

The king of Pontus, a renowned man of letters, mastered 22 languages and was the center of cultural life in his kingdom. An unmatched collector of art works, he presided over a court noted for its Greek men of letters, but that he loved the sensual life just as well is evident by the fact that he awarded prizes to both the greatest poets and the greatest eaters in his kingdom. According to the credulous Pliny, Mithridates came to an ironic end. All his days he had guarded himself against poisoning by accustoming his body to small amounts of poison, rendering himself immune by gradually increasing their daily doses. Then, weary of his son's treachery, he decided to commit suicide and found that he had mithridatized himself too well. No poison in any amount worked, for he had total immunity. He had to have a slave stab him to death.

Molière (Jean-Baptiste Poquelin; 1622–1673)

Moron, as a designation for a feebleminded person, is said to be one of two words ever voted into the language. It was adopted in 1910 by the American Association for the Study of the Feebleminded from the name of a foolish character in Molière's play *La Princesse d'Elide*. (The unit of electric current called an ampere or amp, named for French scientist André Ampère, had been voted into the language at the International Electrical Congress held in Paris 29 years earlier.)

As a child Molière lived in a house on a Paris street that was decorated with sculptures representing a group of monkeys playing. The monkey had long been the traditional emblem of the comic actor.

Voltaire tells us that Molière was no good as an actor in dramatic roles because he suffered "from a kind of hiccup which was quite unsuited to serious roles...[but which] served to make his acting in comedy the more enjoyable."

Molière invented the French comedy of manners with *Les précieuses ridicules* (*The Pretentious Young Ladies*) in 1659. Legend holds that during the first performance on November 18th Molière worried about how the play would be received until a woman rose in the audience and cried, "Courage! Courage! Molière, this is good comedy!"

Molière's *Tartuffe* (1664), which has to this date been performed more often than any other French play, is an exposure of the hypocritically pious; this apparently included a great number of real-life clergymen, considering their reaction to the play. The archbishop of Paris, for example, threatened with excommunication anyone who read, heard or performed it, and another clergyman cried that "[Molière] should be burned at the stake as a foretaste of the fires of hell."

Though he distrusted and satirized doctors, Molière got along well with his own physician, Monsieur de Maurvilan. Asked why, he replied: "We reason with one another; he prescribes remedies; I omit to take them and I recover."

On February 10, 1673, Molière appeared in his last play, *Le malade imaginaire* (*The Imaginary Invalid*), playing the part of Argan, a hypochondriac who had twice pretended death. Just as he uttered the word "*Juro*") ("I swear") when Argan took the Hippocratic oath as a physician, he began coughing convulsively. Hiding his discomfort, he completed the play, but once he got home he began coughing more violently, burst a blood vessel in his throat and choked to death on his own blood.

Molière could not be buried in a consecrated grave because he was connected with the theater, thought to be an evil institution at the time. Tradition has it that his patron Louis XIV let him be buried in a churchyard anyway, but 14 feet down—just beyond the depth that the church consideed consecrated ground.

∇ ∇ ∇

Ferenc Molnár (1878–1952)

The Hungarian dramatist and novelist, whose translated plays were great hits in the United States, had a surefire way to solve the problem of unwelcome callers to his house. He instructed his secretary to say: "Sorry, he's not in. He left just a moment ago, and if you rush down the street I'm sure you'll catch him."

A friend took Molnár to the theater on complimentary tickets, but the playwright had enough of the play after one act and started to leave. "You can't walk out," his friend whispered. "We're guests of the management." Molnár thought for a moment and then got up again. "Where are you going now?" his friend demanded. "To the box office," explained Molnár, "to buy two tickets so we can leave."

Molnár headed for his beloved Café Central as soon as he got back to Budapest, only to be told that his stunning mistress had been sleeping with other men while he was gone. his friends spared him no details about her escapades and Molnár listened to their accounts attentively. "It's all right," he finally said with a smile. "She goes to bed with others because she loves them. But for money—only with me!"

∇ ∇ ∇

Theodor Mommsen (1817–1903)

A friend asked the German historian and archaeologist for his opinion of Napoleon III's *History of Julius Caesar*—was it suitable to give to his son? "How old is the boy?" Mommsen asked.

"Fourteen."

"Good, give it to him right now. One more year and he'll be too old for it."

∇ ∇ ∇

Michel Eyquem de Montaigne (1533–1592)

The great Montaigne, who wrote on the importance of the classics in education, himself learned to speak Latin before he learned French.

The French author's handwriting was so bad that he was forced to hire secretaries to transcribe his work. But one secretary had handwriting worse than his own, and as a result parts of Montaigne's Italian journal remain unintelligible today.

Montaigne, who invented the word essay and almost the essay form itself, was a man who "spoke to popes," a man who was in love with books, *"meas delicias,"* or "my delights," as he called them. He once described his library in the tower of his chateau: "The form of it is round, and hath no flat side but what serveth for my table and chair; in which...manner at one look it offers me the full sight of all my books...There is my seat, there is my throne. I endeavor to make my rule therein absolute, and to sequester that only corner from the community of wife, of children, and of acquaintance."

He chose as the motto on his seal: *Que sais-je?* (What do I know?) As the inscription for his library he had: I do not understand; I pause; I examine.

A bad memory had its advantages, he observed: "One cannot be a good liar; one cannot tell long stories; one forgets offenses; and one enjoys places and books a second time around."

"...there should be some legal restraint aimed against inept and useless writers as there is against vagabonds and idlers," Montaigne proclaimed in 1588. "This is no jest. Scribbling seems to be a sort of symptom of an unruly age."

Montaigne for many years collected cases of strange deaths and hoped that he would not die without at least uttering some interesting last remark. As it happened, he died paralyzed from an attack of gout, unable to move or speak a single word to his wife or the priest at his bedside.

∇ ∇ ∇

Federigo da Montefeltro (1422–1482)

One of the most civilized and literate of rulers, Duke Federigo ruled the tiny principality of Urbino in the Apennines. His court was a citadel of culture complete with 30 copyists continually transcribing Greek and Latin manuscripts for his library. A scholar who wrote poetry, he once captured a town by forging a letter of surrender from its ruler.

Charles-Louis de Secondat, Baron de La Brède et de Montesquieu (1689–1755)

The French philosopher and author was a friend of the witty Lord Chesterfield and no slouch as a wit himself. During a debate, a rather obtuse opponent declared, "I will bet my head that you are wrong!" Replied Montesquieu: "I accept it. The smallest trifle has its value among friends."

Shortly before his death, exhausted by his labors, he nevertheless told a friend, "Study has been for me the sovereign remedy against all the disappointments of life. I have never known any trouble that an hour's reading would not dissipate."

▽ ▽ ▽

Comte Robert de Montesquiou-Fezensac (1855–1921)

Edmond de Goncourt, the famous diarist, recorded in his journal how this French poet had his first love affair with a female ventriloquist, "who while he was straining to achieve his climax would imitate the drunken voice of a pimp."

The poet, a bisexual who had Sarah Bernhardt as a mistress for a time, was an odd character who wore thick makeup and frequently took his gold tortoise with him on his walks (only Nerval, who had a pet lobster, beats him in this regard). It is said that Proust patterned Baron Charlus on the rich count, who spent his entire fortune pampering his male lovers, and that Montesquiou-Fezensac's death was caused by the shock of recognizing himself as the baron's prototype. (See also GÉRARD DE NERVAL.)

▽ ▽ ▽

James Graham Montrose (1612–1650)

The gallant Marquess of Montrose, a royalist general and poet, lost 1,000 of his 1,200-man army in a shipwreck when sailing to Scotland from France and was captured by Scottish Covenanters a few months later. Imprisoned in Edinburgh Castle, he scratched his famous poem beginning "My dear and only love" on his prison window the night before he was hanged. The story of his heart's burial is one of the strangest in literature. Recovered from his body, which had been buried by the roadside outside Edinburgh, his heart was enclosed in a steel box and sent to his father, then in exile. Lost or stolen on its journey, it was years later discovered in a curiosity shop in Flanders. Brought by a member of the Montrose family to India, his heart was then stolen for use as an amulet by a native chief. Once more regained by the family, it was, perhaps finally, lost in France during the Revolution, 139 years after his death.

Hegesippe Moreau (1810–1838)

So poor was this French lyric poet that for a long period he lived in a cholera hospital during a cholera epidemic in order to obtain food and shelter. Only after he had sold the copyright to his poems for a loaf of bread and died in a poorhouse at the age of 28 did his work become popular.

∇ ∇ ∇

Philippe de Mornay (1549–1623)

The French Protestant leader invented sauce Mornay for King Henry IV. Made with fish broth, the white sauce is enriched with Parmesan and Gruyere cheese and butter. Popularly known as the Protestant Pope, Mornay was Henry's right-hand man until the king converted to Catholicism and the Seigneur Duplessis-Mornay fell out of favor. After Henry's assassination, Louis XIII finally retired Mornay as governor of Saumur because of his opposition to the government's rapprochement with Catholic Spain. Mornay's spiritual writings and organizing abilities strongly influenced the development of a Protestant party in France.

∇ ∇ ∇

Abbé Arthur Mugnier (1853–1944)

Abbé Mugnier, a friend of Proust and other literary lights, had original ideas for a Catholic priest. One time a prospective convert asked him if he believed there was a hell. "Yes, because it is a dogma of the church," he replied, "but I don't believe anyone is in it."

∇ ∇ ∇

Amir Mu'izzi (d. 1147)

The Persian Sultan Sanjar gathered around him a celebrated group of poets who often wrote panegyrics to him. These men included Amir Mu'izzi, called "the King of Poets" in his day. Unfortunately this lyric king, though he wrote his sultan the most stirring panegyrics of all, never received the type of rewards that Sanjar was noted for giving. One morning while out hunting with Sanjar he was accidentally killed by a stray arrow from the sultan's bow.

∇ ∇ ∇

Multatuli (Edward Douwes Dekker; 1820–1887)

The Dutch novelist, one of the leaders of the "Eightiers," who fought Dutch romanticism and sentimentality in literature during the 1880s, had among the most interesting of pen names. His pseudonym Multatuli translates as "I have suffered much."

Lady Murasaki no-Shikibu (978–1031?)

Lady Murasaki finished her great novel, whose title literally translates as "Gossip About the Genji" but is often called "Tales of the Genji," in about 1001 A.D., the whole filling 54 books or 4,234 pages. Paper was very expensive at the time, and after she bought all she could afford, a contemporary charged that "she laid sacrilegious hands upon the sacred sutras of a Buddhist temple, and used them for manuscript papers." Nevertheless, her book has come to be regarded as the first important novel written anywhere in the world.

∇ ∇ ∇

Gasparo Murtola   See GIOVANNI BATISTA MARINI.

∇ ∇ ∇

Alfred de Musset (1810–1857)

George Sand angered the French author in many little ways but he hated worst her habit of getting up immediately after they had enjoyed a long night of love and sitting right there in the bedroom working on her latest novel. His lover would never put him before her work, Musset knew, and he could do nothing about it. His anger turned to hate when George Sand left him for another man and he finally wrote the pornographic novel *Gamiani* about her.

The poet's famous "Ballade à la lune," which compared the moon shining above a church steeple to the dot above an *i*, was actually written as a parody of French romantic poetry at the time. But to the 19-year-old poet's delight it was taken seriously and hailed as a work of genius.

"Monsieur, they tell me you boast of having slept with me," a vain actress told the poet.

"Pardon me," replied Musset, "but I have always boasted of the exact opposite."

∇ ∇ ∇

Benito Mussolini (1883–1945)

Like Nero before him the Italian dictator imagined himself a great writer. No one else ever recognized artistic qualities in him, certainly not his teachers, who found him incorrigible. Mussolini was expelled from the first school he ever attended, a religious academy in Faenza run by priests. When only nine he hit a teacher with an inkpot, stabbed a pupil with a knife and was dismissed from the school.

While editing the Socialist newspaper *L'Avanti* in 1909, Mussolini, a journalist by profession, wrote a steamy novel entitled *The Cardinal's Love* that was serialized in the paper. Awash with purple prose and morbid observations, the novel nonetheless proved very popular. Unfortunately, Mussolini chose to devote himself to politics instead of purple prose, and never wrote another book.

"Youth," he remarked on his 50th birthday, "is a malady of which one becomes cured a little every day."

∇ ∇ ∇

Abbad al-Mutamid (1068–1091)

Mutamid's passions were stronger than those of most poets. The Spanish poet-king preferred the company of poets to that of generals and often gave his favorite writers as much as a thousand ducats, an immense sum at the time, for an epigram. He, in fact, married a slave girl named Rumay Riyya because she wrote excellent verses, and was her passionate lover until the day he died. Yet his cruelty was barbarous. Once he hacked to pieces a lifelong friend who insulted him and he made it a practice to grow flowers in the skulls of his slain enemies.

His love of poetry was so great that after he was deposed and sent as a prisoner to Tangier he gave the last 35 ducats he had in the world to a local poet who sent him some verses asking for a gift. Some of the time in chains, he wrote poetry until his death:

> And we—that dreamed youth's blade would never rust,
> Hoped wells from the mirage, roses from the sand—
> The riddle of the world shall understand
> And put on wisdom with the robe of dust.

∇ ∇ ∇ ∇ ∇ ∇ ∇ ∇ ∇

Vladimir Nabokov (1899–1977)

Nabokov told one interviewer that he extensively rewrote all of his work from the time he began writing: "I have rewritten—often several times—every word I have ever published. My pencils outlast their erasers."

He never showed his work until it was finished. "Only ambitious nonentities and hearty mediocrities exhibit their rough drafts," he once said. "It is like passing around samples of one's sputum."

Aside from his widespread literary fame, Nabokov is remembered as the inventor of the Russian crossword puzzle.

When he was asked which historical events he would most like to see portrayed on film, he included in his list: "The Russians leaving Alaska, delighted with the deal. Shot of a seal applauding."

An editor offered him $200 for 2,000 words on the question "Does the writer have a social responsibility?" Wrote Nabokov in reply: "My answer to your questions...is NO. You owe me 10 cents, Sir."

∇ ∇ ∇

Muhammad al-Nadim (c. 987)
In 987, at a time when the culture of Islam was perhaps the greatest in the world, the Arab author wrote his *Index of the Sciences*, a critical bibliography of all the books in Arabic on any branch of knowledge, along with biographies of their authors. Not one in a thousand of the vast number of books he named is known today.

∇ ∇ ∇

Naevius (c. 270–199 B.C.)
One of the earliest Latin poets, Naevius supposedly invented the historical drama, and his *Bellum Punicum* is the first known Roman epic. He is said to have originally been a Roman soldier imprisoned for a time for his abuse of officials. Some scholars feel he should share with Livius Andronicus the title "Father of Roman Literature." In any case, his self-composed epitaph reads: "If immortals may weep for mortals, the Muses weep for the poet Naevius; after his death, they forgot how to speak Latin at Rome."

∇ ∇ ∇

Israel Ben Moses Najara (fl. late 16th century)
The Hebrew poet's religious poems were written with such intense emotion that they were compared to love poems. This, and the fact that he set some of the lyrics to Arabic melodies that had been associated with ribald themes, caused many holier-than-thou critics to condemn them. But their beauty prevailed over the years and they won their way into the prayer book, living long after their critics had become dust.

Napoleon Bonaparte (1769–1821)

Napoleon was asked if he thought the pen mightier than the sword. "A journalist," he replied, "is a grumbler, a censurer, a giver of advice, a regent of sovereigns, a tutor of nations. Four hostile newspapers are more formidable than a *thousand* bayonets."

Though an avid reader of thousands of books, the French emperor disdained the literary life. "You live too much with literary people," he once wrote to his brother Joseph. Another time he opined: "I regard scholars and wits the same as coquettish women; one should frequent them and talk with them, but never choose one's wife from among such women, or one's ministers from among such men."

The present code of regulations of Paris's Théâtre-Français, home of the Comédie-Française, was actually drawn up by Napoleon while among the burning ruins of Moscow on October 15, 1812.

An anonymous wit said the name of the newspaper for which Napoleon wrote many unsigned articles should be changed from *Le Moniteur Universel* (*The Universal Monitor*) to *Le Menteur Universel* (*The Universal Liar*).

Ideas came so fast to him that he had to write rapidly—so rapidly that even he could not decipher his own scrawl. His only alternative was to dictate all his letters and speeches.

On board H.M.S. *Bellerophon* he was asked what he would do to amuse himself during his exile on St. Helena. "Whatever shall we do in that remote spot?" he replied. "Well, we will write our memoirs. Work is the scythe of time."

▽ ▽ ▽

Natsume Soseki (1867–1916)

Japan's most popular modern novelist, Soseki was a humorous but very neurotic man who came close to insanity in his life and probably died as a result of stomach ulcers. He was especially unhappy in the last years of his marriage, as one might expect of a man said to have capriciously chosen his bride solely because, though she had rotten teeth, "she made no attempt to hide them."

▽ ▽ ▽

Joachim C. Neander (1650–1680)

It is seldom noted (no English dictionary records the derivation) that the word *Neanderthal*, for "a primitive backward person," is from the name of a gentle poet—and a learned, pious churchman to boot! The early forms of *Homo sapiens* called *Neanderthals* were so named because of the first skeletons of them recognized as a distinct group of archaic humans was found in the Neander Valley (the Neander Thal) near Dusseldorf, Germany, in 1856. But the Neander Valley had been named for the German poet and hymn writer Joachim Neander, a schoolmaster who wrote the beautiful hymn on the glory of God in creation, "Lo Heaven and Earth and Sea and Air!" There is further irony in the fact that the poet's great-grandfather's name had been *Neuman*, but he had changed it to *Neander* in the 16th century at a time when Germany was undergoing a rebirth of learning and many were translating their names into Greek. Thus, traced to its ultimate source, *Neanderthal*, which today means a primitive and brutal man, translates as "the man from the valley of the new man (the man of the future)"!

∇ ∇ ∇

Jawaharlal Nehru (1889–1964)
The Indian leader preferred rather unusual working conditions while writing. "All my major works have been written in prison," he told a reporter. "I would recommend prison not only to aspiring writers but to aspiring politicians, too."

∇ ∇ ∇

Nejati (d. 1508)
As a young poet Nejati concocted a scheme to win the attention of the Ottoman ruler Sultan Mohammed II. He wrote an ode praising Mohammed and attached it to the turban of the sultan's favorite chess partner. Mohammed read the poem while playing chess, sent for Nejati and made him an official of his court, where the poet wrote some of the favorite lyrics of his time.

∇ ∇ ∇

Nikolai Alekseyevich Nekrasov (1821–1877)
Bog is the Russian word for God. In 1930 one million copies of a school textbook containing a poem by Nekrasov with the word *Bog* in it were printed by the Soviet government. Then someone discovered, to the horror of the Kremlin, that *Bog* was spelled with a capital letter thoughout the poem. Reducing *Bog* to *bog* required resetting type in 16 pages of each of the million books printed, but the change was made, despite the expense, so that "the books reached the Soviet children uncontaminated." Despite the efforts of Soviet censors, the Russian language remains rich in references to God, such expressions as "God knows," "God save us," "Oh, my God" and "Praise God" being quite common. In fact, former Soviet President Leonid Brezhnev invoked the name of God in a speech calling for peace.

Nero (37–68 A.D.)

After Nero killed his pregnant wife, Poppaea, by kicking her in the stomach, he found a boy, Sporus, who resembled her, had him castrated, married him in a formal ceremony and "used him in every way like a woman." Quipped an anonymous wit: "One can only wish that Nero's father had such a wife."

That Nero fiddled while Rome burned is essentially true, though he probably sang and played the harp, not the fiddle, while regarding the spectacle with cynical detachment. The spindle-shanked, potbellied despot somehow found the courage to cut his throat when the Praetorian Guard revolted against him and he heard that the Roman Senate had decreed his death. Nero thought himself a great poet and expired crying, "Oh, what an artist dies in me!"

∇ ∇ ∇

Pablo Neruda (1904–1973)

The Chilean poet, born Neftalí Ricardo Reyes Basualto, took the pseudonym Pablo Neruda in 1920. Only 16, with a father who didn't like the idea of his writing poetry, he picked the name at random from a newpaper to disguise his first efforts. He did not know that the name he chose was that of one of the most beloved of Czech poets, Jan Neruda (1834–91), whose monument stands in Prague. Later the Chilean legally adopted his pseudonym.

Neruda once recalled the joy, excitement and fear of his first sexual experience, with a woman he did not know and never saw. After threshing wheat with a gang of farm laborers he slept with them that night on a "mountain of straw." In the dark night, he remembered,

> "Suddenly a hand slid over me...than an avid mouth clung to mine and I felt a woman's body pressing against mine, all the way down to my feet...Little by little my fear turned into intense pleasure...How difficult it is to make love, without making noise, in a mountain of straw burrowed by the bodies of seven or eight other men, sleeping men who must not be awakened for anything in the world (for any one might be the husband). And yet we can do anything, though it may require infinite care. A little while later, the stranger suddenly fell asleep next to me, and worked into a fever by the situation, I started to get panicky. It would soon be daybreak, I thought, and the first workers would discover the naked woman stretched out beside me...But I also fell asleep. When I woke up, I put out a startled hand and found only a warm hollow, a warm absence. Soon a bird began to sing and the whole forest filled with warbling..."

In an address to the Armenian Society of Writers, Neruda told of his fascinating visit to the well-stocked zoo in Evian, France. Replying to his speech, the president of the society said: "Why did Neruda have to go visit our zoo? This visit to the Society of Writers would have been enough for him to find all the animal species. Here we have lions and tigers, foxes and seals, eagles and snakes, camels and parrots."

Neruda's "dark and gloomy but essential book" (his words) *Residencia en la Tierra* was found next to the body of at least one suicide in Chile. The poet could never forget that a boy from Santiago killed himself at the foot of a tree, leaving his book open at the poem "Significa Sombras" ("It Means Shadows").

∇ ∇ ∇

Gérard de Nerval (1808–1855)
The French poet was found in the Palais-Royal, leading a lobster along at the end of a blue-ribbon leash. When the gendarmes asked him why a lobster instead of a dog, he replied, "Because it does not bark and knows the secrets of the sea." Nerval had to be sent to an asylum at Montmartre. He later committed suicide, hanging himself from a lamppost by his mother's apron strings. (See MONTESQUIOU-FEZENSAC.)

∇ ∇ ∇

Nguyen Dinh Chieu (1822–1888)
As a young man, the Vietnamese poet passed the examinations to become a government official in Hue, but fell ill and lost his sight on his way back home. After becoming a teacher, the blind poet wrote many patriotic poems while collaborating with the leaders of the anti-French revolt. It is said that when he learned of the final defeat of the anticolonist forces, he died of a broken heart.

∇ ∇ ∇

Nguyen Trai (1380-1442)
The Vietnamese poet's verses are the oldest in his language to have survived. Nguyen Trai, who sometimes used the pseudonym Uc Trai, was a very close adviser of two successive kings and even wrote their letters for them. Other courtiers plotted against him, however, and had him executed for allegedly planning regicide.

∇ ∇ ∇

Friedrich Wilhelm Nietzsche (1844–1900)
The great German philosopher attributed his breakdown in 1888, which marked the end of his productive life, to both overwork and the lack of recognition. "My health is really quite normal," he wrote to his sister, "only my soul is so sensitive and so full of longing for good friends of my own kind. Get me a small circle of

men who will listen to and understand me—and I shall be cured." But he was never to have friends or disciples in his lifetime.

Early in 1865, Nietzsche, traveling in Cologne, was taken to a brothel by a duplicitous sightseeing guide. He found it difficult to extricate himself from what he found to be an extremely uncomfortable situation. "Suddenly," he later recalled, "I found myself surrounded by a half-dozen creatures in tinsel and gauze, looking at me expectantly. I stood speechless for a while. Then I instinctively went to a piano as if to the only soul-endowed being in the place and struck a few chords. That dispersed my shock and I escaped to the street."

∇ ∇ ∇

Vaslav Nijinsky (1890–1950)
Late in 1918, as madness crept near him, the gret dancer Vaslav Nijinsky began to keep a diary. According to one biographer, "For hours and hours, day and night, he wrote and wrote," and as he hovered over the border of madness, probably knowing he would never dance again, he made these observations about writing:

> I do not write for my own pleasure—there can be no pleasure when a man spends all his free time on writing. One has to write a great deal to be able to understand what writing means. It is a difficult occupation—one gets tired of sitting, having the legs cramped, the arm stiff. It spoils the eyes and one does not get enough air; the room gets stuffy. From such a life a man dies sooner…People who write a great deal are martyrs…"

∇ ∇ ∇

Nizami (c. 1140–c. 1202)
Having written some 20,000 distichs over his lifetime, Nizami ranks among the most prolific of Persian poets. When he dedicated his first epic masterpiece to the Persian monarch in 1176 his ruler was so impressed that he bestowed upon him for life all the revenue of two large villages.

∇ ∇ ∇

Victor Noir (1848–1870)
This revolutionary French journalist was killed in a duel with Pierre N. Bonaparte, a cousin of Napoleon III. Sudden death caused an erection of his penis, and since his bronze statue was made exactly as he had lain on the field of honor, it shows the unmistakable bulge. For over a century now, women have visited his tomb in Paris's Père Lachaise cemetery, considering it a fertility symbol.

Nostradamus (Michel de Nostredam; 1503–1566)

The French physician and astrologer, whose rhymed prophecies still enjoy some popularity, wasn't always successful at predicting things in his own time. Young Charles IX would live a full 90 years, he predicted in 1564. Ten years later Charles died at the age of 24.

▽ ▽ ▽

Abu Nuwas (Hasan ibn Hani; c. 756–810)

Recognized as the greatest Arab poet of his time, the Persian-born Abu Nuwas wrote more than 5,000 poems over his relatively short career. His sobriquet Abu Nuwas, "Father of the Curl," derived from his abundant curly locks. He was much admired for his wine songs and his sometimes cynical and "immoral," though always genial, love poems. Though his style was seemingly effortless it was achieved at high cost. At the beginning of his career Abu Nuwas spent a year alone in the desert, eating and drinking little, in order "to gain purity of language." His adventures are described in *The Thousand and One Nights*.

▽ ▽ ▽ ▽ ▽ ▽ ▽ ▽

Adam Gottlob Oehlenschläger (1779–1850)

When Jens Baggesen condemned the romantic Danish poet's work as ignorant, Oehlenschläger's friends silenced the critic by challenging him to a duel with the poet in the form of a debate in Latin. The critic declined.

▽ ▽ ▽

José Olmedo (1782–1847)

Standing in a plaza in Guayaquil, Ecuador, is a statue honoring José Olmedo, who, like most poets, struggled to survive all his life. Looking closely, however, you might notice a resemblance to someone else. You would be right. The statue really represents the English poet Lord Byron and was purchased secondhand because the town wouldn't spend enough money to have an Olmedo statue commissioned, reasoning perhaps that one poet was the same as the next anyway.

Caliph Omar (fl. 642 A.D.)

Caliph Omar has traditionally been regarded as history's greatest book-burner. Reasoned the caliph before his followers burned the 400,000 manuscript volumes in the Alexandrian library: "Either these books conform to the Koran or they do not. If they do, they are not needed; if they do not, they are positively harmful. Therefore, let them be destroyed."

(Today, however, this story is regarded as without foundation; part of the library is said to have been accidentally burned when Caesar was besieged in Alexandria.)

∇ ∇ ∇

Porphirius Optatianus (fl. 305–337)

The poet, a prefect under Constantine, is sometimes called the most mannered of Roman poets, his work noted for its acrostics, palindromes, figure-poems, etc. One of his poems includes several of these devices. The first four lines are composed of two, three, four and five syllables, respectively. The fifth line is rhapalic—that is, the first word of the line has one syllable, the second two, and so on. The sixth line contains all the parts of speech and the seventh and concluding line is a palindrome.

∇ ∇ ∇

Ordericus Vitalis (1075–c. 1143)

Before the advent of printing monastic copyists were urged on in their onerous task of copying manuscripts by the assurance from their superiors that God would forgive one of their sins for every line they copied. According to the Norman chronicler Ordericus Vitalis, one monk he knew had so many sins that he "escaped hell by the margin of a single letter."

∇ ∇ ∇ ∇ ∇ ∇ ∇ ∇ ∇

Pa Chin (Ba Jin; b. 1904–?)

The Red Guards imprisoned the great Chinese novelist as a "stinking intellec-tual" and assigned him to pouring night soil into septic tanks. According to a fellow writer who labored with him: "As the mixture of excrement and urine was noisly poured into the pool, foul water would splash. After a while on the job, Ba Jin's face would look like a spotted cat…"

∇ ∇ ∇

Marcus Pacuvius (c. 220–130 B.C.)

Considered by Cicero to be Rome's first tragic poet, Pacuvius, who lived until about 90, cetainly ranks among the oldest of active playwrights. He was writing plays at least until the age of 80.

∇ ∇ ∇

Caecina Paetus (fl. c. 40 B.C.)

When this Roman senator and philosopher was condemned to kill himself by the emperor Claudius, his wife, Arria Major, "taught him how to die." Arria took his dagger first and stabbed herself. Dying, she withdrew the dagger from her heart and handed it to her husband, saying, "It doesn't hurt, Paetus."

∇ ∇ ∇

Pamphilus (fl. 12th century)

Pamphilus, seu de Amore was the title of an erotic love poem of the 12th century, but nothing is known about its author Pamphilus except his name in the title. No more than a few pages in length, these Latin verses grew so popular during the Middle Ages that they became the best-known love poem of their time. Just as the small book containing *Aesop's Fables* came to be familiarly called *Esopet* in French, the little poem became known as *Pamphilet*, the English spelling it as *Pamflet*, and eventually *Pamphlet*. By the 14th century any small booklet was called a *pamphlet* and within another 300 years the word had acquired its sense of a "small polemical brochure," the transition completed from sensuous love poem to political tract. (See also PROCOPIUS.)

∇ ∇ ∇

P'an Yüeh (c. 247–c. 300)

Though he died relatively young the Chinese poet left behind a sizable body of work. P'an, said to be as famous for his good looks as his talent, was also an ambitious man fond of backbiting. Unfortunately, when a clique he had criticized came to power he was marked for death. The poet, his entire family of 20 or more people, and many of his friends were executed in the public marketplace.

Paracelsus (Philippus Theophrastus Bombastus von Hohenheim; 1493?–1541)

Write off as entertaining but untrue the old story that *bombast* for inflated speech on trivial subjects comes from the real name of the egotistical Swiss physician, alchemist and writer Paracelsus—Philippus Theophrastus Bombastus von Hohenheim. Paracelsus was certainly bombastic, but the word derives from a form of cotton. Bombast was cotton used as a padding or stuffing for clothes in days past, the term deriving from the word *bombyx*, for "silkworm or silk," which was applied to cotton as well. Just as stuffing or padding in clothing was called *bombast*, so was padded, stuffed, inflated speech—this figurative use of bombast was first recorded in 1589, not long after the word was first used in its literal sense.

Paracelsus did invent the word "tartar" so commonly used in toothpaste ads today. "All diseases can be traced to a coagulation of undigested matter in the bowels," he wrote. He called these acids of putrefaction "tartar" because their deposits in joints, muscles and other parts of the body "burn like hell, and Tartarus is hell." He went on to say that "Doctors boast of their [knowledge of] anatomy, but they fail to see the tartar sticking to their teeth."

Up until the 19th century ailing people still made pilgrimages to the grave of Paracelsus in Salzburg, believing they would be miraculously cured by his spirit there.

▽ ▽ ▽

Blaise Pascal (1623–1662)

In his short life the French philosopher not only wrote his *Pensées* and other famed literary works; he made great contributions to mathematics and physics as well. Few are aware that he was also a gifted inventor. Pascal invented a calculating machine, a hydraulic press, and a syringe. But he did not invent the wheelbarrow as has been claimed; its invention dates back at least three centuries before his birth.

A traditional story has Pascal's father forbidding him to study mathematics because he thought the 11-year-old's passion for the subject would detract from his other studies. He relented, however, when he discovered the boy writing on a wall with a piece of coal the proof that the three sides of a triangle equal two right angles.

While driving a carriage pulled by four horses Pascal had an accident that nearly killed him when the horses plunged into the Seine, leaving his carriage dangling over a parapet above the water. He claimed on recovering that he had had a vision of God while unconscious, believing in it so fervently that he recorded his vision on parchment that he ever after kept sewn in his coat lining:

> The year of grace 1654.
> Monday, Nov. 23rd,…from about half past six in the
>   evening to half an hour after midnight.
> The late
> God of Abraham, God of Isaac, God of Jacob,
>   not the philosophers and the scholars.
> Certainty, certainty, feeling, joy, peace.
> God of Jesus Christ
> He is not to be found except by ways taught in the Gospel.
> Grandeur of the human soul.
> Just Father, the world has never known you, but I have
>   known you.
> Joy, joy, joy, tears of joy…
> My God, will you abandon me?…
> Jesus Christ
> Jesus Christ…
> I was separated from Him, I fled Him, renounced Him,
>   crucified Him.
> May I never be separated from him…
> Reconciliation sweet and complete.

∇ ∇ ∇

Boris Pasternak (1890–1960)

Shortly after he was awarded the Nobel Prize for literature in 1958, a shameful political campaign (stemming from his anti-Stalinism) was launched against him in the Soviet Union and the Russian poet and novelist was forced to decline the prize. Pasternak, according to Russian poet Andrei Voznesensky, survived the darkest years of communism because for some unknown reason Stalin had given the order, "Don't touch this village idiot."

∇ ∇ ∇

Paul IV (1476–1559)

The first papal *Index auctorum et librorum*, or index of books banned by the Catholic Church, was issued by Paul IV in 1559. Thousands upon thousands of books were burned that year throughout Italy—10,000 in one Venice bonfire alone—under a papal law that one former monk called "the finest secret ever discovered for…making men idiotic." But then this ascetic pontiff loved to burn all things heretical and spared no book or body. "Even if my own father were a heretic," he declared, "I would gather the wood to burn him." When Paul IV died, all Rome celebrated for close to a week, pulling down his statue, dragging it through the city and dumping it in the Tiber.

∇ ∇ ∇

Georges Perec (1936–1982)
Among the French author's unusual works was a novel in which the letter *e*, the most common vowel, wasn't used, and another in which *e* was the only vowel used. He also wrote an anagrammatic poem using only the 10 commonest letters in the alphabet—*e, s, a, r, t, i, n, u, l* and *o*. He claimed that a palindrome he wrote of 5,000 characters was the longest in the world.

∇ ∇ ∇

Peregrinus (d. 165)
Scornful of life, the Cynic philosopher, who had tried and abandoned Christianity, committed suicide by building and lighting his own funeral pyre before an assemblage at Olympia and leaping into it to be burned alive.

∇ ∇ ∇

Periander (c. 600 B.C.)
Included among the Seven Sages of Greece, the famous tyrant of Corinth was a wise ruler who encouraged poetry, music and all the arts. Once he was asked, "What is the largest thing in the smallest container?" He replied: "Good sense in a human body."

∇ ∇ ∇

Charles Perrault (1628–1703)
In the French raconteur's 1697 version of the fairy tale "Sleeping Beauty," the princess is awakened by a kiss from the handsome prince. But his tale is the first ot use a kiss. Perrault's story is, in fact, based upon the old romance *Perceforest* in which the prince discovers the sleeping beauty and rapes her before he leaves.

∇ ∇ ∇

Petrarch (Francesco Petrarca; 1304–1374)

It was the day when the sun's heavy rays
  Grew pale in the pity of his suffering
    Lord
When I fell captive, lady, to the gaze
  Of your fair eyes, fast bound in love's
    strong cord.

Laura of Petrarch's immortal love poems was no figment of the poet's imagination. According to tradition, the poet laureate of Rome wrote his poems for Laura, the daughter of Audibert de Noves and the wife of Count Hugo de Sade, an ancestor of the French nobleman who gave us sadism. Petrarch never revealed the real Laura's identity, guarding his secret jealously, but he wrote that he saw her for the first time in the church of St. Clara at Avignon on April 6, 1327, and that this first sight of her inspired him to become a poet. In the 18th century the Abbé de Sade identified her as the wife of Hugo de Sade, who bore the old man 11 children before dying of the plague in 1348 when she was only 40. But his identification is not certain. It is only known that Laura was a married woman who accepted Petrarch's devotion but refused all intimate relations. Their platonic love inspired the long series of poems, 366 in all, that are among the most beautiful amorous verse in literature, the most famous the sonnet in praise of their first meeting quoted above. The Italians call this collection of lyrics the *Canzoniere* and it is titled *Rime in Vita e Morte di Madonna Laura*. Petrarch died long after his Laura (whoever she was). Lord Byron put the whole affair in a more humorous perspective when he wrote in *Don Juan*: "Think you, if Laura had been Petrarch's wife,/He would have written sonnets all his life?"

The only one Petrarch ever loved nearly as much as his Laura was the cat who became his companion during the last lonely years of his life. When the poet died in the Euganean Hills, his cat was killed and mummified. Petrarch is believed to have previously written the inscription under its niche saying that in his heart this cat was "second only to Laura."

Petrarch pitied the corseted Renaissance women, most of whom wore corsets that could be tightened by turning a key. "Their bellies," he once said, "are so cruelly squeezed that they suffer as much pain from vanity as the martyrs suffered for religion."

Petrarch is said by one biographer to be "the most completely musicked poet in world literature." By the 16th century every line of his lyric poetry was set to music; in fact, some of his most popular stanzas were made into songs over a dozen times.

A man supremely confident of his place in history, Petrarch once noted, in Latin: "It seems apparent that I have lived with princes, but in truth it was the princes who lived with me."

An old story claims that Petrarch apparently died in 1344 during the plague years and was laid out for 24 hours in accordance with local law. After 20 hours he suddenly sat up in bed and instead of being buried lived another 30 years.

When the poet did die, villagers found him slumped over the books and papers on his desk, pen in hand. He had previously written: "I desire that death find me ready and writing, or, if it please Christ, praying and in tears." In his will he left 50 florins for Boccaccio to buy a cloak so that he would be warm in the winter.

∇ ∇ ∇

Gaius Petronius (d. 65 A.D.)

The Roman author turned down an invitation from Nero to attend an orgy featuring 100 naked virgins. "Tell the emperor," he told the messenger, "that one hundred naked virgins are not one hundred times as exciting as one naked virgin."

∇ ∇ ∇

Philemon (361?–263? B.C.)

In ancient Greece only Menander was more highly regarded than Philemon as a comic dramatist, but only fragments of Philemon's plays remain today. Plutarch says that Philemon journeyed to Egypt and on the way fell into the hands of King Magas of Cyrene, whom he had once satirized. Magas frightened him and treated him with much contempt, finally freeing the poet with a contemptuous present of toys fit only for a child. There are several accounts of Philemon's death, but the most popular one has him dying of laughter over a joke he had just made.

He won more prizes than his rival Menander, who is much favored by critics today, but this was probably because he was the first playwright to raise to an art form the use of a personal claque that applauded and cheered him.

Living to be almost 100, the playwright worshiped the work of his great predecessor Euripides, who had lived a century before him. "If I could be sure that the dead have consciousness," he once said, "I would hang myself to see Euripides."

∇ ∇ ∇

Philetas (fl. 4th century B.C.)

The extreme thinness of this Alexandrian poet and tutor of Egypt's Ptolomey I was a cause of ridicule. It is said that he was so thin that he had to put lead as ballast in his shoes (or attach leaden balls to his shoes) to keep from being blown away.

Phrynichus (fl. 512–476 B.C.)

Some ancient writers regarded Phrynichus as the real founder of tragedy, and the Greek tragedian was probably the first to introduce a separate actor, as distinct from the chorus leader, which laid the foundation for stage dialogue, as well as the first to introduce women characters on stage (these played by men in masks). Phrynichus's most famous play was the *Capture of Meletus* (c. 493), which dealt with the fall of Athens' sister city to the Persians. The audience was moved to tears by the play, but in a time when playwrights were expected to write only about the accepted myths and legends of the early Greeks, Phrynichus was fined 1,000 drachmas for his innovation and forbidden ever to present the play again. One theory has it that the Athenian statesman and commander Themistocles secretly arranged to have the author write the play to stir up the Athenians to go to war against the Persians.

▽ ▽ ▽

Pablo Picasso (1881–1973)

The great Spanish painter was the author of one play, the little- known *Desire Caught by the Tail*. One of his stage directions instructs that the character Tart "go to the front, face the audience and urinate and syphilize for a full five minutes."

▽ ▽ ▽

Pindar (522?–443 B.C.)

Pindar received the equivalent of $10,000 for the processional song in which he wrote the lines "renowned Athens, rich, violet-crowned, worthy of song, bulwark of Hellas, god-protected city." When he died, his seventh Olympian ode (to Diagros of Rhodes, winner of the Olympian Games boxing match) was inscribed in golden letters on a temple wall in Rhodes. In 335 B.C., over a century after his death, Alexander the Great ordered the poet's house spared during the destruction of Thebes.

So sweet were Pindar's songs that the Greeks of his day invented a tale explaining his power to move them: "One day as he slept in the fields, bees gently settled on the young poet's lips and deposited there an everlasting honey."

Pindar lived until the age of 80. It is said that 10 days before his demise he sent to the oracle of Ammon the question "What is best for man?" The Egyptian oracle replied with one word: "Death."

Luigi Pirandello (1867–1936)

The Italian novelist did not much value his Nobel Prize and gave his medal to the state to be melted down. After receiving the coveted award, he sat behind a typewriter while he talked to the press; reporters noticed that he was typing out the word "buffoonery."

Pirandello's concern with insanity and its relation to sanity and reality stemmed in great part from the problems in his personal life caused by his wife's incurable madness. When his wealthy family lost its fortune, the author's wife lost her mind, and after 17 years he finally had to put her into a nursing home because her delusions that he was having a sexual relationship with their daughter threatened the child's safety.

Of his own work he said:

> I think that life is a very sad piece of buffoonery; because we have in ourselves, without being able to know why, wherefore or whence, the need to deceive ourselves constantly by creating a reality (one for each and never the same for all) which from time to time is discovered to be vain and illusory...My art is full of bitter compassion for all those who deceive themselves; but this compassion cannot fail to be followed by the ferocious derision of destiny which condemns man to deception.

∇ ∇ ∇

Alexis Piron (1689–1773)

The French dramatist and epigrammatist, called a "machine à sailles" (a machine that makes witticisms) by Grimm, was cornered by a would-be author who proceeded to begin reading him an entire five-act play. Piron listened politely, but soon found a way to escape from a work so blatantly lifted from other authors. He began to bow to each quotation he recognized as another author's effort and soon the would-be playwright asked him why he was bowing so much. Said Piron, "Why that is the way I am accustomed to greeting old friends when I run into them."

"These are the best verses I have ever written," a would-be poet told Piron. "Please read them and put a cross before each of the few lines that could possibly be improved." A few days later Piron returned his manuscript. "Why, I don't see a single cross on my papers!" the man exclaimed, obviously proud of himself. "No," Poiron said dryly. "I didn't want to make a graveyard of it."

Dimitry Ivanovich Pisarev (1840–1868)

Pisarev, who ended his life a suicide by drowning, was a Russian nihilist who believed that the only criterion in judging literary works was their social usefulness. His constant slogan was "Boots are better than Shakespeare."

∇ ∇ ∇

Placentius (fl. 16th century)

This 16th-century Dominican monk wrote a poem of 253 verses called *Pugna Porcorum* in which every word begins with a *p*, the first line translating as "Praise Paul's prize pig's prolific progeny."

∇ ∇ ∇

Gustave Planche (1808–1857)

The most loyal of George Sand's many lovers was French critic Gustave Planche. In 1843 Planche actually fought, and won, a duel with another critic who had written that the novelist's *Lélia* was an obscene work.

∇ ∇ ∇

Plato (c. 428–c. 348 B.C.)

Legend has it that Plato's real name was Aristocles and that he was called by the aptronym Plato because of his broad shoulders.

It's said that the philosopher Cleombrotus killed himself after reading Plato's *Phaedo* "so that he might enjoy the happiness of the future life so enchantingly described." The *Phaedo* is a dialogue narrating the discussion that took place between Socrates and his friends during the last hour of his life. This work also influenced the Roman Stoic philosopher Cato, Caesar's chief political rival, when he committed suicide by falling on his sword after realizing that his cause against the Caesarians was hopeless. Cato had spent all of the last night of his life reading Plato's *Phaedo*.

One story has Diogenes visiting the well-appointed house of the aristocratic Greek philosopher, where the floors were covered with the richest carpets, and stamping his foot in scorn.

"Thus do I tread on the pride of Plato!" he cried.

"With greater pride," Plato calmly added.

Titus Maccius Plautus (254–184 B.C.)

Among the most popular of Roman playwrights, Plautus was a robust, jolly man who is said to have written some 130 plays. His name is perhaps the best fate ever bestowed upon a playwright of broad comedy, translating literally as Titus the flat-footed clown.

▽ ▽ ▽

Pliny the Elder (Gaius Plinius Secundus; 23–79 A.D.)

Although Rabelais calls Pliny a liar, his *Natural History* is rather what one critic described as "a lasting monument to Roman ignorance." His attempt "to give a general description of everything that is known to exist throughout the earth" deals with 20,000 topics, but is more a grabbag of superstitions and absurdities, with occasional pieces of truth, than an encyclopedia. One of the most industrious if not the most credible of authors, Pliny, according to his nephew, owed his vast body of work to his "unequaled capacity to go without sleep." He would usually retire at 9 or 10 o'clock in the evening and rise to begin his work between midnight and 1 a.m., never sleeping later than 2 a.m. He constantly read and wrote, even while bathing and eating, and took no time for naps. He always traveled from place to place in a sedan chair accompanied by a stenographer. As his nephew said, "He once reproved me for walking. 'You need not have lost those hours,' he said, for he counted all time lost that was not given to study." Over 2,000 books were referred to in his *Natural History* alone.

"No book is so bad," he told his son, "but some good might be got out of it."

His adopted son Pliny the Younger described how his foster father died during the eruption of Vesuvius. Pliny the Elder had been in command of the fleet at Misenum and sailed in a light vessel to investigate the eruption, dictating his observations under a hail of stones. The next night he was awakened by friends when his house began to rock alarmingly and they fled out into the open with pillows around their heads to protect them from falling rocks. "Now it was day elsewhere," Pliny the Younger writes, "but there night darker and denser than any night...It was decided to go out upon the shore...There Pliny lay down upon a cast-off linen cloth, and once and again asked for cold water, which he drank. Then flames and a smell of sulfur announcing the approach of flames, aroused the others to take to flight and raised him. Supported by two slaves he got upon his feet, but immediately collapsed, his breathing, I gather, being obstructed by the thickening vapor which closed up his throat—naturally weak and narrow and frequently inflamed. When day returned...his body was found intact and uninjured, covered as he had been dressed. The appearance of the body suggested one sleeping rather than dead."

Plotinus (205–270)

The Greek philosopher, so spiritual, wrote one contemporary, that "he seemed to be ashamed to be in a body," refused to have his portrait painted. He explained: "It is bad enough to be condemned to drag around this image in which nature has imprisoned me. Why should I consent to the perpetuation of an image of this image?"

▽ ▽ ▽

Po Chu-i (742–846)

The simple stoic poet was for generations the best-loved bard of the Chinese people. In order to keep his poems—and he wrote over 3,000—understandable to the common man, Po Chu-i is said to have read each one to an old peasant woman after he finished it and simplified any word or image that she could not understand.

▽ ▽ ▽

Gaius Asinius Pollio (76 B.C.–5 A.D.)

Not only was Pollio the discoverer and patron of Virgil, but also, with his great book collection, he founded Rome's first public library. The author of many tragedies and erotic poems, he is also said to have been the first poet to recite his own works to an audience, for better or worse introducing the world to poetry readings.

▽ ▽ ▽

U Ponnya (1812–1867)

The Burmese poet and playwright was appointed court poet after being a monk for many years of his life. His sharp wit and sardonic outlook did not please one of the king's ministers, however, and the minister conspired to have him put to death. His most popular poem, now called "the immortal song" in his country, was composed a few minutes before he was assassinated.

▽ ▽ ▽

Porphyry (233–c. 304)

This Greek historian and scholar was originally named Malchus. But as a young man he studied under the witty Cassius Longinus. Noting that his name, Malchus, meant king (in Greek), his tutor changed it to Porphyrius, or Porphyry, meaning "clad in purple," a joking allusion to the color of royal or kingly robes.

Abbé Prévost (Antoine-François Prévost d'Exiles; 1697–1763)
Abbé Prévost's immensely popular romances enabled this former soldier and Benedictine monk to support himself entirely by his pen in an age when not many could do the same. He lived an exciting life well into his old age; even his death was out of the ordinary—if we are to believe the probably apocryphal tale told by his niece of his demise. She held that Abbé Prévost was walking in the Chantilly woods when stricken with apoplexy. A doctor found him, thought him dead, and cut him open on the spot to ascertain the cause of his death. It developed that this autopsy was the cause of his death—he had been alive before he was cut open.

∇ ∇ ∇

Priscian (c. 500)
A professor in Constantinople, Priscian wrote a number of books, including an immense Latin grammar in 18 volumes that became one of the most famous textbooks of medieval times. In fact, though this work, written in 526, is long forgotten, Priscian's name is still remembered through the phrase *to break Priscian's head*, meaning to break a rule in grammar.

∇ ∇ ∇

Procopius (d. 562?)
To this secretary to Emperor Justinian's General Belisarius we owe the word anecdote as we know it today. Justinian, Byzantine emperor from A.D. 527 to 565, wrote a book of brief tales about life in his court. These true stories were satirical, scandalous and sometimes off-color. Justinian—better known for the Justinian legal code—probably didn't intend them for publication, but they were published by Procopius as a supplement to his history of the times. Procopius entitled the book *Anekdota*, a Greek word meaning "unpublished, secret." The title of the book later became the term anecdote, meaning a brief, factual story like the ones *Anekdota* contained. (See also PAMPHILUS.)

∇ ∇ ∇

Marcel Proust (1871–1922)
The small, rich, shell-shaped cakes called madeleines are doubtless the most famous pastry in all literature. They are said to be named for their inventor, Madeleine Paulmier, a 19th-century pastry cook of Commeray, France. It was on a visit to his mother that Marcel Proust was served the scalloped *petite madeleine*, "so richly sensuous under its severe religious folds," whose taste brought back the flood of memories resulting in his eight-volume masterpiece *À la Récherche*

du Temps Perdu. One cynic has called Proust's work "the tale of a man who fell in love with a cookie."

Proust was as sensitive to scents as he was to taste. One time a friend called and he asked him to take his perfumed handkerchief out of his jacket pocket. "Celeste," he then told the maid, "take the gentleman's handkerchief and put it in another room. My dear friend, the last time you were so good as to come and see me...I was obliged to take the chair you sat in and keep it out in the courtyard for three days: it was impregnated with scent."

The novelist, like Joyce after him, would blend many real-life people into one of his characters. Proust's character Bergotte in *À la Récherche du Temps Perdu*, for example, may be based mainly on French author Anatole France, but Bergotte has characteristics Proust borrowed from at least a dozen real-life people, including novelist Alphonse Daudet, historian Ernest Renan, critic Jules Lemaître, novelist Paul Bourget, and critic John Ruskin, to name just a few.

Prout's character Aimé in *À la Récherche du Temps Perdu* (1913–27) was suggested by the monocled Olivier Dabescat, headwaiter at the Ritz. Dabescat never failed a gourmet with enough money. Once he even served elephant's feet (Dumas, *q.v.*, has a recipe for it) to a rich American, having an elephant at the Paris zoo slaughtered for this purpose.

The novelist's minor character the Princesse de Sagan gives her name to the present day best-selling French author Françoise Sagan, whose real family name is Quoirez. She took the pseudonym so that her romantic books would not embarrass her conservative parents.

Like Swinburne in England before him, Proust was a good man to keep away from when in the midst of a temper tantrum. He was in the habit of taking his friends' hats off their heads, especially top hats, and crushing the chapeaux by jumping up and down on them.

Everyone knows the story of Proust lining the walls of his bedroom with cork to reduce the noise and dust, and in the last years of his life rarely leaving this room. Proust did have chronically weak lungs and suffered from asthma and hayfever, but his hypochondria made his illnesses worse than they were in reality. The author would go to extreme lengths to avoid catching pneumonia, which he ironically died of. When he ventured out to attend his brother's wedding, for example, he dressed in so many layers of clothing that he couldn't fit in a pew and was forced to watch the entire ceremony standing in the rear of the church.

His hypochondriacal habits forced Proust to write in bed most of the time protected from illness with blankets, hot water bottles, fumigation powder and medicines in his cork-lined bedroom. He always had dozens of pens at hand. For if he dropped one on the floor, he dared not pick it up, fearing that germs might contaminate him or dust might aggravate his asthma.

In the last five months of his life Proust ate nothing except café au lait, according to the artist Paul-César Helleu, who painted his portrait as he lay dying. "Oh! it was horrible," Helleu recalled with almost ghoulish glee to an art dealer, "but how handsome he was! You can't imagine how beautiful it can be, the corpse of a man who hasn't eaten for such a long time, everything superfluous is dissolved away. Ah, he was handsome, with a beautiful thick, black beard. His forehead, normally receding, had become convex...Ah, but he was beautiful!"

As he lay on his death bed Proust instructed a servant to bring him the manuscript page where he had described the death agonies of one of his characters. "I have several revisions to make here, now that I am in the same predicament," he explained.

In his last days he wrote in bed, living on ices and beer—delivered by the Ritz—as he raced time trying to finish his great work. On his last night, unable to move his pencil, he dictated to his housekeeper as long as he could. "Celeste," he finally said, "I think what I've made you take down is very good. I shall stop now. I can't go on." The next afternoon he died.

∇ ∇ ∇

George Psalmanazar (1679?–1763)

Psalmanazar was a pseudonymous literary faker whose real name still isn't known. A Frenchman, he fashioned his pseudonym from that of the biblical character Shalmaneser. Claiming to be a native of Formosa (Taiwan) and even inventing a complete "Formosan" language that he spoke, he attracted the attention of Scottish army chaplain William Innes, who saw through his imposture but became his confederate. Innes "converted" him in order to get credit for a "conversion" and in 1703 Psalmanazar went to London, where guillible authorities hired him to teach "Formosan" at Oxford and write a dictionary of "Formosan." The following year the impostor wrote *The Historical and Geographical Description of Formosa*, which described the odd customs of the "Formosans"— e.g., that they ate only raw meat, including the flesh of executed criminals; and that they annually offered as a sacrifice to the gods 18,000 hearts cut from the breasts of boys under the age of nine. In 1706 Catholic missionaries to Formosa exposed Psalmanazar and after a time he confessed his fraud, renounced his past life in 1728 and went on to become an accomplished scholar. But there remained something of the impostor in this friend of Dr. Johnson. The title of his autobiography, published posthumously in 1764, was *Memoirs of———Commonly Known by the Name George Psalmanazar.*

∇ ∇ ∇

Ptah-hotep (c. 2650 B.C.)

Some have bestowed the title of "the first philosopher" on this Egyptian governor of Memphis and prime minister to the king under the Fifth Dynasty. In any case, after he retired from office he wrote for his son a manual of wisdom, which, written 2,300 years before Confucius, Socrates and Buddha, is the oldest known work of philosophy. Among his instructions to his son: "Be not proud because thou art learned; but discourse with the ignorant man as with the sage. For no limit can be set to skill, neither is there any craftsman that possesseth full advantages. Fair speech is more rare than the emerald that is found by slave-maidens among the pebbles...Live, therefore, in the house of kindliness, and men shall come and give gifts of themselves..."

∇ ∇ ∇

Ptolemy I (323–283 B.C.)

Ptolemy Soter founded one of the most famous libraries in history in Alexandria, Egypt. This vast depository, which contained 700,000 volumes at its peak, was gradually destroyed beginning with Caesar's invasion in 47 B.C. and finally by the Arabs in 391. The Arabs are said to have burned the books to heat the city's 4,000 public baths, claiming that they were unnecessary, for all the knowledge needed by humanity was in the Koran, but this story is probably untrue.

∇ ∇ ∇

Ptolemy II (309–246 B.C.)

Seventy-two authors gave their "name" to the word Septuagint. Tradition has it that Ptolemy II, who reigned from 285 to 246 B.C., had the laws of the Jews translated into Greek by 72 scholars, 6 from each of the 12 Jewish tribes, in a period of 72 days on the island of Pharos. The translation became the earliest Greek version of the Old Testament, later erroneously named the Septuagint from the Latin *septuaginta*, which means 70—not 72. Scholars believe that the translation was made in Alexandria at this time, but not at Ptolemy's request, not by 72 Jewish scholars, and not in 72 days. Nevertheless, the fable about "the seventy" is responsible for the word.

Ptolemy III (282?–221 B.C.)

In order to enlarge the famous Alexandrian library, which his grandfather Ptolemy I had begun, Ptolemy required that the original of every book brought into the city be given to the library after a copy was made for its owner. He lived in an age when collecting old books was so popular that there were specialists who dyed and spoiled new manuscripts in order to sell them as antiquities. He himself borrowed rare manuscripts from Athens, leaving today's equivalent of some $250,000 as security, only to keep the originals and send back copies—telling the Athenians to keep the deposit.

∇ ∇ ∇

Alexandr Pushkin (1799–1837)

Russia's greatest poet, of black ancestry, came from an ancient aristocratic family. His maternal great-grandfather had as a child been kidnapped from his village in Africa and given as a present to Peter the Great. The kidnapped child rose in the czar's court to become the famous Russian General Abram Petrovich Hannibal.

Pushkin, of whom Czar Nicholas once said, "I have just been speaking with the most intelligent man in Russia," was extremely popular among the Russian people, not only because he was Russia's greatest poet, but for his liberal views, which had caused him to be banished to the south of Russia early in his career. When he was killed in a duel over his wife with the adopted son of the Dutch minister to Russia, his body had to be smuggled out of Moscow during the night to prevent inevitable rioting at his funeral.

∇ ∇ ∇

Pythagoras (b. 580 B.C.)

The Greek thinker Pythagoras is said to have coined the word *philosopher* from the Greek words for love and wisdom. Up until this time philosophers were called *sophists*, "wise men." Said Pythagoras: "No man, but only God is wise. Call me rather, a philosopher, a lover of wisdom."

Francisco Gómez de Quevedo y Villegas (1580–1645)
Quevedo, though disabled by a club foot and notoriously poor eyesight, was as much feared for his sharp sword as his satirical pen. He knew no peace in his lifetime. Having killed at least three men in duels, he was forced to flee to Italy. There he was jailed three years for his part in a political plot. Recalled from a 10-year exile by Philip IV in 1621, he resumed cutting opponents with both his rapier and wit. But he finally went too far, and was accused of leaving an anonymous petition in verse under Philip's napkin at dinner one night. He was arrested, his health was broken by four years' imprisonment, and he died two years after being released.

∇ ∇ ∇ ∇ ∇ ∇ ∇ ∇ ∇

François Rabelais (c. 1494–1553)
According to a traditional tale, the French writer once had no money to pay his hotel bill or to get to Paris from a small town many miles away. Filling three packets with brick-dust, he labeled them "Poison for the King," "Poison for Monsieur," and "Poison for the Dauphin." His landlord immediately informed on this "poisoner" and he was transported by the police to Paris, where he explained his joke and was set free.

When he was ill one time Rabelais asked to be wrapped in his *domine* (or hooded cape), because, he punned, *"Beati qui in Domino moriuntur* (Blessed are they that die in the Lord)."

Rabelais, who drank deep as any man of life as well as wine, had as his bywords: "Let her rip," "The appetite grows by eating" and "Do what thou wilt." His last words are said to be: "Ring down the curtain, the farce is over…I go to seek the great perhaps."

A traditional story says that Rabelais left this one-sentence will: "I owe much. I possess nothing. I give the rest to the poor."

Jean Racine (1639–1699)

"What story did you base your religious drama *Athalie* upon?" the actress Marie Champmele asked the French playwright. "It is from the Old Testament," Racine replied. "Really," said Champmele—"from the *old* testament? I always thought there was a new one."

The best of his tragedies, *Phèdre* (1677), was driven from the stage when a rival theatrical company with powerful connections presented another *Phèdre* written by Nicolas Pradon just a week later. Racine wrote very little for the rest of his life after this disappointment.

"The applause I have met with," said Racine to his son, "has often flattered me a great deal; but the smallest critical censure...always caused me more vexation than all the pleasure given me by praise."

▽ ▽ ▽

Petrus Ramus (Pierre de La Ramée; 1515–1572)

From the beginning of his career Ramus tried to break the Aristotelian tradition among French scholastics; his master's thesis, which he defended against the faculty a full day at the University of Paris, was entitled "Whatever was said by Aristotle is false." He met a horrible end during the massacre of St. Bartholomew's Day in 1572. Two assassins—unknown to this day—broke into his study, shooting and stabbing him while he prayed. After they threw him out the window, students dragged his still-live body to the Seine and tossed it in. He may still have been alive when others dragged his body out and hacked it to pieces.

▽ ▽ ▽

Raphael (Raffaello Sanzio; 1483–1520)

The great Italian artist is known to have written love sonnets on the backs of his drawings for his *Disputa*, frescoes in the Vatican. Raphael's amorous exploits were legendary in his own time. He had dozens of mistresses in his short lifetime, and the woman he had promised to marry reputedly died of a broken heart while he dallied with the others. Raphael himself is said to have died after indulging in which Vasari called "an unusually wild debauch."

▽ ▽ ▽

Oscar von Redwitz (1823–1891)

This German poet and dramatist may not have written of suffering as well as Goethe or Rilke, but he certainly suffered more—at least in his mind. Probably history's greatest literary hypochondriac, the baron is said to have visited a doctor *every day* of his life from the time he was 40, complaining of fully *10,000* different ailments or symptoms.

∇ ∇ ∇

Max Reger (1873–1916)
The German composer received a terrible review from newspaper critic Rudolf Lewis. He immediately replied: "I am sitting in the smallest room in my house. I have your review before me. Soon it will be behind me."

∇ ∇ ∇

Regiomontanus (Johann Müller; 1436–1475)
Regiomontanus predicted a lunar eclipse for February 29, 1504, in his book *Ephemerides*. Columbus had the book with him at that time, a time when the Jamaican Indians were reducing their food supplies to his stranded crew so drastically that the men were beginning to starve. Remembering Regiomontanus's calculation, the explorer told the Jamaican Indian chief that God was angry at the Indians for letting his men starve and would punish them that night by blotting out the moon. The Indians scoffed until the eclipse came and then they quickly brought more food. Columbus then told them that he had prayed to God to restore the moon if they would always adequately feed the crew.

∇ ∇ ∇

Mathurin Régnier (1573–1613)
"Every woman is to my taste," this court poet once remarked to France's Henry IV, and it is said that as a result he not only contracted syphilis but also was old and gray before turning 30. Though he remained young and vigorous in his verse, Régnier died when only 39, writing his satirical epitaph shortly before:

> I have lived without a thought,
> letting myself go sweetly
> by nature's sweet law;
> and I know not why
> death should think of me,
> who never deigned to think of her.

∇ ∇ ∇

Theodore Reinking (fl. 17th century)
The Danish author of *Dania ad Exteros de Perfidia Suedorum* (1644), a tract bitterly condemning the Swedish occupation of Denmark, was thrown into prison by the

Swedes and after several years in jail given the "choice" of being beheaded or eating his words, that is, his entire critical book. Reinking of course chose the latter alternative and the Swedes were civilized enough to let him eat his bitter pages "boiled in broth."

∇ ∇ ∇

Erich Maria Remarque (1898–1970)

Remarque once noted in a letter these differences in novels among various nationalities: "American novel—two people want each other from the beginning but don't get each other until the end. French novel—two people get together right at the beginning, but from then on don't want each other anymore. Russian novel—two people don't want each other or get each other, and for the next 800 pages they brood about it."

Interviewed by a *New York Times* reporter on January 27, 1946, the German novelist recalled: "My father, a good man, told me 'Never lose your ignorance; you cannot replace it.'"

∇ ∇ ∇

Jules Renard (1864–1910)

"Writing," the French author once observed, "is the only profession where no one considers you ridiculous if you earn no money."

∇ ∇ ∇

Nicolas-Edme Restif de La Bretonne (1734–1806)

The French novelist, called in his time "the Rousseau of the gutters" and whose work reflects his overactive libido (he claimed he had had 15 mistresses by the time he was 15) as well as his passion for female feet (he is literature's first recorded foot fetishist), wrote rambling but accurate stories. His descriptions of even the incidental characters he drew from life were so realistic that the people who had been portrayed often cursed him as he passed them by in the streets of Paris.

∇ ∇ ∇

Jean Paul Richter (1763–1825)

The German author, more popular than Goethe in his day, aimed a sarcastic shaft at windy German philosophy when he quipped: "Providence has given to the English the empire of the sea, to the French that of the land, and to the Germans that of the air." When Richter died in 1825 an unfinished essay on the immortality of the soul was found on his desk.

Peter Riga (c. 1200)

The lipogram—a composition in words from which a specific letter is deliberately omitted—has been known since ancient Greek and Roman times. Riga's allegorical Biblical poem *Aurora* is noted for its "lipogrammatic" manner. In one passage of 23 lines the letter *a* doesn't appear in the first line, the letter *b* in the second, and so on.

∇ ∇ ∇

Jacques Rigaut (1899–1929)

Ten years before his death, at the time poet Jacques Vachet committed suicide, Rigaut condemned himself to die and chose the exact date and time when he would take his own life. In the interim the surrealist writer abandoned literature and married an American girl, but he carried out his death plan exactly as he had predicted it when the time came.

∇ ∇ ∇

Rainer Maria Rilke (1875–1926)

The experience of the greatest German lyric poet of the 20th century should hearten the most massively blocked writer. Rilke began his famous *Duino Elegies* well before World War One, but abandoned the poems and did not return to them until 1922, fully 10 years later, completing the entire cycle in a feverish 18 days.

"I never read anything concerning my work," he wrote to a friend. "I feel that criticism is a letter to the public which the author, since it is not directed to him, does not have to open and read."

∇ ∇ ∇

Arthur Rimbaud (1854–1891)

The French poet wrote some of the poems in his collected works before he was 15. His poem "Le Bateau Ivre," which is now hailed as a pioneer of the French symbolist movement, was written when he was only 16.

Rimbaud in his quest to "be modern completely" claimed that he "invented the color of the vowels." "*A* is black," he said, "*E* white, *I* red, *O* blue, and *U* green." He did not give a color for the schwa.

It is said that Rimbaud had stolen something from friends and one of them, a giant of a man, angrily reprimanded him. Rimbaud, facing up to his accuser, replied, "I do not fight with horses!"

While walking in the woods with a friend, Rimbaud scraped his forehead against a tree trunk. "Are you bleeding?" his friend asked. "It's nothing," Rimbaud said, "it's the thorn of thought." It has been suggested that he meant that his radical ideas were like a crown of thorns to him. In any case, his conversational phrase later inspired Paul Valéry to write in *Mauvaises Pensées*: "Man is on the cross of his body. His overburdened head is pierced by the deep thorns of his crown of thoughts."

Dr. Antoine Cros explained in a letter to a friend just how far Rimbaud went in the interests of "the rational deranging of the senses" that Rimbaud felt was one of the keys to a poet becoming a "seer." Wrote Cros:

> The three of us (Rimbaud, Verlaine, and myself) were in the Café du Rat Mort (Place Pigalle), when Rimbaud said: "Lay your hands on the table. I want to show you an experiment." Thinking it to be some kind of joke, we stretched out our hands. Then, drawing an open knife from his pocket, he made a fairly deep cut in Verlaine's wrists. I had enough time to withdraw my hands, and wasn't wounded. Another day, I was in the café with Rimbaud. I left the table for a moment, and, when I came back, I saw that my beer contained a sulphurous liquid that Rimbaud had just poured into it.

After Rimbaud abandoned literature, becoming a vagabond in Europe and Africa, he regarded it as little more than a filthy joke. Once a friend told him he had acquired a large number of rare books. "Buying books, especially books like that, is completely idiotic," Rimbaud told him. "You've got a head on your shoulders that should replace all books. All books are good for is to stand on shelves and conceal the leprous condition of old walls!"

In 1889 Rimbaud encountered a traveler who asked him if he wasn't the same Rimbaud who had written poetry in his youth. He was that same man, Rimbaud admitted. As for the poetry, he declared, it was, "Hogwash. Pure hogwash."

∇ ∇ ∇

Ottavio Rinuccini (1562–1621)

The Italian poet has the distinction of having written the lyrics for the first true opera known to history. *Dafne*, music by Jacopo Peri, was performed in 1597 before a group of music lovers called the *camerata* at the home of the wealthy Jacopo Corsi in Florence.

∇ ∇ ∇

Guiraut Riquier (1230–1294)

Riquier is said to have been "the last of the troubadours." When he saw the end of the troubadour era coming in France, he mournfully confessed, "song should express joy, but sorrow oppresses me, and I have come into the world too late." He died a few days after.

∇ ∇ ∇

Comte de Rivarol (Antoine Rivaroli; 1753–1801)

Asked his opinion of a two-line poem, the French author read it and commented: "Very nice, but there are dull stretches."

∇ ∇ ∇

Diego Rivera (1886–1957)

A great practical joker, the Mexican painter and muralist was the subject of a novel by Ilya Ehrenburg entitled *The Extraordinary Adventures of Julio Jurenito*. One of his favorite hoaxes was to pose as a cannibal who ate human flesh because it constituted the only healthy diet. Backing his theory with fictitious endorsements by prominent medical people, Rivera would highly recommend his human flesh diet, even supplying his dupes with recipes for cooking people of all ages.

∇ ∇ ∇

José Rizal (1861–1896)

The Philippine poet was a revolutionary executed by the Spanish government in 1896 on a charge of treason. He was one of those few poets who compose their best poems in their last moments on earth, writing down his famous *"El Último Adios"* ("The Last Farewell") just before he was shot.

∇ ∇ ∇

Jules Romains (Louis-Henri-Jean Farigoule; 1885–1972)

The French author's novel or "novel-cycle," as he described it, *Men of Good Will*, was published in 14 volumes from 1933 to 1946. Totaling 4,959 pages and 2,070,000 words, it is generally considered the longest important novel ever published.

∇ ∇ ∇

Pierre de Ronsard (1524–1585)

A weak, sickly man, French king Charles IX was at heart a poet. His love for Ronsard's poetry inspired this verse:

> We both wear diadems; but I my crown
> Received as king, you, poet, made your own;
> Your lyre, which charms with concourse of sweet sounds,
> Subdues the soul, while flesh my empire bounds.

It softens hearts, holds loveliness in fee.
I can give death; you, immortality.

▽ ▽ ▽

Joseph Henry Rosny (Joseph-Henri-Honoré Boëx, 1856–1940; and Séraphin-Justin-François Boëx, 1859–1948)

The pseudonym Joseph Henry Rosny was adopted by the two Boëx brothers listed above in the early 1880s when they began collaborating on novels together. The French authors wrote almost a score of books with scientific backgrounds and were designated by Goncourt as original members of his academy. Theirs is one of the few literary collaborations in which the collaborators wrote under one assumed name.

▽ ▽ ▽

Jean-Baptiste Rousseau (1671–1741)

This French poet and playwright was denied admission to the Café Laurent, frequented mostly by literary men, for his libelous verse. This did not silence him, for about 10 years later, in 1712, he was prosecuted for defamation of character. When he didn't appear in court to defend his biting literary epigrams, he was condemned to perpetual exile. Banished from France, he wandered Europe until his death almost 30 years later.

▽ ▽ ▽

Jean-Jacques Rousseau (1712–1778)

The Swiss-French moralist wrote in *Emile* (1762) of his scheme of education in which the child is allowed to develop fully in natural surroundings protected from the baleful influences of civilization. Seventeen years earlier, however, he had taken as his life-long mistress (he finally married her in 1768) Thérèse le Vasseur, a maid at a hotel where he was staying, and had five children by her, all of whom he sent to a foundling hospital soon after their births. When he became famous as a moralist, his refusal to face his guilt about his children helped cause his nervous breakdown.

Emmanual Kant began reading Rousseau's *Emile* early one morning. The philosopher became so engrossed in the book that he forgot to take his daily walk.

Rousseau told the following story in *Emile*: "'My Lord—I must live'—once said a wretched author of satire to a minister who had reproached him for following so degrading a profession. 'I fail to see why,' replied the great man coldly."

His novel *Julie, ou La Nouvelle Héloïse* (1761) was so popular that copies could not be printed fast enough, readers even renting it from others for 12 sous an hour.

Late in his life he felt great guilt for abandoning his family. In his last year he saw a child playing outside in the sunshine and, in his own words, went to his room where he "wept and expiated."

In the last 15 years of his life Rousseau became increasingly paranoid, fleeing from one country to another. Real threats existed: an order for his arrest in France for his criticism of the church; the official burning of his books in Geneva; Voltaire's anonymous pamphlet condemning him as a hypocrite and heartless father; a mob stoning his house in Motiers...But he imagined many more "conspirators" from whom he fled. His life seemed to become an effort to defend himself or justify himself to the world. He insisted on reading interminable extracts from his *Confessions* in Parisian drawing rooms until one hostess had to have the police ask him to desist. His final act to justify himself was his *Dialogues: Rousseau Juge de Jean-Jacques*, which he tried in 1775 "to place under God's protection" on the high altar of Notre Dame. But when he found that the iron grill surrounding the choir prevented him from doing so, he felt that God Himself had joined his persecutors and fell into a deep depression that only relented a little in the last few years that he lived. (See also MARQUISE DU CHÂTELET.)

∇ ∇ ∇

Rudagi (Farid-eddin Mohammed 'Abdallah; c. 870–954)

It is said that Rudagi, his pen name taken from his home village of Rudag in what was then Persia, became "the first great literary genius" of his country despite the fact that he was totally blind since birth. In any case, over 1,300,000 brilliant verses have been attributed to him, as well as many epic masterpieces. But time was cruel to the poet: only 52 of these verses survive.

∇ ∇ ∇

Olof Rudbeck (1630–1702)

Something of a chauvinist, this Swedish professor and author tried to prove in one book that the Biblical Garden of Eden was located in the Land of the Midnight Sun. Not content with this, he went on to "prove" in his *Atlantikan* that Sweden had been the locale of Plato's Atlantis.

Leopold von Sacher-Masoch (1835–1895)

Sacher-Masoch, famous for his masochistic novels, actually was the "slave" to a number of mistresses and two wives before he died, even signing a contract with a mistress that read in part: "Herr Leopold von Sacher-Masoch gives his word of honor to Frau Pistor to become her slave and to comply unreservedly...Frau Pistor, on her side, promises to wear furs...when she is in a cruel mood." Furs so fascinated him that they became prominent in his most widely read novel, *Venus in Furs,* and his first marriage was marked by a private ceremony in which he wore white tie and tails and his bride took her vows in a long fur coat. A prolific, talented novelist who had published several scholarly histories and had once been a professional actor, Sacher-Masoch became a leading literary figure of his time. But he finally suffered a complete breakdown before turning 50; his second wife committed him to an asylum after he had tried to kill her on several occasions. In a fitting ending to his bizarre life, his wife officially announced that he had died, even mourning him, 10 years before his actual death. The pre-Freudian neurologist Richard von Krafft-Ebing probably first used Sacher-Masoch's name to describe his ailment, and the word *masochism* was first recorded in 1893.

∇ ∇ ∇

Marquis de Sade (Comte Donatien-Alphonse-François; 1740–1814)

Physically, at least, Comte Donatièn-Alphonse-François de Sade seems to have been one of the beautiful people, a handsome, little man. Actually, various descriptions of the miniature aristocrat exist. One writer gives him "blue eyes and blonde well kept hair," another "a delicate pale face from which two great black eyes glared," a third tells us that he was "of such startling beauty that even in his early youth all the ladies that saw him stood stock still in rapt admiration." Unfortuantely, there is no authentic portrait of de Sade, but one might expect the probable descendant of the Laura made famous in Petrarch's (*q.v.*)immortal love poems four centuries before to present a striking appearance.

From 1777 on, de Sade spent all but 13 of his remaining 37 years in prison or in the lunatic asylum at Charenton. While imprisoned he began writing the novels and plays that give his name to the language. The *120 Days of Sodom* (1785), in which 600 variations of the sex instinct are listed, *Justine, or Good Conduct Well Chastised* (1790), and *The Story of Juliette, or Vice Amply Rewarded* (1792) are among his works replete with myriad descriptions of sexual cruelty. Never able or willing to reform, de Sade died at the age of 74, while still at Charenton, where he wrote and directed fashionable plays performed by the inmates, many of whom he corrupted in the process. Sometimes his insights were deep and remarkable, but his was in the main the disordered, deranged mind reflected in his life and licentious work. *Sadism*, the derivation of satisfaction or pleasure from the inflicting of pain on others, can be sexual in nature or stem from a variety of motives, including frustration or feelings of inferiority. De Sade's life indicates that many such causes molded his twisted personality.

When de Sade's *Justine or the Misfortunes of Virtue* was published in 1791, it became popular for a time among mothers, misled by its title, who purchased it for their daughters to read "as an object lesson."

Full of self-hate, de Sade wrote in his final testament: "The ground over my grave should be sprinkled with acorns so that all traces of my grave shall disappear so that, as I hope, this reminder of my existence may be wiped from the memory of mankind."

De Sade's last will and testament also requested that he be viewed in his open casket for at least 48 hours so that there would be no chance he could be buried alive.

▽ ▽ ▽

Sa'di or Saadi (Muslih ud-Din; 1184?–1291)
Though he believed that "the ringlets of the lovely are a chain on the feet of reason," the sensual Persian philosopher-poet outlived two wives by the time he was 50. He wrote all his major works from his 50th birthday until the time he died at well over 100, having added such colorful phrases to the world's language as "dead men tell no tales" and "I complained that I had no shoes until I met a man without feet."

▽ ▽ ▽

Saint-Evremond, Charles de Marguetel, Seigneur de (1610–1703)
Though he lived till the age of 90 and achieved the rare honor for a French author of being buried in Westminister Abbey, the Seigneur de Saint-Evremond was a hypochondriac of the first rank. Once he remarked, "Without Monsieur Descartes's philosophy, which says, 'I think, therefore I am,' I should scarcely believe myself to be; that is all the benefit I have received from studying that famous man."

▽ ▽ ▽

Charles-Augustin Sainte-Beuve (1804–1869)
Writing of poet Alfred de Vigny, Sainte-Beuve invented the term "ivory tower" for one who cuts himself or his work off from reality. The pertinent part of the poem, *Pensée d'Août*, reads as follows:

Hugo, stern partisan
... fought under armor,
And held his banner high in the midst of the tumult:
He holds it still; and Vigny, more secret,
As if in his tower of ivory, retired before noon.

Few writers have been more conscientious than the French critic, whose dedication has been compared to a Benedictine monk's. "I am accustomed incessantly to call my judgments in question anew, and to re-cast my options the moment I suspect them to be without validity," he wrote. His love of truth left him little time for living. "I never have a holiday," he once complained. "On Monday toward noon I lift up my head, and breathe for about an hour; after that the wicket shuts again and I am in my prison cell for seven days."

"I challenge you to a duel," an author told Sainte-Beuve. "You may have the choice of weapons."
"I choose spelling," Sainte-Beuve said. "You're dead."

Sainte-Beuve held an open umbrella throughout his pistol duel with a Monsieur Dubois. When asked why, the French literary critic replied, "I was resigned to being killed but not to catching cold."

▽ ▽ ▽

Louis-Antoine Sainte-Just (1767–1794)
This French author is well-known for his revolutionary writings, but the first work of the *enfant terrible* of the Terror, as he has been called, was an erotic poem of 20 cantos celebrating rape, the rape of nuns being most highly recommended. He met his end with Robespierre on the guillotine.

▽ ▽ ▽

Jean-François de Saint-Lambert   See MARQUISE DU CHÂTELET.

▽ ▽ ▽

George Sand (Amandine-Aurore-Lucie Dupin; 1804–1876)
The French author's first husband, Baron Casimir Dudevant, a retired army officer and no angel himself, separated from her in 1831 after nine years of marriage. But all his life he believed that his suffering from her affairs was unequaled in all France. (He claimed, for example, that her lover in one affair slept in the same bed with Sand and her 4-year-old daughter.) Indeed, 40 years later, just before his death, Dudevant wrote the emperor claiming that the pain

he suffered as George Sand's husband entitled him to the Legion of Honor—he had suffered for the glory of French literature! (See also ALFRED DE MUSSET.)

Someone called her "a terrible cow full of ink." She wrote, customarily, from 10 at night until five in the morning, always writing *à la diable*, that is, never with any plot or plan of action.

After leaving her lover, poet Alfred de Musset (*q.v.*), she lived with witty lawyer and author Jules Sandeau, with whom she had collaborated on a novel that they signed Jules Sand, which eventually yielded her pen name. She left Sandeau when she returned unexpectedly from a trip and found another woman in their apartment. Finally, she tried to get Musset back again and cut off all her hair and sent it to him as a token of penitence. He never forgave her, however, and refused to see her when on his deathbed.

After composer Franz Liszt broke with her he described what he thought was her use, or abuse, of men: "George Sand catches her butterfly and tames it in her cage by feeding it on flowers and nectar—this is the love period. Then she sticks her pin into it when it struggles—that is the congé (discharge) and it always comes from her. Afterwards she vivisects it, stuffs it, and adds it to her collection of heroes for novels."

"My heart is a cemetery!" she once wrote to her friend and confessor Sainte-Beuve. Years, and many men, later her discarded lover Jules Sandeau heard the remark and commented: "A necropolis!"

∇ ∇ ∇

George Santayana (1863–1952)
The Spanish-born philosopher, who taught at Harvard for many years, was an honest but kind man. "It is part of prudence," he once observed, "to thank an author for his book before reading it, so as to avoid the necessity of lying about it afterward."

∇ ∇ ∇

Santo Kioden (1761–1816)
Japanese fiction writers in Santo's time were classed with actors as among the lowest ranks of society. Santo had to earn his living as a seller of quack medicines and tobacco pouches, for most publishers of the time considered an invitation to dinner enough payment for a book (even in this enlightened age more than one novelist has claimed that his advance didn't equal the cost of the lunch at which he and his publisher celebrated the contract signing). Finally, Santo Kioden

married a harlot and with her help wrote a book on Tokyo brothels, which did rather well. However his next work, *An Edifying Story Book* (1791), was a piece of pornography that got him in trouble. The authorities tried him under Japan's indency law and sentenced him to 50 days in his home, handcuffed so that he could not write a word. Poor Santo reformed and went back to starving.

∇ ∇ ∇

Sappho (mid-7th century B.C.)
Lesbos, a Greek island in the Aegean Sea off the west coast of Turkey, was a center of civilization in the seventh and sixth centuries B.C. There Sappho, the most famous poetess of her time, taught the arts of poetry to a select group of young women. The legend has never been proved, but the romantic ardor of some of Sappho's lyrical poems probably accounts for the tradition that she and her followers engaged in homosexual love, female homosexuality being named for the Lesbians, or residents of Lesbos. The word Lesbian (with a capital) designates any inhabitant of the island, which is noted for its rich soil as well as its sardine and sponge fisheries. Here Epicurus and Aristotle once lived and the philosopher Theophrastus was born. Sapphism, from Sappho's name, is a synonym for lesbianism. The poetess, according to legend, threw herself into the sea when spurned by the handsome youth Phaon, but the story is generally regarded as pure invention. Sappho may have married and had a son. Her simple, passionate verse, characterized by matchless lyricism and vivid use of words, originally formed nine books, but only fragments of these survive today. The "Tenth Muse," as she was known, used the four-line verse form now called sapphic in her honor, and is noted for her careful control over meter.

Sappho's verse totaled nine books, consisting of about 12,000 lines. In 1073, however, Constantinople church authorities publicly burned all her work. All her poems would have been lost forever if in 1897 two English scholars hadn't discovered coffins made of papier-mâché at Oxyrhynchus in the Fayum. The coffins had been made of the scraps of old books, and among the scraps were some poems by Sappho.

∇ ∇ ∇

Francisque Sarcey (Sataní Binet; 1827–1899)
The French critic attended a play in which a mechanical asp raised its head from a box and hissed. Later, when asked his opinion of the play, he replied, "I agree with the asp."

Victorien Sardou (1831–1908)

The following happened to the French playwright at a literary dinner party:

Sardou knocked over his wine glass and the woman at his side sprinkled salt on the stained tablecloth; Sardou tossed some of the salt over his shoulder to ward off bad luck.

The salt hit the butler in the eyes.

The butler rubbed his eyes and dropped a platter of chicken on the floor.

The family dog began devouring the chicken and choked on a chicken bone.

The son of the house tried to loosen the chicken bone from the dog's throat.

The dog bit the boy's finger.

The boy's finger had to be amputated.

∇ ∇ ∇

Jean-Paul Sartre (1905–1980)

Besides Erik Karlfeldt the only laureate to refuse the Nobel Prize voluntarily was Jean-Paul Sartre, who, in declining in 1964, said: "It is not the same thing if I sign Jean-Paul Sartre or if I sign Jean-Paul Sartre, Nobel Prize winner. A writer must refuse to allow himself to be transformed into an institution, even if it takes place in the most honorable form." (In 1958 Russian author Boris Pasternak was forced to decline the award by the Soviet Union, which considered the Nobel "a reactionary bourgeois award.")

∇ ∇ ∇

Monsieur Sauton (fl. early 19th century)

Monsieur Sauton is remembered only for originating or first systematizing the body of hired applauders called a claque that operated in Paris theaters. In 1820 Sauton opened an office in Paris to ensure the success of dramatic pieces for a price. Theater managers could order the required number of *claqueurs*: these divided into *commissaires*, who memorized the plays and were quick to point out their merits to others in the audience; *rieurs*, who laughed at the jokes and puns; *pleureurs*, who cried at appropriate times; *chatouilleurs* to keep the audience in good humor; and *bisseurs* to cry *bis* (encore).

∇ ∇ ∇

Joseph Justus Scaliger (1540–1609)

Called in his day "the bottomless pit of erudition," Scaliger was learned in all known areas, and some consider him the greatest master of general erudition who ever lived. It was Scaliger who established the first systematic chronology of ancient history, and it was he who first suggested that Christ was born in 4 B.C.

Paul Scarron (1610–1660)

Born terribly deformed and almost completely crippled, with quack remedies for syphilis later destroying his nervous system, the French poet once described himself for his readers: "I am going to tell you as nearly as possible what I am like. My figure was well made, though small. My malady has shortened it by a good foot. My head is rather large for my body—My face is full, while my body is that of a skeleton. My sight is fairly good, but my eyes protrude, and one of them is lower than the other...My legs and thighs formed at first an obtuse, next a right, and finally an acute, angle; my thighs and body form another; and with my head bent down on my stomach I resemble not badly the letter Z. My arms have shrunk as well as my legs, and my fingers as well as my arms. To sum up, I am a condensation of human misery."

Scarron became an abbé when 19 years old. A possibly apocryphal story says that when he was about 30, serving his canonry at Le Mans, he for a lark tarred and feathered himself like a carnival freak. On discovering this the people of Le Mans chased him into a swamp where he had to hide until their rage subsided and where he contracted a rheumatism that made his pain even worse. In any event, from the age of 30 on, Scarron lived in a state of pain so severe that he was only able to endure life with the aid of opium.

Despite his misery, he presided over the most famous salon in Paris, his body held by a box from which only his head and arms protruded. His wit was so treasured that people continued to come when his mounting debts forced him to charge his guests for dinner.

What dowry can you bestow upon your beautiful young bride? a friend asked the impoverished poet. "Immortality," replied Scarron.

"For my sister's bitch," ran the dedication to a collection of Scarron's poems, which he had dedicated to his sister's dog. Scarron and his sister had a falling-out while the book was being printed. The poet could not eliminate the dedication as he wanted to, so in the book's errata he noted: "For 'my sister's bitch' read 'my bitch of a sister.'"

Scarron composed his own epitaph shortly before his death:

He who lives here
Awoke more pity than envy,
And suffered death a thousand times
Before losing life.
Passing, make here no noise,
Take care not to wake him;

For this is the first night
That poor Scarron sleeps.

▽ ▽ ▽

Giovanni Virginio Schiaparelli (1835–1910)

In 1877 the Italian astronomer and scientific writer observed faint lines on Mars through his telescope and in his treatise on the subject called them *canali*, Italian for "channels." But his English translator erroneously translated *canali* as "canals," a word carrying a strong connotation of something manmade, which *canali* doesn't. In any case, the long search by astronomers for life on Mars, suggested by such "manmade canals," was probably inspired by this poor translation of Schiaparelli's work.

▽ ▽ ▽

Johann Christoph Friedrich von Schiller (1759–1805)

Schiller was one of the founders of modern German literature, with only Goethe overshadowing him in his time. Forced to become a doctor, while serving in military school against his wishes, Schiller finally rebelled and lived as a fugitive for a while. A poet, dramatist, historian and philosopher, he also wrote ballads, many of which became German favorites. Schiller was an idealist who hated tyranny in any form and his philosophy influenced Einstein and Schweitzer among other famous Germans. The *Wallenstein* trilogy (1795) and *William Tell* (1804) were used by Beethoven in the chorale finale to his Ninth Symphony.

Schiller often inspired himself to write by smelling a drawerful of rotten apples he kept in his desk. So great a favorite with the people was he that a German dish called Schillerlocken—curled chips of smoked fish—is named after the poet's curly locks.

▽ ▽ ▽

Friedrich Ernst Daniel Schleiermacher (1768–1834)

"My lecture audiences are composed mainly of students, young women and soldiers," the German philosopher once said. "Students come because I'm a member of the Board of Examiners. The young women come because of the students. And the soldiers come because of the young women."

▽ ▽ ▽

Heinrich Schliemann (1822–1890)

The celebrated German archaeologist who excavated or rediscovered Troy was a businessman who did not turn to archaeology until he was almost 50. However, Schliemann was always "a man mad about Homer" and the myths of ancient

Greece, a self-educated man who spoke eight languages fluently. According to a biographer, he baptized his children, named Andromache and Agamemnon, "by laying a copy of the *Iliad* upon their heads and reading a couple hundred of Homer's hexameters aloud." The buried treasure he uncovered in the graves of Troy (actually it proved to be the city below Troy) was the richest ever found to that day and Schliemann lived in great wealth until his death on Christmas morning 1890.

Schliemann, who knew at least 12 foreign languages as well as he knew German, once explained how he learned Greek: "In order to acquire quickly the Greek vocabulary, I procured a modern Greek translation of *Paul et Virginie*, and read it through, comparing every word with its equivalent in the French original. When I had finished this task I knew at least one-half the Greek words the book contained; and often repeating the operation I knew them all, or nearly so, without having lost a single minute by being obligated to use a dictionary...Of the Greek grammar I learned the declensions and the verbs, and never lost my precious time in studying its rules; for I saw that boys, after being troubled and tormented for eight years and more in school with the tedious rules of grammar, can nevertheless none of them write a letter in ancient Greek without making hundreds of atrocious blunders. I thought the method pursued by the school-masters must be altogether wrong...I learned ancient Greek as I would have learned a living language."

∇ ∇ ∇

Arthur Schopenhauer (1788–1860)
The German philosopher had been studying a plant in a public garden for an inordinately long time. A police officer, his suspicions aroused, approached him and demanded, "Who are you?" Schopenhauer looked the man in the eye, scratched his chin and contemplated his words for several moments. Finally, he said slowly, "If you could only answer that question for me, I'd be eternally grateful."

∇ ∇ ∇

Christian Friedrich Daniel Schubart (1739–1791)
For a few satirical references in his newspaper *Deutsche Chronik* to the Duke of Wurttemberg and his mistress Shubart was imprisoned without trial for 10 years in the fortress of Blaubeuren. The duke provided for the care of his wife and children and when he was released in 1787 the poet and gifted musician was appointed master of music to the Court.

Albert Schweitzer (1875–1965)

While the great German humanitarian and author was traveling in America two women asked him, "Have we the honor of speaking to Professor Einstein?"

"No, unfortunately not," he told them. "Though I can quite understand your mistake, for he has the same kind of hair I have. But inside, my head is altogether different. However, he is a very old friend of mine—would you like me to give you his autograph?" He then wrote on a slip of paper: "Albert Einstein, by way of his friend, Albert Schweitzer."

▽ ▽ ▽

Aleksandr Scriabin (1872–1915)

The Russian composer aspired toward a fusion of the arts, and his *Divine Poem* (1903) tries to unite music and philosophy. His many artistic experiments were cut short when he died an untimely death at only 43. He died of blood poisoning after picking a pimple on his lip.

▽ ▽ ▽

Magdeleine de Scudéry (1607–1701)

Mademoiselle de Scudéry, known as Sappho in her influential salon, published her books under her beloved brother Georges' name, but proudly claimed all her witticisms. When Madame de La Fayette—who had a long-term affair with La Rochefoucauld— published her pioneering psychological novel *La Princesse de Cleves* (1678), Sappho remarked: "Monsieur de La Rochefoucauld and Madame de La Fayette have written a novel, which I am told is admirably done…They are no longer of an age to do anything else together."

▽ ▽ ▽

Sei Shonagon (b. 965?)

Little is known about this Japanese court lady except that she served as lady-in-waiting to Empress Sadako. Her only known work, *Makura no Soshi* (*The Pillow Book*) is the first example of the Japanese genre called *zuihitsu* (random notes), a huge collection of notes, lists, descriptions, sketches and anecdotes. Its title is probably a generic term describing an informal book of notes people recorded their thoughts in before retiring and kept in the drawers of their wooden pillows.

▽ ▽ ▽

Selim the Grim (Selim I; 1467–1520, reigned 1512–1520)

Unlike their counterparts in the west, Islamic rulers have traditionally been noted for their ability as poets over the ages. Twelve sultans and numerous princes are recorded among the 2,200 Ottoman poets said to have won fame in the last 600 years. Even such an unlikely candidate as Sultan Selim the Grim (Selim I), whose military genius made Egypt a province of the Ottoman Empire, devoted much of his time to his rhymes, leaving Suleiman the Magnificent not only a great empire but a royal book of his collected poems.

∇ ∇ ∇

Lucius Annaeus Seneca (c. 4 B.C.–65 A.D.)

There are a good number of rich writers alive today, but probably none of them—neither those rich from their works or by inheritance—has a fortune comparable to that of Seneca, history's richest author. The greatest of the Roman philosophers, tragic poet and tutor and adviser to the young Nero, Seneca has been called one of the most lovable hypocrites in history. He turned to writing after inheriting his father's fortune and for years was Italy's leading author, statesman and winegrower, his fortune finally totalling 300 million sesterces, perhaps over $100 million in today's money. It is said that at one point in his life Seneca suddenly called in all the provincial loans he had made (at usurious interest rates) and caused a financial panic and insurrection in Britain. The philosopher was denounced as a hypocrite, adulterer and critic of luxury "who displays 500 dining tables of cedar and ivory," yet he did live ascetically— sometimes existing for long periods on wild apples and running water for fear of being poisoned. He ate little and drank no wine, and when he died it was discovered that his body was emaciated from undernourishment. His generosity was demonstrated after the great fire of A.D. 64 when he donated most of his fortune to rebuild Rome.

Trying to curb Nero's cruelties, Seneca once warned him, "However many you put to death, you will never kill your successor."

Ghostwriting was common enough in Greek and Roman times. Following the example of such Greeks as the orator Lysias and many others before him, Seneca ghostwrote speeches for Nero and a number of Roman officials.

Nero sentenced Seneca to commit suicide after charging him with plotting to make Piso emperor. But Seneca wasn't afraid of death and had suffered so much from asthma (the gasping breaths of which he described as "practicing how to die") and weak lungs all his life that he had often considered suicide. Before his death he wrote to his friend Lucilius: "This is one reason why we cannot complain of life; it keeps no one against his will...You have had veins cut for the purpose of reducing your weight. If you would pierce your heart, a gaping wound is not necessary; a lancet will open the way to freedom, and tranquility can be purchased at the cost of a pinprick...Wherever you look, there is an end to troubles. Do you see that precipice?—it is a descent to liberty. Do you see that river, that cistern, that sea—freedom is in their depths...But I am running on too long. How can a man end his life if he cannot end a letter?...As for me, my dear Lucilius, I have lived long enough. I have had my fill. I await death. Farewell."

After Nero ordered him to take his life Seneca asked the centurion guarding him for tablets to make his will. "When this was refused," Tacitus writes, "he turned to his friends and said that, since he was prevented from rewarding their services, he would leave to them the one thing, and yet the best thing, that he had to leave—the pattern of his life...At the same time he reminded his weeping friends of their duty to be strong...what had become of the philosophy which through so many years they had studied in the face of impending evils?...Then he embraced his wife and, with a tenderness somewhat in contrast to his fortitude, entreated her to moderate her grief and not nurse it forever, but in the contemplation of a well-spent life to find honorable consolation for the loss of her husband."

Seneca drank hemlock after his veins were opened and he was put in a warm bath to ease his pain, playfully sprinkiling his servants with water. His wife, Paulina, tried to die with him but Nero ordered that her wrists be bound and the flow of blood stopped.

∇ ∇ ∇

Aloys Senefelder (1771–1834)
As a youth in Munich in 1796, Senefelder accidentally discoverd what is now called lithography when he scratched his mother's laundry list on a stone. It later occurred to him that words and pictures could be engraved on a stone from which copies could be printed.

∇ ∇ ∇

Rezsoe Seres (1899–1968)
During the Great Depression, American singer Paul Robeson introduced an English version of a melancholy song called "Gloomy Sunday," then quite popular in Europe. The dirgelike tune became a great hit in America, too, though it reportedly set off a wave of suicides, leading some radio stations to ban its playing. "Gloomy Sunday," composed by Hungarian songwriter Rezsoe Seres, experienced similar troubles in its native land. Hungarian officials particularly objected to the song's climax ("My heart and I have decided to end it all"), blamed it for a sharp increase in suicides and finally prohibited its performance anywhere. It isn't unusual for songs to have a depressing effect on suicide-prone

individuals. Seres, an unhappy man to begin with, became even more morose with this rejection. He felt that he'd never be able to write a second hit, and never did. No one can say how many of the composer's remaining days were dismal, but Rezsoe Seres finally took his own life on January 13, 1968, shortly after his 69th birthday. He leaped out of his apartment house window in Budapest—on what weather reports indicated was indeed a gloomy Sunday.

∇ ∇ ∇

Michael Servetus (Miguel Serveto; 1511–1553)
The Spanish physician and author was the first to discover that some of the blood circulates through the lungs. Condemned for his religious beliefs by both the Catholic Church and leaders of the Reformation, he was finally tried in Geneva by John Calvin's order and burned at the stake; his last book bound to his side, Servetus shrieked in agony for over half an hour before he died. The Catholics later burned him in effigy.

∇ ∇ ∇

Clodius Servius (c. 100 B.C.)
The famous scholar was so devoted to the work of the great Roman comic playwright Plautus that he was said to be able to recognize any line of the author's (in his more than 20 plays) by its sound.

∇ ∇ ∇

Shapur or Sapor I (241–272)
A man of great learning, the Persian king was a patron of the arts who wanted to give up his throne and become a philosopher. This at a time when his coffers were filled with the equivalent of over half a billion dollars, when 10,000 knights might accompany him wherever he might go, and when the royal crown was so heavy with gold and jewels that it had to be suspended by unseen wires at an invisible distance from his head. Before he could do as he wished, however, he was drawn into foreign wars that occupied him until his death.

∇ ∇ ∇

Shimazaki Toson (1872–1943)
Toson was the first established Japanese writer to become an expatriate, fleeing to Paris in 1913. He fled there after he made pregnant a young niece who had come to help with his children after his wife had died three years earlier. Though he thoroughly enjoyed the life of a Parisian, and wrote about it for the Tokyo *Ashai*, the novelist returned home to Japan at the outbreak of World War I and more than fulfilled his familial obligations over the remaining years of his life.

Emperor Sigismund (1366–1437)

Today we wouldn't name even a Fowler anything like "Jacob the Scourge of Grammar," as Giles Jacob (1686–1744), author of the *Lives and Characters of English Poets*, was called in his day. Yet the Scourge himself wouldn't have contradicted German Emperor Sigismund, who like Caesar considered himself above grammar. This story is told of Sigismund in Carlyle's *Frederick the Great*: "At the council of Constance, held in 1414, Sigismund used the word *schisma* as a noun of the feminine gender (*illa nefanda schisma*). A prig of a cardinal corrected him saying, 'Schisma,' your highness, 'is neuter gender.' Whereupon the emperor turned on him with ineffable scorn, and said 'I am king of the Romans, and what is grammar to me?'"

∇ ∇ ∇

Silius Italicus (25–101 A.D.)

An informer under Nero, Silius loved the poems of Virgil so much that he made pilgrimages to his tomb in Naples. Though he wrote, in Pliny the Younger's words, "with more pains than genius," he has the distinction of being the author of the longest poem in the Latin language—the 17-book epic *Punica*, on the Second Punic War. Silius starved himself to death on learning that he had an incurable disease.

∇ ∇ ∇

Antonio José da Silva (1705–1739)

Considered the best Portuguese playwight of his day, da Silva was arrested with his mother in 1726 for being a Jew. His mother was burned at the stake, but he was released upon renouncing his religion. Thirteen years later he was charged with secretly practicing Judaism and burned at the stake himself. On the day of his execution one of his plays was being performed in Lisbon.

∇ ∇ ∇

Guido Postumo Silvestri (1479–1521)

Pope Leo X richly rewarded poets who pleased him, presenting one versifier with 500 ducats for an epigram. Silvestri, a nobleman, wrote an elegiac poem about Italy's happiness under the pope, which Leo liked so much that he returned all of the poet's confiscated estates and made him his boon companion. He treated Silvestri too well, however, for the poet is said to have died of overeating at one of his lavish dinners.

Georges Simenon (1903–1989)

The Belgian-born novelist wrote hundreds of what he called "commercial" novels, among them his famous Inspector Maigret mysteries, but considered them inferior to his "pure" or "non-commercial" works. When working on these, which took him eleven days each to write, he spoke to no one, didn't take a phone call, lived "just like a monk." Before beginning he would cancel all appointments for eleven days and have a complete physical examination from his doctor. Once he started, working from the barest of outlines sketched on the back of a 7 x 10 envelope, he would become the main character in his story, driving that character to his limit. He once explained that this was why his "pure" novels were so short. After eleven days it was impossible to go on: "It's physical. I am too tired."

∇ ∇ ∇

Simonides (c. 556–c. 468 B.C.)

In his essay "Should Old Men Govern?" (yes, they should, he concludes), Plutarch tells us that Simonides kept winning the prize for lyric poetry almost up to the year when he died at 88 or so and was buried with a king's honors. The worldly Simonides might be called the first professional writer, for he wouldn't use his muse without getting gold and was the first Greek to write poetry and eulogies to order for payment. Aristophanes quipped that the poet would "go to sea on a hurdle to earn a groat" (an English coin worth four cents), but Simonides insisted that poets had as much right to eat as any one else.

"Poetry is vocal painting," he said, "just as painting is silent poetry."

His popularity as a poet was so great that he alone was able to prevent a battle between the armies of Theron and Hieron by personally appealing to these leaders.

∇ ∇ ∇

Alcibiades Simonides (b. 1818)

Simonides was a brilliant Greek scholar and author who fooled kings and archaeologists with his forgeries of literary documents. But he was caught red-handed by an illiterate old gardener. Simonides had insisted that an "ancient manuscript" had been buried in a box under a fig tree in a Turkish pasha's garden. The gardener, however, testified that he had planted the fig tree only 20 years before, that the soil was thoroughly dug up at the time and there had been no sign of a box.

Egill Skalla-Grímsson (c. 910–980)

The Icelandic author's greatest poem was "Head Ransom." He wrote it in 948 after being captured by his enemy Eirík Bloodaxe, ruler of York. Old Bloodaxe told him he would spare his life if he wrote in one night a magnificent poem honoring him. This proved just the inspiration he needed.

$$\nabla \ \ \nabla \ \ \nabla$$

Socrates (469–399 B.C.)

Legend has made Socrates' wife, Xanthippe, the classic shrew, and her name has become proverbial for a quarrelsome, nagging, shrewish wife or woman. In *The Taming of the Shrew* Shakespeare writes: "Be she as foul as was Florentius' love,/As old as Sibyl, and as curst and shrewd/As Socrates' Xanthippe, or a worse,/She moves me not." The gossips in Athens talked much of Xanthippe's terrible temper and she may have literally driven Socrates out into the open and his marketplace discussions. But then Socrates may have been a difficult husband, and by most accounts is said to have been unusually ugly and uncouth in appearance. Xenophon writes that Xanthippe's sterling qualities were recognized by the philosopher, and various historians, including Zeller in his *Vortrage und Abhandlungen* (1875), argue that she had been much maligned, that Socrates was so unconventional as to tax the patience of any woman, as indeed would any man convinced that he has a religious mission on earth.

Socrates' troubles with Xanthippe are legendary. "By all means marry," he is said to have advised someone, according to a traditional story. "If you get a good wife, you will become very happy; if you get a bad one you will become a philosopher—and that is good for every man."

Tradition has it that when Socrates was asked whether it was better for a man to marry or remain single, he replied, "Let him take which course he will, he will repent of it."

The Delphic oracle named Socrates the wisest man in Greece, to which the Athenian philosopher replied, "Since the god proclaims me the wisest, I must believe it; but if it is so, then it must be because I alone of all the Greeks know that I know nothing."

In his *Lives*...Diogenes Laertius wrote: "They say that Socrates, having heard Plato read the *Lysis*, cried out, 'O Heracles! What a number of lies the young man has told about me!' For Plato had set down a great many things as sayings of Socrates which he had never said."

Montaigne tells the following story: "It was pointed out to Socrates that a certain man had been no whit improved by travel. 'I believe it well' said he, 'for he carried himself with him.'"

Strolling in the marketplace, Socrates examined the myriad items offered for sale there. "How many things there are that I do not want!" he exclaimed joyfully.

The philosopher liked to drink, but he drank without getting drunk. If we can believe Xenophon, he said; "So far as drinking is concerned, wine does of a truth 'moisten the soul' and lull our griefs to sleep...But I suspect that men's bodies fare like those of plants...When God gives the plants water in floods to drink they cannot stand up straight or let the breezes blow through them; but when they drink only as much as they enjoy they grow up straight and tall, and come to full and abundant fruitage."

Of superb physical condition, Socrates made a great reputation as a soldier. He is said to be the last Athenian to give ground at Delium, frightening even the Spartans and saving himself by standing fast and glaring at them.

Though many ancient writers treated Socrates like a saint, others vilified him. He was called "ignorant and debauched," "a gadfly," and compared in looks to a satyr, among other insults. He himself said that he had "an unduly large paunch that he hoped to reduce by dancing."

∇ ∇ ∇

Solon (638?–559? B.C.)

Among the great poet and lawmaker's laws was one that canceled all existing debts. Unscrupulous friends learned of this and bought on mortgage large pieces of land, later retaining them without paying the mortgages. It was charged that Solon, too, had profited by his own law, but he proved that he had been a heavy creditor who actually lost money because of his measure.

Solon had strong reservations about the theater and acting. Once, as Plutarch records, he stopped backstage after one of Thespis's performances:

Thespis, at this time, beginning to act tragedies, and the thing, because it was new, taking very much with the multitude, though it was not yet made a matter of competition, Solon...went to see Thespis himself, as the ancient custom was, act; and after the play was done, he addressed him, and asked him if he was not ashamed to tell so many lies before such a number of people; and Thespis replying that it was no harm to say or do so in a play, Solon vehemently struck his staff against the ground: "Ay," said he, "if we honor and commend such play as this, we shall find it some day in our business."

∇ ∇ ∇

Khekheperre-Sonbu (c. 2150 B.C.)

Even this ancient Egyptian savant—of the reign of Senusret II and one of history's earliest known philosophers and authors—complained that nothing new remained for literature. "Would," he lamented, "that I had words that are unknown, utterances and sayings in new language, that hath not yet passed away, and without that which hath been said repeatedly—not an utterance that hath grown stale, what the ancestors have already said."

∇ ∇ ∇

Sophocles (496–406 B.C.)

Sophocles' sons are said to have summoned him to court in his old age (he lived to be 90) so that a jury might find him incompetent to manage his estate on the ground of senility. After he read them the play he had just finished, *Oedipus at Colonus*, the jury sided with him, reasoning that no man in his dotage could write such a work. They even escorted him home as an honor. A similar story is told of the great diva Luisa Tetrazzini, whose children tried to have her declared incompetent in her late years. The judge dismissed the case after she sang an aria for him in court.

"If I am Sophocles I am no dotard," he told his accusers at his trial, "and if I dote I am not Sophocles."

Few if any writers have dominated a national literature for as long as Sophocles did in his day. Of his 118 plays, 20 won the esteemed first prizes at the Dionysian and Lenaean festivals. He won his first prize when only 25 and his last 60 years later when an old man of 85.

Tradition has it that because of his weak voice Sophocles was the first poet not to appear in his own plays.

He found fault with fellow dramatist Euripides for "representing men as they are, not as they ought to be."

Among the earliest of writers to be honored as an athlete as well as an author, this son of a swordmaker was renowned as a ballplayer and won a prize as a wrestler. After the battle of Salamis, the handsome Sophocles was chosen to lead the youths of Athens in a nude victory dance.

An old apocryphal story holds that he died when his breath failed him because he had no time to pause while reading a long passage from his tragedy *Antigone*.

∇ ∇ ∇

Sotades (3rd century B.C.)

Only a few fragments of Sotades' satirical poetry remain, but nothing remained of Sotades himself when the satirized Ptolemy II got through with him. The Alexandrian poet, said to be the inventor of the palindrome and the peculiar Sotadic meter that bears his name, directed his coarse, scurrilous satires against the kings of Egypt and Macedonia. Ptolemy II took exception and had him sewn up in a sack and thrown to the fishes in the sea.

∇ ∇ ∇

Benedict (Baruch) Spinoza (1631–1677)

The philosopher, born in Holland though of Portuguese origin, held that the love of God involves the love of our fellow creatures. Apparently these did not include spiders, for it's said that his favorite entertainment was catching two spiders, confining them together in a small space, and watching them fight to the death.

When the brothers Jan and Cornelius de Witt were hacked to pieces by a monarchist mob in 1672 Spinoza made a placard advertising his disgust with "the very lowest of barbarians," as he called the mob. He was on his way out of the house to post his sign at the scene of the crime when his friend Van der Spych, with whom he was staying, locked the door and refused to let him out. If Van der Spych hadn't physically restrained him he would surely have been slaughtered by the mob, just like the brothers de Witt.

∇ ∇ ∇

Ssu-ma Ch'ien (c. 145–90? B.C.)

The greatest historian of ancient China was also a poet and an astrologer who reformed the Chinese calendar. He became grand historian in 108 B.C. after the death of his father. Toward the end of his life Ssu-ma was convicted of some unknown offense and told that his punishment would be castration. His prosecutors agreed to let him commit suicide to escape this horrible punishment, but he refused—so that he could complete the *Shih Chi*, his encyclopedic history of the whole known world, which became the model for Chinese historians.

Madame de Staël (Anne-Louise-Germaine, Baronne de Staël; 1766–1817)

"Here I am between wit and beauty," said a young man sitting with Madame de Staël on one side of him and the lovely Madame Récamier on the other. "Quite so," said the French author, "and without possessing either."

Talleyrand, it was rumored through all Paris, had been caricatured as an old woman in Madame de Staël's book *Delphine*. The caricature is all but forgotten to history, but not the French statesman's remark to Madame de Staël when he met her soon after the book's publication. "That is the book, is it not," Talleyrand said to her, "in which you and I are exhibited in the disguise of females."

Napoleon made her an enemy for life when he answered her question, "Who is the greatest woman, alive or dead?" Replied Bonaparte, who had a low opinion of women, "The one who has made the most children."

One time Napoleon was so rash as to call the regulars at her salon "ideologues." She quickly branded him an "ideophobe."

When Napoleon, tired of such remarks as "He is a Robespiere on horseback," banned her from Paris, she traveled throughout Europe writing her books and trying her best to overthrow him. Fourteen years passed before the Allies defeated Napoleon at Leipzig in 1814 and she could return home.

She made her lover, French author Benjamin Constant, sign this pledge of love with her.

> We promise to consecrate our lives to each other; we declare that we regard ourselves as indissolubly bound to each other; that we will share forever, and in every respect, a common destiny; that we will never enter into any other bond; and that we will strengthen the bonds now uniting us as lies within our powers.
> I declare that I am entering into this engagement with a sincere heart, that I know nothing on earth as worthy of love as Madame de Staël, that I have been the happiest of men during the four months I have spent with her, and that I regard it as the greatest happiness in my life to be able to make her happy in her youth, to grow old peaceably by her side, and to reach my term together with the soul that understands me, and without whose presence life on this earth would hold no more interest for me.

Although both were unfaithful, they remained bonded psychologically all their lives. When Constant read her his *Adolphe*—a short novel whose heroine, based upon her, dies at the end—she fainted in his arms.

Joseph Vissarionovich Stalin (1879–1953)

It is often forgotten that the communist leader was a writer, the author of five books and the first editor of *Pravda*. Born Iosif Vissarionovich Dzhygashvili he took the last name Stalin, "man of steel" in Russian, on joining the Russian revolutionary movement. Ironically enough his first book was an argument in favor of "self determination" for oppressed nations.

∇ ∇ ∇

Stendhal (Marie-Henri Beyle; 1783–1842)

"Whilst writing the *Chartreuse [de Parme]*," the great French novelist once confided, "in order to acquire the correct tone I read every morning two or three pages of the Civil Code."

He took his pseudonym from the small German town that was the birthplace of Johann Joachim Winckelmann, the German classical author who strongly influenced Goethe, Schiller and so many other European writers. But his first pen name, used on his first book, a study of music, was L. C. A. Bombet. He possibly changed this because reviewers criticized him for borrowing heavily from other authors.

He scribbled on a manuscript in 1840: "It is the nobility of their style which will make our writers of 1840 unreadable forty years from now."

Independent of all schools and influences, he wrote for posterity. "I take a ticket in the lottery," he told a friend early in the 1830s, "the grand prize of which may be summed up as—to be read in 1935." He won, of course, and is in fact more read today than in his own time.

Late in his writing life, only a year or so after he had finally gained recognition—when Balzac hailed him as a great novelist—he finally signed a lucrative contract with the *Reveue des Deux Mondes* for "nouvelles." Just after he signed he fell dead of apoplexy on the boulevard outside.

In his diary he tells of how, when visiting Florence in 1817, he felt ill in the presence of all the great works of art around him, especially the frescoes in the Church of Santa Croce. His heart beat irregularly, he feared he would fall down if he walked and he felt his life draining away from him. Only when he left the church and sat down on a bench to read poetry did he feel better. Today his experience is shared by scores of travelers in Florence every year, so many that psychiatrists have dubbed the phenomenon "the Stendhal syndrome."

Stendhal chose for the epitaph on his tombstone: "Here lies Henri Beyle, Milanese; he lived, he wrote, he loved." ("Quì giace, Arrigo Beyle Milanese; visse, scrisse, amò.")

∇ ∇ ∇

Daniel Stern (Marie-Catherine-Sophie de Flavigny Agoult; 1805–1876)

Another woman who took a man's name as her nom de plume, like George Sand and George Eliot, the French comtesse was married to Comte Charles d'Agoult and was active in George Sand's Paris salon. She became Franz Liszt's mistress and they had three children, their second child, Cosima, becoming the wife of Richard Wagner. Breaking her liaison with Liszt, she left their home in Switzerland and returned to Paris, where she gathered about her a billiant group of writers and activists, including Heine, Sainte-Beuve, de Vigny and Chopin, and also took a militant part in the Revolution of 1848.

∇ ∇ ∇

Stesichorus (c. 640–c. 555 B.C.)

Plato, among others, wrote that the Greek lyric poet was struck blind for slandering the beautiful Helen (the daughter of Zeus and "the face that launched a thousand ships") by writing that she had accompanied the god Paris to Troy. When he recanted and wrote that it was not Helen but her phantom that accompanied Paris, the poet's sight was restored. Of all Greek poets Stesichorus was said to be most like Homer but of all his 26 books only 50 lines survive, so his greatness can only be calculated, in the words of our scholar, "as astronomers infer the presence of an indiscernible star." Another legend says the poet was assassinated at Catania in Sicily.

∇ ∇ ∇

August Strindberg (1849–1912)

The Swedish playwright's misogyny and oppressive pessimism (Robert Benchley onced called him "Smiles" Strindberg) had no one cause. It was certainly motivated by the fact that his father married his housekeeper after she had given him three sons. (Strindberg's 1886 autobiography was entitled *The Son of a Servant*.) Each of the playwright's three wives was mentally unbalanced, which no doubt also contributed to his hatred of women, especially the excesses of his second wife, Frida, an Austrian woman who for a time ran an illicit nightclub in London. Ezra Pound once recalled the notorious Madame Strindberg dismissing a customer from her table at the club. "Sleep with you, I will," she cried, waving him away, "but talk to you—never! One must draw a line *somewhere*."

When his first marriage failed and his wife Siri left him, Strindberg imagined that feminists were persecuting him and had won his wife over to their side. Seeking to dispel an imaginary rumor that his marriage ended because he was less than a man, he hired a doctor to come with him to a bordello and measure his erect penis, which proved of a perfectly normal length.

∇ ∇ ∇

Ercole Strozzi (1471–1508)

This rich Italian poet married poet Barbara Torelli in 1508 and 13 days later he was horribly murdered, his killer or killers stabbing him 22 times, his death one of literature's oldest unsolved mysteries. His wife wrote this touching poem to him:

> Why may I not go down to the grave with thee?
> Would that my fire might warm this frigid ice,
> And turn, with tears, this dust to living flesh
> And give to thee anew the joy of life!
> Then would I boldly, ardently, confront
> The man who snapped our dearest bond, and cry,
> 'O cruel monster! See what love can do!'

∇ ∇ ∇

Herman Sudermann (1857–1928)

The German dramatist was persuaded to make up with his enemy, playwright Richard Voss. "Herr Sudermann," Voss said as they shook hands, "I wish for your next play the same success as you wish me." Sudermann threw up his hands in desperation: "Did you hear that? There he goes again!"

∇ ∇ ∇

Sugawara Michizane (845–903)

Few if any partrons of the arts have been honored like this Japanese nobleman. Sugawara Michizane's patronage of literature in the Golden Age so endeared him to his countrymen that he became worshiped in future gneerations as the god of letters and a school holiday was declared in his honor on the 25th of every month.

∇ ∇ ∇

Eugène Sue (1804–1857)

The mistress of the French novelist directed in her will that a set of books be bound with her skin. This was done and as recently as 1951 a special edition of Sue's *Vignettes: les Mystères de Paris*, its cover made from skin taken from the woman's shoulders, sold for $29 at Foyle's, the famous London bookstore. (See also CAMILLE FLAMMARION and MAURICE HAMMONEAU.)

∇ ∇ ∇

Aleksandr Petrovitch Sumarokov (1718–1777)

Sumarokov, who directed the first Russian national theater, considered his greatest rival to be the all-knowing man of letters Mikhail Lomonósov, called "the first Russian university" by Pushkin. Solely to demonstrate his superiority as a poet, he published a book containing both his own odes and those of Lomonósov. The demonstration, however, proved just the opposite.

∇ ∇ ∇ ∇ ∇ ∇ ∇ ∇

Rabindranath Tagore (1861–1941)

The Indian poet was so gentle a spirit that when he walked and rested in the woods "squirrels climbed upon his knees and birds perched in his hands." Like the great 11th-century poet Tulsi Das, he is said to have been able to communicate with the creatures of the forest.

∇ ∇ ∇

Amra Taraja (d. 570 A.D.)

The Persian poet was buried alive because a single couplet in a long poem he wrote was critical of the king.

∇ ∇ ∇

Torquato Tasso (1544–1595)

Tasso, a child prodigy, was famous for his poems and learning when only 10. But the Italian poet was paranoid from an early age and it may be that Alphonso II locked him up in a madhouse for seven years because of his dangerous conduct at the court of Ferrara, conduct that included trying to stab a servant he suspected of eavesdropping on his conversation with the Princess Lucrezia. This is probably the truth, but the old story, immortalized by Milton, Goethe and Byron, has it that the handsome poet feigned madness to protect the reputation of the Princess Leonora after news of an affair he had with her came to light. In any case, Tasso was released from the madhouse of St. Anna (see Delacroix's famous picture of him) in 1586, on the condition that he would leave Ferrara, and he began wandering Europe from court to court, "wandering like the world's rejected guest." Though he was honored wherever he went, his poems having preceded him, his work never brought him a penny, not even his great epic *Gerusalemme Liberata* (1575). According to one biographer, his life was "a veritable odyssey of malady, indigence and misfortune" and he died in a Roman monastery before the Pope could present him the crown of bay leaves that Petrarch had worn before him.

▽ ▽ ▽

Alessandro Tassoni (1565–1635)
Since Tassoni's famous poem "The Rape of the Bucket" lampooned a powerful Italian nobleman, no one would print it. But word of it spread quickly and soon people were paying scribes large sums to copy the original manuscript for them, making the poem a "bestseller" even before it was printed in France and smuggled into Italy.

▽ ▽ ▽

Terence (Publius Terentius Afer; 180–c. 159 B.C.)
So far as is known Terence was an African slave whose master, Terence Lucanus, recognized his talent and freed him, the playwright later taking his name in gratitude. He became the most respected playwright of his time; one of his plays was performed twice in the same day, a rarity then, and earned him 8,000 sesterces. Unfortunately, he died of a sudden illness, possibly when he was as young as 21.

▽ ▽ ▽

Terpander (fl. 7th century B.C.)
Legend has it that the Greek poet of Lesbos, who replaced the lyre of four strings by one of seven strings, was singing one of his own beautiful songs when someone threw a fig at him that entered his mouth and lodged in his windpipe, "choking him to death in the very ecstasy of song."

▽ ▽ ▽

Thales (640?–546 B.C.)
Diogenes Laertius tells us that Thales died "while present as a spectator at a gymnastic contest, being worn out with heat, thirst and weakness [brought on by the match], for he was very old."

One of the Seven Sages or Seven Wise Men of ancient Greece, Thales was asked what was very difficult. He replied with the famous apothegm, "To know thyself." Then asked what was very easy, he replied, "To give advice."

∇ ∇ ∇

Theophrastus (c. 371–c. 287 B.C.)

The Greek philosopher's original name isn't known. So eloquent was this pupil of Aristotle that he is remembered only by the name his master gave him, Theophrastus—meaning that he spoke like a god.

∇ ∇ ∇

Catherine Theot (1725–1794)

This French visionary preacher and pamphleteer believed that she was the mother of God and changed her name (Theot) to *Theos*, God. She was guillotined during the French Revolution—not for heresy but for her support of Robespierre, whom she had called "her well-behaved son" and "the forerunner of the Word."

∇ ∇ ∇

Thespis (fl. 6th century B.C.)

A *thespian* is, of course, an actor, and as an adjective the word means "pertaining to tragedy or dramatic art." Both words pay tribute to the first professional actor. According to legend, Thespis was a Greek poet of the late sixth century B.C. who recited his poems at festivals of the gods around the country; he is even said to have created the first dialogue spoken on the stage in the form of exchanges between himself as an actor reading his poems and responses by a chorus. Thespis is probably a semilegendary figure, his name possibly an assumed one. The popular story that he went around Attica in a cart in which his plays were acted is of doubtful authenticity, but may be partly true.

∇ ∇ ∇

Letwè Thondara (1723–1799)

The Burmese poet served six kings as court poet, judge and minister before being exiled to a penal settlement in 1764 for alleged crimes against the crown. While imprisoned he wrote a series of poems lamenting his miseries and longing for his family and the capital city. The poems were so beautiful that when the king finally read them, he ordered the poet recalled to his court.

Publius Paetus Thrasea (d. 66)

Nero ordered the Stoic philosopher and Roman senator to commit suicide after he had written a laudatory biography of the emperor's enemy, Cato. (Nero also felt that Publius did not sufficiently appreciate his emperor's poems or singing.)

∇ ∇ ∇

Thucydides (c. 460–c. 400 B.C.)

Tradition has it that the Greek historian was assassinated, which would make him one of the few authors in history, and the only major one, to die in this way. His history of the Peloponnesian War does break off abruptly (in about 411 B.C.), but is nevertheless one of the greatest historical works of all time.

∇ ∇ ∇

Hans Wilhelm von Thummel (d. 1824)

Thanks to his unusual burial place the German poet is still alive in a sense (aside from his works), despite the fact that he died over a century and a half ago. Von Thummel was buried in the hollow of an oak in Noebdentz, Germany, and the tree containing his body is still growing.

∇ ∇ ∇

Ananta Thuriya (1112?–1173)

A Burmese courtier, Thuriya was suspected of disloyalty by King Narapatisithu and sentenced to die. A few months before his execution he wrote a soul-stirring poem of four stanzas that was taken to the king, who immediately pardoned him on reading it. But the pardon came too late; Thuriya had been beheaded before word of it was received. His poem, however, has traditionally been regarded as "the immortal lines" that established the standard form of Burmese verse.

∇ ∇ ∇

Timotheus of Miletus (447–357 B.C.)

The Greek poet and musician increased the number of strings in the lyre, among other technical innovations. Yet conservative elements denounced him so bitterly that he decided to take his own life. The playwright Euripides, however, persuaded him that all Greece would soon sing his praises and he abandoned his suicide plan. He lived until the age of 90, a legend in his time.

∇ ∇ ∇

Marcus Tullius Tiro (fl. c. 63 B.C.)

Marcus Tullius Tiro, the man who invented the & sign, or ampersand, introduced it as part of the first recorded system of shorthand. A learned Roman freedman and amanuensis to Cicero, Tiro invented "Tironian notes" about 63 B.C. in order to take down his friend's rapid dictation. Though a rudimentary system, Tiro's shorthand saw wide use in Europe for almost a thousand years, outlasting the Roman Empire. The & sign, sometimes called the Tironian sign in Tiro's honor, was a contraction for the Latin *et* or "and." Taught in Roman schools and used to record speeches made in the senate, Tiro's system was based on the orthographical principle and made abundant use of initials. Tiro also wrote a lost biography of Cicero, a number of the great orator's speeches, and even some of Cicero's letters to Tiro!

∇ ∇ ∇

Tokutomi Roka (1868–1927)
A highly eccentric man, though not mad as his detractors claimed, the Japanese novelist often beat his wife with a stock, a practice far more scandalous in Japan than it has been in the West up until relatively recent times. A great admirer of Tolstoy, another eccentric, he journeyed to Russia to pay homage to the great author. The two men took a walk together and Tolstoy stopped to urinate in the snow. To the Russian's apparent displeasure, Roka carried hero worship too far and immediately emulated him.

∇ ∇ ∇

Ernst Toller (1893–1939)
Toller was imprisoned by the Nazis in 1933 for his "subversive" writings. In jail he was literally forced to eat his own words— in this case almost an entire volume of one of his anti-Nazi books. The revolutionary German poet and dramatist, unable to bear the changes in his life, committed suicide after he fled to America.

∇ ∇ ∇

Count Leo Tolstoy (Count Lev Nikolaevich Tolstoy; 1828–1910)
Tolstoy liked to make a point about his art by telling this story about the Russian painter Brulov:

> One day, in correcting a sketch made by one of his pupils, Brulov added a stroke or two with his own brush, and immediately put the breath of life into what had been a very mediocre piece of work. "But my sketch is entirely changed," said the pupil, "and all you've done is add a few strokes to it."
>
> "The reason for that," answered Brulov, "is that Art entered the thing just where those strokes began."

The author tried to teach his wealthy disciple, Chertkov, the proper humility and chastised him for always traveling first instead of second class. The next time Chertkov left Moscow the obedient pupil hired an entire second-class coach for himself.

Tolstoy went so far in his vegetarian beliefs that he refused to serve meat to anyone in his house. When his sister-in-law demanded chicken one evening, he trussed a live chicken to a dining-room chair. He then handed her an axe and told her to kill it if she wanted to eat it.

Tolstoy considered sex "degrading," but despite his ascetic beliefs, his prodigious sexual drive lasted at least until he turned 80, as his wife records in her diary.

He was not the most perceptive of drama critics. He told an amused Chekov: "Your plays are even worse than Shakespeare's."

Tolstoy based Fyodor Ivanovich Dolokhov in *War and Peace* on his uncle Fyodor Ivanovich Tolstoy, a character who could hardly be exaggerated. A duelist who killed 11 men, Fyodor Ivanovich was covered ankle to neck with tattoos. In his adventurous lifetime this libertine and gambler even commanded a round-the-world naval expedition on which the crew mutinied and put him ashore in the Aleutians. One wild story has it that, abandoned there, he made love to a female ape, which he then ate.

The Kreutzer Sonata used Tolstoy's own marriage as its basis and for its bitter conclusion that "We were two convicts serving life sentences of hard labor welded to the same chain." Nevertheless, he gave his wife, Sonya, the manuscript to copy.

Tolstoy's wife also copied the huge manuscript of *War and Peace* seven times in pen and ink, often having to use a magnifying glass to understand his handwriting.

Traveling in a wild region of the Caucasus, Tolstoy was befriended by a devout Circassian chief who wanted to hear about the world outside his mountains. After Tolstoy went on at length about the outside world, the chief insisted: "But you have not told us about the greatest general and ruler of the world. We want to know something about him. He was a hero. He spoke with a voice of thunder, he laughed like the sunrise, his deeds were strong as the rock and as sweet as the fragrance of roses. He was so great that he even forgave the crimes of his greatest enemies and shook brotherly hands with those who had plotted against his life. His name was Lincoln and the country in which he lived is called America...Tell us of that man."
Word of Abraham Lincoln had reached even this remote area.

Only a few days before his death from a heart attack, the novelist had a violent argument with his wife over a secret will he had made renouncing his copyrights. I will leave, he threatened his wife: "I will go somewhere where no one can interfere with me!"

Tolstoy refused to be converted to the Russian Orthodox church as he lay on his deathbed. "Even in the valley of the shadow of death, two and two do not make six," he told the priest.

∇ ∇ ∇

El-Aama et Toteli (d. 1057?)

The Blind Poet of Tudila, as El-Aama et Toteli was known, was honored like no other poet of his age. One time the venerated Spanish poet read his poems at a Seville poetry competition and all the other poets present tore their verses to pieces without reciting them.

∇ ∇ ∇

Ben Trovato (forever flourishing)

Ben Trovato isn't an author or authority of any kind. The words come from the Italian phrase *Si non è vero, è ben trovato* (If it is not true, it is well invented), so it has often been used humorously as the authority for a good story that really isn't true—*ben trovato*, in other words, has over the years become the quoted scholar Ben Trovato.

∇ ∇ ∇

Ts'ai Lun (ca. 105 A.D.)

It is said that this Chinese printer or literary man was the first to invent a convenient, inexpensive, writing material. His paper, so important to the development of literature, was made from tree bark, hemp, rags and fish nets. The emperor rewarded him with a high office, but unfortunately Ts'ai got involved in an intrigue with the empress and when this affair was discovered "went home, took a bath, combed his hair, put on his best robes, and drank poison."

∇ ∇ ∇

Tu Fu (713–770)

One of China's supreme poets, Tu Fu's bad luck began when he was captured by a gang of robbers, severely beaten and held prisoner for a year. Though he escaped in rags and reached the emperor's palace, where he was given an official post, he soon fell into disfavor with his ruler and was dismissed. While he struggled for a living digging roots for food and selling firewood, he saw his children die of hunger. He took to wandering through China, trying to find food to eat, writing his most beautiful lyrics all the while. Floods finally forced him into an abandoned temple where he went without any food for 10 days. Local officials who found him decided to honor the poet. They gave him a great feast, at which he reportedly died of overeating.

∇ ∇ ∇

Tulsidas (1532–1623)

Legend, supported by passages in his writings, has it that the greatest and most celebrated of Hindi poets was abandoned as an infant by his parents because he had been born under an unlucky conjunction of the stars. He was then found and adopted by a wandering holy man with whom he visited all the sacred places in India during his early years. The text of Tulsi's famous poem *Tulsi-krit Ramayan* is, according to one authority, better known among Hindus in upper India than the Bible is among Christians in England.

∇ ∇ ∇

Ivan Turgenev (1818–1883)

His short story *First Love* told of a young aristocrat who fell in love with the nineteen-year-old daughter of a neighbor and began courting her, only to find that she was his father's mistress. The tale was based on his own experience at the age of thirteen when he feel in love with Catherine Shakovskoy, the nineteen-year-old daughter of Princess Shakovskoy, who had a country villa next to the Turgenev's. Strongly attracted to Catherine, he found that she was his father's devoted mistress and that he treated her like a slave.

Other young love affairs were more successful. While dining at Flaubert's he told the following story: "When I was a very young man I had a mistress, a miller's wife from the outskirts of St. Petersburg, whom I used to see when out hunting. She was charming, pale as dawn with a cast in one eye, which is quite common among our people. She would take nothing from me. Then one day she said to me, 'You must give me something.' 'What do you want?' 'Bring me some soap.' I brought her the soap. She took it and went away, then came back and blushing said to me, holding out her perfumed hands, 'Kiss my hands like you kiss the hands of the ladies in the drawing rooms in St. Petersburg.' I threw myself at her fet. I can tell you, there had been no moment of my life more precious than that one."

Turgenev constantly feuded with Dostoyevsky, sometimes bitterly. One evening when the Russian novelist entered the room, Dostoyevsky turned his back on Turgenev and looked out the window. "Come over here," a mutual friend said to Turgenev, trying to ease the tension, "I want to show you a fine statue." Turgenev turned and pointed at Dostoyevsky. "Well," he said loudly, "if it looks anything like him, please count me out." (See DOSTOYEVSKY for more on their quarreling.)

He collaborated with the poet Nekrassov on and circulated an epigram directed at Dostoyevsky, who was to become his archrival in Russian literary circles. Dostoyevsky doesn't seem to have heard the epigram but most of Moscow's literary folk did:

A harmless braggart, his features full of woes,
Knight-errant Dostoyevsky by name,
This new arrival is literature's shame,
Like a swelling pimple upon its nose.

He never changed his opinion of Dostoyevsky, later telling a friend that *Crime and Punishment* was "something in the manner of a colic prolonged by an epidemic of cholera. God preserve us!" But then he (at least at first) had a low opinion of Tolstoy's *War and Peace*, too. "To me this is a truly bad, boring failure of a novel," he wrote to a friend.

While visiting Turgenev at his home, Tolstoy was invited to look at the proofs of the author's *Fathers and Sons*. To Turgenev's chagrin Tolstoy fell asleep after reading a few pages.

Though Turgenev was a big, powerful man, stories circulated that he was a coward. He is supposed to have been traveling at sea when his ship caught fire. "Save me, save me!" he cried out to a sailor. "I am the only son of a rich widow!" No help was needed, as it turned out; the ship beached and all the passengers waded ashore.

Not only was his book *A Sportsman's Sketches* (or *Notebook*) a protest against sefdom. Turgenev also wrote a laudatory obituary on Gogol that accomplished the same purpose. For this he was temporarily exiled to his estate by the government.

Among his literary remains was found a paper with the words: "Don't forget me, but do not call me to mind either, in the midst of daily cares, pleasures and needs…I do not want to disturb your life, I do not want to impede its quiet course."

∇ ∇ ∇ ∇ ∇ ∇ ∇ ∇ ∇

Sigrid Undset (1882–1949)

The daughter of a famous Norwegian archaeologist, the author of *Kristin Lav-ransdatter* (1920–22) was intensely nationalistic, even wearing national costume when at home. A very industrious writer, she converted to Roman Catholicism in 1924. Four years later when she was awarded the Nobel Prize, she told reporters who called on her: "I have not time to receive you. I am busy studying scholastic philosophy."

∇ ∇ ∇

Honoré d'Urfé (1567–1625)

It is said that the French novelist wrote his long pastoral romance *Astrée* (1610–19) out of disappointment over his wife, Diana. The aptly named lady preferred hunting to sex and in fact not only ate at table with her hunting dogs but also slept with them, which would be enough to keep any husband up writing.

∇ ∇ ∇ ∇ ∇ ∇ ∇ ∇

Jacques Vaché (1895–1919)

Few critics have been as immoderate as Vaché, one of the founders of dadaism, which flourished from 1916 to 1921. The dadaist author once climbed up on the stage of a Paris theater, pulled out a revolver and threatened to shoot anyone in the audience who applauded the play, which he disliked. Vaché, a good friend of André Breton, committed suicide at the age of 24 to show his contempt for modern society.

Paul Valéry (1871–1945)

The French poet and essayist liked to tell of the year he was rumored to be the strongest candidate for the Nobel Prize in literature. On the morning that the choice was being made in Stockholm, a nervous Valéry took a long walk with his dog. On returning, he asked his secretary, "Were there any phone calls?

"Yes, sir, you had a call from Stockholm a few minutes ago."

"What did they say?" Valéry asked excitedly.

"It was a Swedish newspaperwoman who wanted to know your views on the women's suffrage movement."

Valéry never did win the prize.

Said Valéry in criticizing the literary radicals of his day: "When one no longer knows what to do to astonish and survive, one offers one's pudenda to the public gaze."

∇ ∇ ∇

Cesare Lucilio Vanini (1585–1619)

Sentenced to death by the king of France for his so-called atheistic writings, the Italian freethinker supposedly left his cell to walk to the execution site, saying, "Let us go, let us go cheerfully to die like a philosopher." It seems impossible that he could have, for his death sentence, which he had already seen, read in part that he was "to be delivered into the hands of the executioner...who shall draw him on a hurdle, in his shirt, with a halter about his neck, and bearing upon his shoulders a placard with the words 'Atheist and Blasphemer of the Name of God'; he shall thus conduct him before the principal entrance to the church of St. Stephen, and being placed there on his knees...he shall ask pardon from God, from the King, and from Justice for his said blasphemies. Afterward he shall bring him into the Place of Salen, bind him to a stake there erected, cut off his tongue and strangle him, and afterward his body shall be burned...and the ashes thrown to the wind." Such was the end of the wandering philosopher who gave himself the name Julius Caesar and would answer to no other.

∇ ∇ ∇

Marcus Terentius Varro (116–27 B.C.)

"The most learned of the Romans," as Quintilian called Varro, was a poet, satirist, antiquarian, jurist, geographer, grammarian and scientist. Varro also appears to have been the most prolific of Roman authors, having written some 620 volumes (equivalent to 75 books today), including one of the earliest illustrated books. Though he lived 89 years, he was always rushed to complete his work, as he affirms in words written when he was over 80: "If I had leisure, Fundania, I would have written for you more conveniently what I will now set forth as best

I can, considering that I must make haste, since, as the saying goes, if man is a bubble, still more so is an old man. My eightieth year warns me that I must collect my baggage before I depart from life."

∇ ∇ ∇

Guiseppe Verdi (1813–1901)
Within the space of little more than a year, from 1838 to 1840, The Italian composer and interpreter of Shakespeare lost his infant daughter, Virginia, his son, Ichilio, and his first wife, Margherita. Yet, all alone, his young family wiped out, living in a state of despair bordering on a mental breakdown, he worked on the words and lyrics of the comic opera *Un Giorno di Regno*, commissioned by the director of La Scala.

Verdi's opera *Rigoletto*, containing the famous melody "La donna e mobile" ("The woman is flighty"), was abused by many critics as "uninspired" and "puerile and queer" for some 10 years before being generally recognized as a masterpiece, though the public loved it from the first time it was performed in 1851 at the Venice Theater in Venice, Italy. One newspaper critic went so far as to say that to even discuss it "would be a loss of time and space."

As he lay dying in a Milan hotel room officials ordered that all wagons in the city have their wheels covered with straw so that they would not disturb him when passing by his window.

∇ ∇ ∇

Angelo Vergecio (fl. 15th century)

Here lies Nolly Goldsmith, for shortness called Noll,
Who wrote like an angel and talked like poor Poll.
— David Garrick

Isaac D'Israeli, in his *Curiosities of Literature* (1791–93), says that the phrase "to write like an angel" originally had nothing to do with literary style, but referred to fine penmanship. According to the prime minister's father, a "learned Greek" named Angelo Vergecio immigrated to Italy and then to France, where his beautiful handwriting attracted attention; Francis I, in fact, modeled a Greek typeface on it. "To write like an Angelo" became synonymous with exquisite calligraphy, and Angelo was shortened to Angel at which point the meaning was expanded to include literary style. A good story even if it can't be confirmed.

Paul Verlaine (1844–1896)

After an argument with his lover, avant-garde poet Arthur Rimbaud (*q.v.*), Verlaine shot and wounded the younger poet, serving 10 years in prison for the crime. Breaking with Rimbaud, he became a Catholic, writing some of the best religious poems of all time. Although he lived the rest of his life in poverty, working as a farmer and a teacher, among other occupations, it is said that he was always "as cheerful as a child."

∇ ∇ ∇

Jules Verne (1828–1905)

The French author foresaw the achievements of modern science so well that his fictions were called "dreams come true." One contemporary observed, "For the last twenty years, the advance of the peoples is merely living the novels of Jules Verne."

So accurate was Verne's description of a periscope in *Twenty Thousand Leagues Under the Sea* that a few years later the actual inventor of the instrument was refused permission for an original patent on it.

∇ ∇ ∇

Guarino da Verona (1374–1460)

Legend says that the great Italian scholar mastered Greek while living in Constantinople and then sailed for Venice with a cargo of precious Greek manuscripts. When a box of the manuscripts was lost in a sudden storm "his hair turned white overnight." Guarino, however, lived a long life, possessing all his faculties till the end. He was one of those rare teachers who supported poor students out of his own poor pockets and whose lectures were so popular that students filled his classrooms to overflowing, large crowds of them listening in the halls.

∇ ∇ ∇

Don Vicente (fl. early 19th century)

Legend has it that Don Vicente, a Spanish friar and scholar, murdered five or six collectors to steal a rare book, which makes him a biblioklept as well as a bibliomaniac. The story, according to William Walsh's *Handbook of Literary Curiosities* (1892), is as follows:

> Coming to Barcelona in 1834, Don Vicente established himself in a gloomy den in the book-selling quarter of the town. Here he set up as a dealer, but so fell in love with his accumulated purchases that only want tempted him to sell them. Once at an auction he was outbid for a copy of the *Ordinaciones per los Gloriosos Reyes de Aragon*—a great rarity, perhaps unique. Three days later the house of the successful

rival was burned to the ground, and his blackened body, pipe in hand, was found in the ruins. He had set the house on fire with his pipe, that was the general verdict. A mysterious succession of murders followed. One bibliophile after another was found in the streets or in the river, with a dagger in his heart. The shop of Don Vicente was searched. The *Ordinaciones* was discovered. How had it escaped the flames that had burned down the purchaser's house? Then the Don confessed not only to that murder but others. Most of his victims were customers who had purchased from him books he could not bear to part with. At the trial, counsel for the defense tried to discredit the confession, and when it was objected that the *Ordinaciones* was a unique copy, they proved there was another in the Louvre, that, therefore, there might be still more, and that the defendant's copy might have been honestly procured. At this, Don Vicente, hitherto callous and silent, uttered a low cry.

"Aha!" said the Alcalde. "You are beginning to realize the enormity of your offense!"

"Yes," sobbed the penitent thief, "the copy was not a unique, after all."

∇ ∇ ∇

Gil Vicente (c. 1465–c. 1536)

"The Portuguese Shakespeare" served his country as a virtual poet laureate for over 35 years, crafting his golden lines while making his living as a goldsmith. One time a pedantic critic complained that he continued to use the old forms of verse and not the new forms and meters recently introduced into Portugal from Italy. Replied the poet, "Better an ass that carries me than a horse that throws me."

∇ ∇ ∇

Peire Vidal (c. 1175–1206)

"The maddest man in the world," Vidal's biographer wrote of him. The scatterbrained Provencal troubador went so far as to steal a kiss from his patron's wife in front of his patron, incurring his animosity. He sang sweetly, but among a thousand follies he committed was to dress himself in the skin of a wolf and have himself hunted by a pack of hounds before the country castle of a woman with whom he had fallen in love. He succeeded at great cost in attracting her attention.

∇ ∇ ∇

François-Eugène Vidocq (1775–1857)

In 1827 Vidocq, the founder of the *Sûreté*, the criminal investigative bureau of the Paris police, wrote the first book on crime by a professional detective. Both Vidocq and his book influenced generations of mystery writers, from Poe, who based Chevalier Dupin on him, to Agatha Christie, who modeled Hercule Poirot on the real-life detective. Balzac (*q.v.*) made use of his friend Vidocq in many books, as did Alexandre Dumas and Victor Hugo. The detective's early days as a criminal gave Dumas the heart of his *The Count of Monte Cristo*. Vidocq's quest for freedom as an escaped convict inspired Hugo to model the character Jean Valjean in *Les Miserables* on him, and he became one of the few men to have both the hero and villain in a novel based upon him, for Hugo used his later career as an implacable manhunter as the basis for Inspector Javert in the same book.

∇ ∇ ∇

Gúdbrandr Vígfússon (1828–1889)
This great Scandinavian scholar and author, born in Iceland, was noted for his phenomenal memory. It was said that if all of the many Eddic poems (a 13th-century compilation of difficult ancient poems) were lost nothing would be lost—because Vígfússon could write them all down from memory.

∇ ∇ ∇

Omar Vignole (fl. c. 1927)
The eccentric Argentine poet frequently led his pet cow through the streets of Buenos Aires, and all of his books featured his inseparable friend, books with titles like, *My Cow and I; What the Cow Thinks* etc. Once Vignole challenged a wrestler called the Calcutta Strangler in Buenos Aires' Luna Park. The Strangler made a fool of him before a huge crowd, tying him into knots. But Vignole had the last word. When his new book *Conversations With the Cow* came out a few months later, it bore the dedication: "I dedicate this philosophical work to the forty thousand sons of bitches who hissed and called for my blood in Luna Park on the night of February 24th."

∇ ∇ ∇

Count de Villamediana (1580–1622)
A great gambler and lover as well as a pungent satirist, the Spanish poet was appointed gentleman in waiting to Philip IV's young wife, Isabel de Bourbon. Villamediana wasted no time in heaping attentions upon her and aroused Philip's jealousy. When a fire broke out while his own masque, *La Gloria de Niguea*, was being performed, the poet carried Queen Isabel to safety in his arms. This proved the king's final provocation and a few days later he had assassins murder the poet as he stepped out of his coach, the crime, of course, going unpunished.

∇ ∇ ∇

Giovanni Villani (c. 1275–1348)
With the Black Death raging all around him, the great Italian historian died at his desk while working on his history of Florence, an early monument of Italian

prose. He was in the midst of the unfinished sentence: "In the midst of this pestilence there came to an end..."

▽ ▽ ▽

François Villon (1431–c. 1463)

The legendary French poet died after being banished from Paris for killing a priest, and various tales have transported him to England and elsewhere on the continent in his last years—at least one story had him dispatched by a gang of cutthroats. For this last charge of murdering a priest, the melodious thief was probably not responsible, but Villon admitted to killing another priest, one Philippe Chermoye, in 1455, after the priest started a quarrel with him and cut his lip with a knife.

▽ ▽ ▽

Virgil (Publius Vergilius Maro; 70–19 B.C.)

The longer the great and very self-critical Roman poet worked on the *Aeneid* the more he regretted that he had ever begun it, its very immensity driving him to despair. While gathering material for his epic poem he contracted a fever and died soon after. A proviso in his will ordered that all 12 books of the *Aeneid* be burned, but Emperor Augustus wisely overrode this, appointing Virgil's friends Varius and Tucca to edit the poem but to add nothing. Later, Virgil's poem became so venerated that it was used to foretell the future. A page, selected by opening a volume at random, supposedly could predict what was to come.

Suetonius said that Virgil paused over every line of the *Aeneid*, "licking it into shape as the she-bear does her cubs." When he finally agreed to read portions of it to Augustus, Mark Antony's widow, Octavia, is said to have fainted on hearing the beautiful passage about her recently deceased son Marcellus. Yet still the poet insisted that he needed at least three more years to polish his masterpiece.

Virgil's poetry was so popular in ancient times that an artificial kind of poem called the *cento*, a "patchwork" or "crazy-quilt" poem, was made by putting together bits of lines of his poems. The form was probably invented by the fourth-century poet Falconia Proba and was then applied to other poets. Centos were often obscene, as in the tour-de-force cento made by Ausonius from Virgil's lines.

When Virgil wrote a distich praising Caesar, the actor Bathyllus claimed to have written the lines. Determined to expose his lie, Virgil penned incomplete verses below the distich and had Caesar ask Bathyllus to complete the lines. He couldn't, was chastised, and henceforth stuck to his pantomime acting, for which his name became a synonym. Virgil supplied the poem's missing words, italicized below:

> Hos ego versiculos fici, tulit alter honores;
> Sic vos non vobis, *fertis aratra boves;*
> Sic vos non vobis, *mellificatis apes;*
> Sic vos non vobis, *vellera fertis oves;*
> Sic vos non vobis, *nidificatis aves.*

The Latin translates as:

> These lines made I, another steals my honors;
> So you for others, *oxen, bear the yoke;*
> So you for others, *bees store up your honey;*
> So you for others, *sheep, put on your fleece;*
> So you for others, *birds, construct your nests.*

In 41 B.C. Octavian and Antony confiscated land in the region near Mantua because the terrain favored their enemies. Roman soldiers seized Virgil's father's farm, threatening to kill the young man. The young poet escaped by leaping into the river Mincio and swimming for his life (becoming probably the first of the great literary swimmers, who include Byron, Poe, Eugene O'Neill and Robert Penn Warren).

Legend has it that Virgil's "pet housefly" was given a funeral that would cost the equivalent of over $100,000 today. Musicians, mourners and eulogists were hired and Virgil's mansion was declared the fly's mausoleum. Later it was discovered that Virgil buried the fly so that he could prevent the state from confiscating his estate and distributing it to war veterans as payment for service—all family cemetery plots and mausoleums being exempt from such confiscation. History confirms that Virgil's property was confiscated and that he got it back, but tells us nothing about his pet housefly. Many medieval legends arose about Virgil, and though this story my be true, it probably has its basis in Virgil's real troubles with his property, plus a story that he allegedly wrote called the "Culex." Spenser wrote a poem called "Virgil's Gnat," based on the "Culex," in which a sleeping shepherd is stung by a gnat, which bites him only to warn him that he is about to be attacked by a serpent. The shepherd kills the gnat and then slays the dragon, but the next night the spirit of the gnat reproaches him for his cruelty and the remorseful shepherd builds a monument honoring the gnat.

Many popular legends about the magical skills of Virgil were told in medieval times, including this final one recounted by an anonymous 19th-century author:

At last, having performed many extraordinary things, Virgil knew that his time was come. In order to escape the common lot he placed all his treasures in a castle defended by images unceasingly wielding iron flails, and directed his confidential servant to hew him in pieces, which he was to salt and place in a barrel in the cellar, under which a lamp was to be kept burning. The servant was assured that after seven days his master would revive, a young man again. The directions were carried out; but the emperor, missing his magician, forced Virgil's servant to divulge the secret and to quiet the whirling flails. The emperor and his retinue entered the castle and at last found the mangled corpse. In his wrath he slew the servant, whereupon a little naked child ran thrice round the barrel, crying, "Cursed be the hour that ye ever came here," and vanished.

Virgil sarcastically criticized the two minor Roman poets Bavius and Maevius in his *Third Eclogue* and Maevius was further criticized by Horace in his *Tenth Epode*, making their names forever synonyms for inferior poets or poetasters. In 1794 William Gifford wrote a fierce satire called *The Baviad* and followed it two years later with *The Maeviad*. The works attacked the Della Cruscan school of poetry, founded by sentimental young English poets living in Florence's famous Accademia della Crusca (Academy of Chaff) and striving to purify the Italian language, to sift away its chaff. By the way, Virgil himself was much criticized in his time; one critic published eight volumes consisting of resemblances between lines in Virgil's poems and by earlier Roman poets.

The motto *e pluribus unum* (Latin for "from many, one") on the obverse side of the Great Seal of the United States may come from a line in Virgil's poem "Moretum," which deals with the making of a salad (reading *color est e pluribus unus*) and which is the first recorded use of the phrase in any form. Another possibility, however, is an expression found on the title page of the British *Gentlemen's Magazine*, widely circulated in the United States for several decades after 1731. The title page of the magazine's first volume shows a hand holding a bouquet over the epigraph, *e pluribus unum*. The expression is as fitting for a bouquet of flowers as it is for a nation composed of separate states. Still another choice is an essay by Richard Steele in *The Spectator* (August 20, 1711), which opens with the Latin phrase *exempta juval spiris e pluribus unus* (better one thorn plucked than all remain). The Continental Congress ordered the President of Congress to have a seal in 1776 and *e pluribus unum* appeared on the first seal, as well as on many early coins. Congress adopted the motto in 1781 and it still appears on U.S. coins as well as on the Great Seal.

∇ ∇ ∇

Bernabò Visconti (1324–1385)

There are several instances of people literally eating their words, the earliest occurring in 1370 when the pope sent two delegates to Bernabò Visconti, ruler

of Milan, with a rolled parchment informing him that he had been excommunicated. Infuriated, Visconti arrested the delegates and made them eat the parchment—words, leaden seal and all. Later, arrested by his nephew, Visconti himself
died in prison.

▽ ▽ ▽

Denus Ivanovitch von Visin (1744–1792)

The Russian playwright took Moscow by storm with his comedy *The Minor*. So
enormously successful was the play that Catherine the Great's lover, Grigori
Potemkin, advised him to "die now, or never write again." Visin never did equal
its success.

▽ ▽ ▽

Walter von der Vogelweide (c. 1170–c. 1230)

This celebrated German lyric poet wandered from court to court singing for his
supper. Often scathingly critical of men, his lyrics were full of the joy and love
of nature. His will instructed that the birds at his tomb be fed daily.

▽ ▽ ▽

Isaac Volmar (fl. late 17th century)

The German author wrote a number of pamphlets poking fun at Bernhard, Duke
of Saxe-Meiningen-Hildburghausen, a former grand duchy in central Germany.
The duke, acting as though nothing had happened, invited Volmar to dinner and
only then indicated that he didn't think the booklets were funny. He forced
Volmar to eat every last page of his prose, uncooked.

▽ ▽ ▽

Comte de Volney (Constantin Chasseboeuf; 1745–1820)

Volney, from whose work Shelley borrowed many ideas for *Queen Mab*, knew
every notable in France, from pre-Revolutionary days to the age of Napoleon,
who made him a count. The French philosopher has the dubious distinction of
being the only philosopher Napoleon kicked in the stomach, the emperor dis-
playing his furious temper during an argument with him.

▽ ▽ ▽

Voltaire (François-Marie Arouet; 1694–1778)

A brilliant mathematician, Voltaire made a fortune (which allowed him ample
time to write as he pleased) by winning a government lottery. Noticing a
miscalculation in the government issuance of the lottery, the French author
formed a syndicate, bought up every ticket and became rich enough on his share

to be independent. Years later, in 1891, history repeated itself when the artist Claude Monet won 100,000 francs in the French national lottery and was able to devote himself entirely to his work.

His pen name is either an anagram for Arouet[e] J[eune], with *U* as *V* and *J* as *I*; or it comes from Veautaire, a small farm near Paris that he inherited from his cousin.

When members of the audience expressed their disapproval of his second play, *Artémire*, on the evening of February 15, 1720, he climbed up on stage and proceeded to argue with them about the play's merits. He failed to convince them, though they did applaud his efforts.

Voltaire told of how a commentator on Lucretius by the name of Creech noted on his manuscript: "*N.B.* Must hang myself when I have finished." Added Voltaire: "He kept his word, that he might have the pleasure of ending like his author (Lucretius). Had he written upon Ovid, he would have lived longer."

It is said that the Chevalier de Rohan-Chabot, encountering him in a theater lobby, intoned, "Monsieur de Voltaire, Monsieur Arouet—what really is your name?" Replied Voltaire: "My name begins with me, yours ends with you." He won that round, but two months later Rohan hired six hoodlums to beat him. Directing them from his carriage, he instructed: "Don't strike his head; something good may yet come out of that."

When a young man Voltaire wrote the most unusual of his works, a poem called "The Padlock" (1716). It was written to his mistress "Mme. B.," never further identified, and the padlock he raged about was a chastity belt her suspicious 70-year-old husband had made Mme. B wear to "lock the free sanctuary," "trouble our good time," and "abuse our desires," as Voltaire put it.

The chapter in his romance *Zadig* in which the philosopher-hero accurately describes by pure deduction a lost horse and dog, though he has seen neither, anticipates the detective story by over a century.

A possibly apocryphal story has it that Voltaire did at least some of his writing in bed, using his naked mistress's back for a desk.

Voltaire participated in an orgy with a group of dissolute Parisians. When invited to participate again, he replied, "No, thank you, my friends. Once: a philosopher; twice: a pervert!"

The philosopher had millions (in today's money) by the time he turned 40. He made most of his fortune not from literature, but by lending money from his lottery winnings to needy noblemen. Voltaire loaned heirs to estates large sums, his only condition being that they pay him 10 percent interest on the principal as long as both the heir and Voltaire lived. It is said that because of his thin, sickly appearance, he had little trouble attracting clients. His income in 1777 alone was perhaps the equivalent of a quarter of a million dollars today. "I saw so many men of letters poor and despised," he once wrote, "that I made up my mind not to become one of them."

When in 1723 he came down with smallpox, which often killed in those days, Voltaire thought the end had come and even made out his will. He later claimed that Doctor Gervais saved his life by making him drink "two hundred pints of lemonade."

Voltaire could hardly get a word in edgewise when Diderot came to visit him, the great encyclopedist speaking from the time he came until he left. As soon as Diderot was out the door, Voltaire observed, "That man is a great wit, but nature has denied him one great gift—that of dialogue."

Meeting him in Brussels, the poet Jean Baptiste Rousseau complimented Voltaire on his verse but criticized him for his impiety. It was at this time that Voltaire took a look at Rousseau's "Ode to Posterity" and made his famous remark: "Do you know, my master, that I do not believe this ode will ever reach its address?"

After reading a copy of the *Discourse* sent to him by Jean Jacques Rousseau, Voltaire replied: "I have received, Monsieur, your new book against the human race...You paint in true colors the horrors of human society;...no one has ever employed so much intellect to persuade men to be beasts. In reading your work one is seized with a desire to walk on four paws. However, as it is more than sixty years since I lost the habit, I feel, unfortunately, that it is impossible for me to resume it ..."

But then he was always jealous of Jean Jacques Rousseau, calling him "A mad dog who bites everybody," among other scurrilities. The first half of Rousseau's *Julie, ou la Nouvelle Eloise* was written in a brothel and the second in a madhouse, he once quipped.

After the first performance of his greatest play, *Mérope*, on February 20, 1743, the audience, many in tears, called for him to go on stage to take their applause, the first time this occurred in the history of the French theater. Some sources say he did so, while others claim he just stood up for a moment in his box.

He sent his great love, Madame du Châtelet, a ring with his portrait engraved in it, accompanied by a poem that translates literally as: "Barier engraves these features for your eyes; do look upon them with some pleasure. Your own are graved more deeply in my heart, but by a greater master still."

When Madame du Châtelet took young Marquis Saint-Lambert as a lover, Voltaire was at first hurt and angry, but he quickly recovered. "My child," he later told an apologetic Saint-Lambert, "I was in the wrong. You are in the happy age of love and delight; enjoy those moments, too brief. An old invalid like me is not made for these pleasures."

Casanova visited the Swiss poet Albrecht von Haller, who told him, "Monsieur Voltaire is a man who deserves to be known, although, contrary to the laws of physics, many people have found him greater at a distance." Several days later Casanova visited Voltaire, who asked him where he last came from. "From Roche," Casanova hold him. "I did not want to leave Switzerland without having seen Haller…I kept you to the last as a *bonne bouche* [a tidbit]," "Were you pleased with Haller?" Voltaire inquired. "I spent the three happiest days of my life with him," said Casanova. "I congratulate you," Voltaire said. "I am glad you do him justice," said Casanova. "I am sorry he is not so fair toward you." "Ah-hah!" Voltaire cried. "Perhaps we are both mistaken."

In 1760 he showed Casanova his collection of about 50,000 letters written to him up until that time. Over the remaining years he was to receive about 50,000 more and the definitive collection of his correspondence fills 98 volumes.

Voltaire was told that Frederick the Great did not intend to keep him at his court too much longer. "I need him another year at most," Frederick reputedly said; "one squeezes the orange, and throws away the peel." The possibly apocryphal remark preyed on Voltaire's mind so much that in October 1751 he wrote to Madame Denis: "I keep dreaming about that orange peel…He who was falling from a bell tower and, finding himself at ease in the air, said 'Good, provided this lasts,' resembles me quite." Despite his fears, Voltaire remained at the court another two years and could have stayed longer.

He did not approve of theological writings. "I have two hundred volumes on the subject," he remarked, "and, what is worse, I have read them. It is like going the rounds of a lunatic asylum."

The bishop of Annecy wanted Voltaire executed for his anticlerical writings. "That rascally bishop still swears that he will have me burned in this world or the other," Voltaire remarked to d'Alembert. "To escape being burned I am laying in a supply of holy water."

A young poet called on Voltaire and asked him if he had any use for "a young atheist ready to serve you." "I have the honor of being a deist employer," Voltaire replied, "but though our professions are so opposed, I will give you supper today and work tomorrow. I can make use of your arms, though not of your head."

The French critic Elie Catherine Fréron (1719–76) made the mistake of attacking Voltaire and the encyclopedists. Voltaire, not a man to be tampered with, let go a barrage of overkill upon him in wicked epigrams, in his tragedies, in the virulent satire *Le Pauvre Diable*, and in an anonymous work called *Anecdotes sur Fréron* (1760). What hurt the critic most was Voltaire's making him the principal character in his comedy *L'Écossaise*. In this comedy Fréron's magazine, *L'Année Littéraire* (*The Literary Year*) is called *L'Ane Littéraire* (*The Literary Ass*). The play also depicts Fréron as a scoundrel, spy, toad, hound, snake, lizard and man with a heart of filth, among other things. Voltaire later circulated a quatrain about the critic: "The other day, down in a valley,/a serpent stung Fréron./What think you happened then?/It was the serpent that died."

Writing to Mademoiselle Quinault, Voltaire was the first to point out what has become almost a literary maxim. "The only reward to be expected for the cultivation of literature," he wrote, "is contempt if one fails and hatred if one succeeds."

In a 1735 letter to a friend, Voltaire said, "Shakespeare is the Corneille of London, but everywhere else he is a fool." Thirty years later his opinion of the Bard was hardly better. "Shakespeare is a savage with some imagination," he wrote in another letter, "but everywhere else he is a great fool."

Remarked Voltaire of Claude-Adrien Helvétius and his book *De l'Esprit*, which was burned publicly in 1758: "I liked the author...but I never approved either the errors of his book, or the trivial truths he so vigorously laid down. I have, however, stoutly taken his side when absurd men have condemned him for the same reasons." These words are probably the basis for the saying "I disapprove of what you say, but I will defend to the death your right to say it," which Voltaire never said and which isn't found before the 20th century.

Feelings were running high against the French when Voltaire visited England in 1727. One day as he walked down the street in London a crowd gathered, shouting at him, "Kill him, hang the Frenchman!" Voltaire calmed them by crying, "Englishmen! You want to kill me because I am a Frenchman? Am I not punished enough in not being an Englishman?"

When James Boswell told him that an Academy of Painting had been established in Scotland but failed, Voltaire replied, "Yes, to paint well it is necessary to have warm feet. It's hard to paint when your feet are cold."

Publishers of Voltaire's complete works seem to have met with incredibly bad luck, at least in the 18th and 19th centuries, leading to a literary tradition holding that it was unlucky to publish his books. The first editor of his complete works, for example, lost a million francs in the stock market and died suddenly of a heart attack in 1798. Within the next 70 years at least eight publishers were ruined financially after publishing complete Voltaires. Four of these became paupers and died suddenly, one being killed by a woman he caught stealing a book, another going blind, and two forced to take jobs as workers in printing plants for the rest of their lives.

Voltaire was not afraid to mock himself. When in 1764 James Boswell asked him if he still spoke English, he replied, "No, to speak English one must place the tongue between the teeth, and I have lost my teeth."

A priest arrived to attend Voltaire on his deathbed. "Who sent you?" the philosopher asked.
"God Himself, Monsieur Voltaire."
"And where are your credentials?" Voltaire demanded.

A very wealthy bachelor of 60 told Voltaire that he had fallen in love with a much younger woman. "I want to marry her," he confided, "but I'm afraid I've ruined my chances by telling her my true age. I should have told her I was fifty."
"On the contrary," Voltaire said, "You should have told her you were seventy."

While working on plans for a new French dictionary shortly before his death, he rivaled Balzac (*q.v.*) in his consumption of coffee, drinking 25 or more cups a day to keep going—so much that he was unable to sleep nights.

He wrote to Monsieur Daniliville:
"I have made but one prayer to God, a very short one: 'O Lord, make my enemies ridiculous.' And God granted it."

"In a hundred years the Bible will be a forgotten book found only in museums," he once predicted, writing from his home in Geneva. A hundred years later his home was owned and occupied by the Geneva Bible Society.

Animals, he believed, have certain advantages over humans: "They never hear the clock strike. They die without any idea of death. They have no theologians to instruct them. Their last movements are not disturbed by unwelcome and unpleasant ceremonies. Their funerals cost them nothing. And no one starts lawsuits over their wills."

What other philosopher has ever equaled his fame? He was the hero of all Europe by the end of his life. In Berlin, according to Frederick the Great, "People tear at one another in the struggle for the busts of Voltaire at the manufactory of porcelain, where they do not turn them out fast enough to meet the demand."

At 84 he attended a performance of his play *Irene* and could barely get into the theater, so crowded with well-wishers was the street. Once inside he was covered with a laurel wreath and the audience stood applauding him for over 20 minutes, crying "Hail Voltaire!" "Hail Sophocles!" "Honor to the philosopher who teaches men to think!" After the play, a huge crowd escorted his carriage home.

∇ ∇ ∇

Gerhard John Vossius (1577–1649)
"Vossius is so learned a man," said Sweden's Queen Christina of the eminent Dutch scholar, "that he not only knows the origins of all words, but their destinations."

∇ ∇ ∇ ∇ ∇ ∇ ∇ ∇ ∇

Count de Waldeck (Jean-Frédéric; 1766–1875)
I have it on the authority of author L. Sprague de Camp that the count published his second book, on archaeology, at the age of 100, which makes him possibly the oldest person ever to publish a book. He lived nine years more, dropping dead at 109, just after turning to look at a pretty girl on the boulevards of Paris.

∇ ∇ ∇

Wang Chieh (c. 868)
Wang Chieh has his place in history as the printer of the world's oldest printed book, which is actually a manuscript roll that was found in the "Caves of the Thousand Buddahas" at Tun- huang, China, in 1907, along with 15,000 more books. The *Diamond Sutra*, as it is called, ends with these words: "Printed on [the

ancient equivalent of] May 11, 868, by Wang Chieh, for free general distribution, in order in deep reverence to perpetuate the memory of his parents." Found in the same library of 15,000 books was the world's first folded book.

▽ ▽ ▽

Wang Ts'an (177–217)
One of the greatest poets of the Han dynasty, Wang Ts'an was also famous for his fabulous memory. The aristocratic Wang was said to have total recall of everything he had seen, heard, felt or read through his lifetime.

▽ ▽ ▽

Zacharias Werner (1768–1823)
A romantic poet and dramatist turned priest, the Viennese writer was converted to Catholicism after a life of dissipation bordering on insanity. One Sunday he gave a sermon on "that tiny piece of flesh, the most dangerous appurtenance of a man's body." On and on he graphically expounded to a blushed and blanched congregation—including several ladies who fainted in the aisles—about all the evils this tiny piece of flesh had caused. Finally, Werner concluded, his voice rising to a shout: "Shall I show you that tiny piece of flesh?" Not a breath could be heard until he cried: "Ladies and gentlemen, behold the source of our sins!" Smiling at last, he stuck out his tongue.

▽ ▽ ▽

Gustav Wied (1858–1914)
Wied's loneliness and the bitter nihilism behind all the masks be put on for the world led to his suicide at the outbreak of World War I. He was, however, among the most humorous of Scandinavian writers. In his book *Knagsted* (1902), one of his eponymous character's creations is a collection of Danish writers' commas.

▽ ▽ ▽

Herman Wildenvey (Herman Portaas; 1886–1959)
The Norwegian poet lived as he chose to live, no matter what anyone said; in fact, one critic was so surprised at the sparkling beauty of his first collection of poems that he quipped, "I suppose he is not such a swine as he makes himself out to be." Wildenvey attributed his happy manner and insouciant humor to "having studied for a year within the given confines of an American theological seminary."

Johann Joachim Winckelmann (1717–1768)

The German classical archaeologist and art historian, the son of a shoemaker, greatly influenced the work of Goethe and Schiller. Winckelmann was murdered while traveling in Trieste. Making friends there with another traveler, Francesco Arcangeli, he made the mistake of showing him gold medallions awarded to him in Vienna. The next morning, Arcangeli stole into Winckelmann's hotel room and tried to strangle him from behind with a noose. When Winckelmann fought free of the rope, Arcangeli stabbed him to death and fled with the gold. He was captured a week later, and although Winckelmann had forgiven him in his dying words, he was executed by being "broken alive on the wheel, from the head to the feet, until your soul departs from your body."

∇ ∇ ∇

Tirupati Winkatakawulu (Diwakarla Tirupati Sastri, 1870–1950; and Cellapilla Wenkatasastri, 1871–1921)

This was the pseudonym of the Indian "twin poets," friends who wrote all their work together for over 25 years and called themselves by one name, the only case known of poets doing this. Great scholars as well as bards, they revived a broad interest in Indian Telugu literature with their many original poems and translations. The "twin poets" were also famous for their phenomenal memories, exhibited in the performance of *satawadhana*, where, according to one biographer, "a hundred interrogators were each given line by line a complete verse of four stanzas on a subject prescribed by each, the hundred verses finally repeated complete [by the twin poets] without missing a syllable." Wenkatasastri continued to write under the pseudonym for 30 years after his fellow poet died.

∇ ∇ ∇ ∇ ∇ ∇ ∇ ∇

Xenocrates (396–314 B.C.)

It is said that Xenocrates "had no mistress but philosophy." Hearing of his reputation for virtue, the beautiful Greek courtesan Phryne decided to test her charms on him. Phryne pretended that she was being pursued and pleaded with Xenocrates to let her take refuge in his house. When night fell she asked the philosopher if she might share his single bed and he granted her this wish, too. Once in bed she enticed him with all her charms and all the tricks she knew, but he remained cold to every entreaty, and she stormed angrily out of his bed and house, telling all who would listen that she had slept with a statue, not a man.

∇ ∇ ∇

Xenophanes (fl. 536 B.C.)

Living over a century, this wandering Greek poet and philosopher laughed at the provincialism and anthropomorphism of all he met. "Mortals fancy that gods are born, and wear clothes, and have voice and form like themselves," he once said. "Yet if oxen and lions had hands, and could paint and fashion images as men do, they would make the pictures and images of their gods in their own likeness; horses would make them look like horses, oxen like oxen. Ethiopians make their gods black and snub-nosed; Thracians give theirs blue eyes and red hair...There is one god, supreme among gods and men; resembling mortals neither in form nor in mind."

∇ ∇ ∇

Xenophon (c. 430–355 B.C.)

The Greek author and military man became a student of Socrates in his youth. The historian Diogenes Laertius tells the story: "Xenophon was a man of great modesty, and as handsome as can be imagined. They say that Socrates met him in a narrow lane, and put his stick across it, and prevented him from passing by, asking where all kinds of necessary things were sold. And when Xenophon had answered him, he asked, again, where men were made good and virtuous. And as Xenophon did not know, Socrates said, 'Follow me, then, and learn.' And from that time forth Xenophon became a follower of Socrates."

∇ ∇ ∇ ∇ ∇ ∇ ∇ ∇ ∇

Marguerite Yourcenar (1903–1987)

Miss Yourcenar changed her name from Crayencour (Yourcenar is an imperfect anagram of her inherited name) early in her career (Voltaire did the same two centuries before). The first woman admitted to the illustrious Académie Française over its four-century existence, she never blamed the academy for not admitting a woman sooner. "One cannot say," she remarked after her induction in 1981, "that in French society, so impregnated with feminine influences, the academy has been a notable misogynist: It simply conformed to the custom that willingly placed a woman on a pedestal but did not officially offer her a chair."

The French writer prepared her own tombstone in the final years of her life. She had everything inscribed on the marker up until the final two digits of the date of her death. A friend was horrified that she had even put 19— on her tombstone. "Why should you not live to the year 2000?" she insisted. "I have no desire to live to the year 2000," Miss Yourcenar said. "The year 2000 is not for me."

▽ ▽ ▽

Yung Lo (fl. early 15th century)

The Ming Emperor Yung Lo oversaw the writing of a 10,000-volume encyclopedia, which an army of scholars began in 1403 and finished 22 years later. Then the emperor arbitrarily decided the work would be too expensive to publish, and what was perhaps the greatest collection of knowledge every gathered was ultimately lost to history. One handwritten copy was passed down for generations, but finally all save 162 volumes were lost in a fire during the Boxer Rebellion of 1900.

▽ ▽ ▽

Saint Yves of Brittany (1253–1303)

The French lawyer, judge and writer on the law was canonized in 1347 because of his zealous protection of the poor and orphans. A humorous medieval Latin verse about him is still quoted today:

> Sanctus Ivo erat Brito,
> advocatus et non latro,
> admirandus populo.

(St. Yves was a Breton, a lawyer, and not a thief, a rare wonder in the eyes of the people.)

▽ ▽ ▽ ▽ ▽ ▽ ▽ ▽

Lazarus Ludwig Zamenhof (1859–1917)

Esperanto, which is far better known than any other artificial universal language, takes its name from the pseudonym chosen by its inventor, Lazarus Zamenhof, when he wrote his first book on the subject, *Linguo Internacia de la Doktoro Esperanto*. Dr. Zamenhof, the "Doctor Hopeful" of the title, was a Warsaw oculist who believed that a world language would promote peace and understanding. He launched his system in 1887 and today the movement has some eight million supporters; from half a million to a million people are capable of speaking Esperanto fluently.

∇ ∇ ∇

Zeno of Citium (c. 335–c. 263 B.C.)
When Antigonus II, trying to tempt Zeno with luxury, invited him to be his houseguest, Zeno sent his pupil Persaeus in his place. The philosopher's life was so consistent with his teachings that the saying "more temperate than Zeno" became proverbial in his lifetime.

Zeno's slave, a learned man, received a beating from his master for stealing. "But it was fated that I should steal," he said, citing the doctrine of determinism. "And that I should beat you," Zeno replied.

To a pupil who talked in class excessively Zeno remarked, "The reason why we have two ears and only one mouth is that we may hear more and talk less."

Shipwrecked on the Attic coast, Zeno lost his entire fortune. Not long after, while sitting at a bookseller's stall reading about Socrates, he remarked "Where are such men to be found today?" Just then the philosopher Crates happened to pass by and the bookseller advised, "Follow that man." Zeno did, soon discovering the joys of philosophy. Later he observed, "I made a prosperous voyage when I was wrecked."

The old story says that the tyrant Nearchos ordered Zeno, founder of the Stoic school of philosophy, to be pounded to death in a large, bowl-shaped container. After suffering this punishment a short time, Zeno told Nearchos he had something important to say to him and when he leaned over to hear better, Zeno bit off his ear. Somehow he was freed and from this tale, true or false, came the proverb "A remark more biting than Zeno's," which yielded the expression "a biting remark."

At his public funeral all Athens honored Zeno as a philosopher who "had made his life an example to all, for he followed his own teaching." But legend holds that death came to him after he tripped and broke a toe when 90. According to this tale, Zeno fell and pounded the ground with his fists, repeating a line from the *Niobe*: "I come, why call me like *this*!" He then "immediately strangled or hung himself."

∇ ∇ ∇

Zoïlus (c. 400–320 B.C.)

This Greek grammarian was chiefly noted for his violent attacks on the works of Homer, mainly against their fantastic elements. So vicious were his attacks that the Greeks gave him the name Homeromastix, "scourge of Homer." But his intemperate attacks were also directed against Plato and Isocrates so that the name Zoïlus came to be generally used of any spiteful critic.

∇ ∇ ∇

Émile Zola (1840–1902)

"I'm a total ignoramus!" Zola once despaired in a letter to his friend Cézanne. Judging by his school record alone this would be true. The French author failed the language and literature portions of the Sorbonne entrance examinations, and when he couldn't get admitted there, failed the written exams for the University of Marseilles. Zola worked as a clerk in Paris until the publication of his first book, *Contes à Ninon*, in 1864. (See HEINRICH HEINE.)

Cézanne was a good friend of Zola's until his novel *L'Oeuvre* insulted the artist and the Impressionists. How could Zola have expected this painter not to be offended? This painter, who had bought a parrot and taught it to say over and over again, "Cézanne is a great painter."

Zola was found dead in his bed on the morning of September 29, 1902. He had apparently died in his sleep, accidentally asphyxiated by the fumes from a defective heating flue. Captain Dreyfus was present at the public funeral accorded him and Anatole France delivered an oration at his grave.

In his eulogy at Zola's funeral Anatole France summed up the great writer and champion of justice as "a moment in the human conscience."

∇ ∇ ∇

José Zorrilla (1817–1893)

The Spanish poet suffered great poverty in his early years as a poet, often not having food to eat for days at a time. Strangely enough, his genius was first recognized and he came into national prominence when he read an elegiac poem at the funeral of fellow author Mariano José de Larra in 1837. He remained in dire straits all his life, however, until in 1889, four years before his death, he was publicly crowned at Granada as Spain's national poet laureate.

Miklos Zrinyi (1620–1664)

The epic poet, a great Hungarian and political hero, had enormous influence on Hungarian poetry, but he believed, in his words, that his true vocation was "to perform great deeds with the sword, rather than to write about them with the pen." His sword failed him, however, when he was killed on a hunt by a charging wild boar.

∇ ∇ ∇

Zuhair (Zuhair Ibn-abi Sulma; fl. 6th century)

One of those rare writers who have lived to be over 100 (his exact dates are unknown), Zuhair is said to have met Mohammed on his 100th birthday. One of the great Arabian pre-Islamic poets, he came from a family of extraordinary poetic power; his father, sister and son all were eminent poets.

∇ ∇ ∇

Stefan Zweig (1881–1942)

When exiled Austrian novelist Stefan Zweig and his wife Lotte committed suicide during World War II, on February 21, 1942, they bathed, dressed in their best, took massive doses of veronal and lay down together to die in their bedroom, leaving beside them a touching "open declaration" that Zweig, that "European of yesterday," had written:

> Before parting from life of my own free will and in my right mind I am impelled to fulfill a last obligation; to give heartfelt thanks to this wonderful land of Brazil which afforded me and my work such kind and hospitable repose. With every day I have learned to love this country more and more, and nowhere else would I have preferred to rebuild my life from the ground up, now that the world of my own language has been lost and my spiritual homeland, Europe, has destroyed itself.
>
> But after one's sixtieth year unusual powers are needed in order to make another wholly new beginning. Those that I possess have been exhausted by the long years of homeless wandering. So I hold it better to conclude in good time and with erect bearing a life for which intellectual labour was always the purest job and personal freedom the highest good on this earth.
>
> I salute all my friends! May it be granted them yet to see the dawn after the long night! I, all too impatient, go on before.

In a vase on the sideboard was a four-leaf clover.

∇ ∇ ∇

Huldreich Zwingli (1484–1531)

As a Catholic priest the great Swiss religious reformer and author had numerous affairs with women parishioners, though he curiously, or gallantly, would have nothing to do with nuns, virgins or married women. His sins caught up with him when one of his conquests bragged of her affair with him and he was forced to make a confession to Rome. When he broke with the Church, the pope ordered his confession of his sins published to discredit him, making Zwingli's reform movement all the harder to sustain.

Zwingli was killed while serving as chaplain during a civil war among Swiss Protestants. Killed in cold blood while he lay slightly wounded on the ground, his corpse was quartered by the public hangman and burned with dung by the enemy soldiers. A great boulder today marks the place where he fell, its inscription reading, "They may kill the body but not the soul."

INDEX